East of Malta, West of Suez

East of Malta, West of Suez

Britain's Mediterranean
Crisis, 1936-1939

Lawrence R. Pratt

*Department of Political Science,
The University of Alberta*

Cambridge University Press
Cambridge
London · New York · Melbourne

Published in co-operation with
London School of Economics
and Political Science

Published by the Syndics of the Cambridge University Press
The Pitt Building, Trumpington Street, Cambridge CB2 1RP
Bentley House, 200 Euston Road, London NW1 2DB
32 East 57th Street, New York, NY 10022, USA
296 Beaconsfield Parade, Middle Park, Melbourne 3206, Australia

Library of Congress Catalog Card number: 75–23534

ISBN: 0 521 20869 6

First published 1975

Printed in Great Britain at
the University Printing House, Cambridge
(Euan Phillips, University Printer)

DA
586
- P67
Cop 2

England's first battlefield is the Mediterranean.

Winston Churchill, March 1939

Contents

Foreword

In the 1880s Britain found herself involved in Egypt, nominally as the representative of the European holders of Egyptian public debts. Ten years later she abandoned her attempt to find an internationally acceptable surrogate for her presence in Egypt and settled down seriously to the occupation, development and modernization of the country. The impulse that drove her to this course was the transformation of the Eastern Mediterranean from a landlocked sea to the first stage of a maritime route which led via the Suez Canal and the Red Sea to the Far East and India, the brightest jewel in the imperial crown. Lord Palmerston had opposed the construction of the Suez Canal as a peril for Britain. In 1914 that peril became real. Britain found herself committed to a war on land against the Ottoman Empire. That war she won; and by the Middle Eastern peace settlement so laboriously thrashed out between Versailles and Lausanne, Britain's area of responsibility expanded to take in Palestine, Transjordan and Iraq with its oil wells and pipe-lines to the Mediterranean.

This process not only committed Britain's exiguous professional army to the protection of new land areas, it also moved the areas of British overseas rule manifestly closer to the spheres of action of the European land forces from which the sea and Britain's naval supremacy had so long protected her. In terms of maritime strategy too, it shifted the areas of main interest to the Royal Navy from the outlets to the Atlantic and the Italo—Tunisian narrows to the Eastern Mediterranean, as had once been done before when Nelson destroyed the French fleet off the Nile, Captain Sidney Smith commanded Acre and General Abercrombie destroyed those whom Napoleon deserted. In those days Britain had occupied Corfu and the Ionian islands as a fleet station in the Eastern Mediterranean. It was only with the threat from Italy in 1935 that the Mediterranean Fleet would return to base at Alexandria. In 1940 Churchill would gamble with Britain's own security, sending the armour essential to Britain's defence against Nazi invasion to the Middle East where General Wavell was, that same winter, to use it to eliminate Italian land power in North Africa. So far had the Middle East come in Britain's order of strategic priorities.

Most historians of twentieth-century British overseas policy knew of

Churchill's decision. Fewer seemed to be ready to apply the normal canons of historical continuity backwards to examine the antecedents of Churchill's decision. Fewer still felt the absence of the Mediterranean dimension — apart from the roles ascribed to the Italian attack on Ethiopia and the Spanish Civil War in the events leading up to Hitler's attack on Poland and and Anglo—French declaration of war on Germany — from the controversy over appeasement.

It is one of the many virtues of Professor Pratt's work that he has explored the strategic anxieties besetting the makers of Britain's external policies in the face of the dictators, arising from the British entrapment in the Eastern Mediterranean and has shown how they dovetail into the parallel anxieties aroused by Hitler's Germany and imperial Japan. He throws considerable light on the varieties of sympathy felt for Italian Fascism in odd, sometimes very odd, corners of the inner circle of advisers and policy-makers, and has thrown into strong relief the essentially imperial and extra-European causes and sources of their anxiety. He throws a good deal of light on the advocates of the avoidance of conflict with Italy, their anti-Americanism, their suspicion of France, their preoccupation with the threat to Britain from Germany and the intolerable strain imposed on them by their consciousness of Britain's weakness in the face of this threat. This strain, he hints, underlay the contrast between their desire to stand up to Germany and the comparatively ignominious efforts they made to appease Hitler's petty Latin imitator. He shows too how a new toughness crept into their thought in 1939, misplaced, as it happened, in view of the lack of French will to act, and any British capacity. In the end the policy of appeasement paid off and Italy remained neutral.

D. C. Watt

Preface

One of history's harshest lessons appears to be reserved for great powers that over-extend themselves.

A great power, it is sometimes said, is almost by definition one that seeks to expand its influence beyond its own national boundaries. But not all great powers practise imperialism. There is a world of difference between a conservative policy attempting to convert legitimate self-interest into influence and an expansionist design that seeks indefinite aggrandizement and an ever-wider dominion, whether in the name of trade and markets, national glory or some civilizing mission. Not surprisingly, the destructive urges that impel empires to expand their spheres of control and plunder beyond their defensive capabilities tend, over the long run, to be the undoing of those empires as well as profoundly disruptive of international stability. Wise and rare are the nations that practise restraint because they understand that sooner or later all empires must confront resistance, whether from within or without, and that the attempt to repress or appease such resistance often only compounds the imperial dilemma. The thankless business of holding an empire together is far more difficult than the earlier, more glorious, task of putting it together.

Few modern nations have confronted a more hopeless prospect of empire-holding than that faced by England in the 1930s. The British Empire was over-extended and under-prepared, resembling a patchwork of interdependent weaknesses. Writing in the shadow of the crisis that exposed the acute nature of the British global predicament, the country's first naval officer confessed in 1936 that the Empire was 'disjointed, disconnected and highly vulnerable. It is even open to debate whether it is in reality strategically defensible.' The tensions in imperial policy between far-flung commitments and scarce military resources had been underlined by Mussolini's invasion of Abyssinia in 1935 and his flaunting of the League of Nations, events that challenged England's traditional paramountcy in the Mediterranean and the security of its line of communications to the Middle and Far East.

This study reconstructs and analyses Britain's unsuccessful effort to restore its security in the Mediterranean in the aftermath of the 1935–6 war scare. In addition, the author has attempted to bring some light to bear on the interdependence of British problems and policies, particularly on the relationship, largely ignored, between appeasement and empire. Any analysis that ignores or discounts the crisis of empire in explanations of the policy of appeasement cannot, in the author's opinion, pass close scrutiny. In many ways the Mediterranean — especially that part of the sea which lies 'east of Malta, west of Suez' — was at the heart of England's pre-war dilemma, and its failure to refashion its traditional security in that region played a decisive role in the ultimate collapse into war and the downfall of the Empire. Despite repeated efforts to remedy weakness in the Mediterranean through appeasement, England's vulnerability presisted and forced the diversion of strategic supplies from home defence. Insecurity in the Eastern Mediterranean and Middle East also crippled Britain's capacity for independent action in the Far East and increased the Empire's reliance on the United States. Appeasement sprang from the exigencies of defending an over-extended, exhausted empire which could not, in the final analysis, be defended.

May 1975

Acknowledgements

Research for this study was carried out in England from 1968 to 1971 and during a second research visit to London in 1973. This research was made possible through the generous financial assistance of the Canada Council.

I am one of a growing number of students of modern international history whose ideas have been deeply influenced by their association with Professor Donald Watt of the London School of Economics and Political Science. Without his intellectual stimulation and personal encouragement this study might not have been completed.

Several other scholars who have worked in the diplomatic and military history of the 1930s in one way or another encouraged me. I would like to extend special gratitude to Professor David Dilks, Captain Stephen Roskill, Professor James Joll, Professor Michael Howard, Professor M. G. Fry, the late Donald McLachlan, Mr Brian Bond, Mr John Lippincott and the late Sir B. H. Liddell Hart.

For permission to consult various collections of private papers I wish to thank the Lady Vansittart, the Viscount Simon, the Viscount Caldecote, Lord Chatfield, the late Sir B. H. Liddell Hart, Professor A. T. Patterson and the late Donald McLachlan. I am also indebted to the following institutions: the University Library and Churchill College Library, Cambridge; the Institute of Historical Research; the British Library of Economics and Political Science, London School of Economics and Political Science; the Reading Room and Manuscripts Room, the British Museum; the Royal Institute of International Affairs, Chatham House; the Douglass Library, Queen's University, Kingston, Canada; the Public Archives of Canada, Ottawa; and the Public Record Office, London.

For assistance in the publication of the manuscript I wish to thank the Publications Committee of the London School of Economics; Dr Grant Davy and Dr Henry Kreisel, the University of Alberta; and Mrs Patricia Williams and Mrs. Bettina Wilkes of Cambridge University Press.

Department of Political Science　　　　　　　　*Lawrence Pratt*
University of Alberta
May 1975

Introduction:
Empire and Appeasement

It can be said, without great risk of exaggeration, that the historiography of the origins of the Second World War has been so heavily orientated towards European events and problems that it could almost be called Germanocentric. There is no clear and satisfactory explanation for this aside from the intuitive and unverifiable remark that the Nazi phenomenon has exerted a strong pull on the academic, as well as popular, curiosity. Of course, it is also true that the interpretative history depends on the availability of primary sources, and until recently historians could tap a wealth of documentation that could be used to study aspects of German policy but was less useful for other areas of research. Beyond these points, however, it may be argued that the emotional impact of the post-war revelations concerning Adolf Hitler's *Reich* shaped in significant ways the historiography of war origins. There emerged a tendency to reproduce and amplify the arguments of the Nuremberg trials for like purposes: to prove Hitler's responsibility and originality and to expose the 'guilty' men' of pre-war Europe who failed either to understand or to stop him. Hitler was Europe's crisis personified, and British and French diplomacy have been seen simply in varying degrees of shared responsibility for their failure to manage this crisis. The appeasement theme and its association with a few key personalities is so characteristic of studies of British foreign policy, for example, that explanation has been reduced in some instances to mere caricature.[1]

In recent years the monolithic 'guilty men' orthodoxy and its 'war-premeditated' thesis have come under attack and historians have been engaged in a search for pluralist analyses.[2] The level of debate on war

[1] For a critique of the 'hanging judge' approach to appeasement, see D. C. Watt, 'Sir Lewis Namier and contemporary European history', *Cambridge Journal* (1954); and on its political origins, D. C. Watt, 'Appeasement: the rise of a revisionist school?' *The Political Quarterly* (1965).

[2] Especially since the publication of A. J. P. Taylor's *The origins of the Second World War* (London, 1961); see also the essays reprinted in E. M. Robertson (ed.), *The origins of the Second World War* (London, 1971); also Watt, 'Appeasement: the rise of a revisionist school?' *op. cit.*

1

origins has been raised, and it should be raised yet again in the near future; for the revision of the fifty-year rule in Great Britain has confronted scholars with a mass of unpublished documents against which earlier assessments will have to be measured. The minutes and papers of the Cabinet, Foreign Office and Committee of Imperial Defence (C.I.D.) and the various collections of inter-departmental correspondence allow the historian to study the British decision-making process in detail to see how policies were evolved, where information, correct or false, was available to policy-makers, and by which premises and assumptions actions were guided. There are great advantages, and it is hoped that our knowledge of the sources of British diplomatic conduct will be much enhanced before further judgements are passed on the state of its moral health. This may be wishful thinking, however, as one writer has already used this new material to 'convict' Neville Chamberlain and to place him before the 'bar of history' on several counts.[3] This is a dubious role for history and one which the present study attempts above all to avoid. The temptation to slide into partisan writing and to look for 'historical responsibilities' rather than explanations, which one historiographer of the Spanish Civil War has noted,[4] still prevails in the debate on the meaning of the 1930s and constitutes the most difficult hurdle for the historian new to the period.

An almost unnoticed, but equally important, historiographical tendency of the continuing study of war origins has been its Eurocentric character. Writers have tended to focus almost exclusively on the German problem, as if it can be seen, or was seen, in a vacuum hermetically isolated from the global crisis of the 1930s. Studies of pre-war British policy have concentrated on the formation of a German line but they have virtually ignored, or relegated to unrelated chapters, London's imperial and extra-European commitments and dilemmas. It is almost as if Britain had suddenly abandoned its overseas interests and maritime traditions in order to commit itself solely to a continental role; whereas, in fact, the tendency (at least before the spring of 1939) was in precisely the opposite direction. With only a few exceptions, existing studies of appeasement suffer not only from a lack of balance, but they also grossly distort the way in which the actual decision-makers perceived the world.[5] One writer has fairly commented that 'there is no

---

3 Ian Colvin, *The Chamberlain Cabinet* (London, 1971), p. 14.
4 'Right and Left in the Spanish Republic', *Times Literary Supplement*, 26 March 1971.
5 Exceptions are W. N. Medlicott, 'The coming of war in 1939', *The Historical*

major discussion of British foreign policy in the 1930s which faces the problems, as the Chamberlain administration had to, as part of a concurrent though rarely concerted attack on Britain's position in Europe, in the Mediterranean and Middle East, and in East Asia and the Pacific'.[6] Research into the interdependence of these problems is needed and an effort must be undertaken to analyse how Britain's imperial dilemmas shaped, and were in turn shaped by, its policies in Europe. In brief, what was the relationship in British policy between empire and appeasement?

The historian who has examined the pre-war papers of Britain's strategists cannot fail to be impressed by the unremitting tension between capabilities and commitments. Aside from its important role in Europe, England managed extensive political and economic interests in both the Far and Middle East, remained heavily dependent upon its non-European trade and its lines of maritime communication, held a number of overseas colonies and bases, and still had important strategic commitments to certain of the Dominions. The dilemma of strategy, as the First Sea Lord once put it with a sailor's candour, was this: 'We are in the remarkable position of not wanting to quarrel with anybody because we have got most of the world already, or the best parts of it, and we only want to keep what we have got and prevent others from taking it away from us.'[7] Yet such a holding operation was an immense undertaking, because the Empire's interests far exceeded its military capabilities, particularly if these were jeopardized on more than one front. Britain's imperial salad days were past, although this was apparent to few in the mid-1930s. The same First Sea Lord admitted after the Abyssinian crisis that the Empire was 'disjointed, disconnected and highly vulnerable. It is even open to debate whether it is in reality strategically defensible.'[8]

These two statements reflect a basic contradiction between the aggrandizing impulse of British imperialism — the desire to control the

---

Association, 1963; D. C. Watt, *Personalities and Policies* (London, 1965), especially essays 4 and 8; in addition, see the editor's introduction in David N. Dilks (ed.), *The Diaries of Sir Alexander Cadogan 1938–45* (London, 1971), pp. 14–15 and 29–30.

[6] Watt, 'Appeasement: the rise of a revisionist school?' *op. cit.* 208.

[7] Admiral Sir Ernle Chatfield to Sir Warren Fisher, 4 June 1934. Lord Chatfield Papers. I am indebted to the present Lord Chatfield and to Professor A. T. Patterson for permission to consult this collection.

[8] Chatfield memorandum on League of Nations reform, August 1936. Chatfield Papers.

'best parts' of the globe — and the material resources needed to realize the desire in the face not only of nationalist oppositions, but, far worse, predatory 'have-not' imperial rivals such as Japan and Italy. Reduced to a one-power naval standard and an army and air force barely adequate for the duties of imperial defence, an over-extended Empire had been confronted by three major powers, all of whom appeared to have hostile intentions:

> We are in a position of having threats at both ends of the Empire from strong military Powers, i.e., Germany and Japan, while in the centre we have lost our traditional security owing to the rise of an aggressive spirit in Italy accompanied by an increase in her military strength. So long as that position remains unresolved diplomatically, only very great military and financial strength can give the Empire security.[9]

Like strategy, diplomacy also worked, to borrow Professor Howard's phrase, within an interdependent global system.[10] Although the Foreign Office did occasionally reflect the compartmentalized perspective of a world divided among area desks and embassies, for the most part this did not apply at senior levels, and when it did the Cabinet or defence committees were usually prompt to intervene. It can be argued as a general proposition that the members of the foreign policy-making élite had the global picture close at hand. To cite a typical document, in March 1938 the Foreign Office, in an appreciation of the international situation following Germany's annexation of Austria, pointed to seven developments since mid-1936 that had transformed England's position in world power politics. These were first, the consolidation of links among Rome, Berlin and Tokyo; second, the Sino—Japanese War; third, the Spanish Civil War; fourth, the Soviet purges and the consequent weakness of the Red Army; fifth, the *Anschluss*; sixth, the dangerous state of Anglo—Italian relations; and seventh, the Palestine crisis in the Middle East. And although the same document anticipated the coming crisis over Czechoslovakia as the most likely cause of war, the outlook in the Empire was uniformly gloomy as well: imperial priorities could

---

9 Chiefs of Staff (sub-committee), 'Review of Imperial Defence', 22 February 1937. C.P. 73 (37). Cab(inet) 24/268. Public Record Office, Chancery Lane and Portugal Street, London. All unpublished references, unless otherwise noted, are from the British government archives held at the Public Record Office.

10 M. Howard, *Studies in war and peace* (London, 1970), p. 124.

gravely undermine England's hand in European affairs.[11] Britain's predicament, in other words, had world-wide dimensions, and European questions and the German menace in particular were only an aspect of that global predicament.

Increasing signs of a formally orchestrated attack from its enemies made the dilemmas seem even worse, but even failing such collusion, it was argued, if Britain attempted to respond to one threat with force it would expose its other interests to probing by some other opportunist. Its weaknesses were thus interdependent. A few ships lost in a Mediterranean war in 1935 might mean the collapse of British sea power in the Far East later on. Conversely, if the fleet was moved to Singapore in January 1938 or June 1939, Italy would have free hands to move against Egypt and Suez. A mere dozen anti-aircraft guns and a squadron of fighters for Egypt in late 1937 would weaken England's position in Europe, a point which also applied during the Munich crisis when British army commitments in Palestine and Egypt were at their pre-war height. The examples could be multiplied. In such circumstances British policy tended to be a search for priorities and constraints rather than dramatic solutions. 'What has to be considered', wrote Neville Chamberlain during the 1932 Shanghai crisis, 'is one set of risks balanced against the other.'[12] Here was a ruling principle of imperial security.

One observer of international affairs, lately of the Foreign Office, was able to arrive at a fairly judicious public estimate of the policy implications of this general weakness. Britain, noted E. H. Carr in late 1937, had too many enemies and could not afford to pursue a policy 'which leads straight to the consolidation of a German—Italian—Japanese bloc confronting the rest of the world'. Couching the options in global terms, Carr saw just two practical strategies:

> Short of a complete reversal of Japanese policy I see no prospect of a lasting agreement between Great Britain and Japan — if only because such an agreement would have to be bought at the price of our friendship with the United States . . . But if we cannot abandon the Pacific to Japan, then we must seek to ease the tension nearer home. Two courses are open to us. We can come to terms with Italy

---

11 Foreign Office note on revised terms of reference for military planning, March 1938. C1651/42/18 [(F.O.371)/21656]. Hereafter all Foreign Office references, unless otherwise noted, are from the F.O. 371 class.

12 Cited in C. Thorne, 'The Shanghai crisis of 1932: the basis of British policy', *The American Historical Review*, 75:6 (October 1970).

— terms which would probably involve the recognition of Italy as the leading Mediterranean Power — in order to withstand German claims; or we can come to terms with Germany in order to re-assert our supremacy in the Mediterranean against Italy.[13]

London's policy-makers perceived their international predicament in the same stark terms and drew approximately the same conclusions. Competing commitments and strained resources were recurring themes in the earliest defence debates of 1933–4, and the coming of the crisis with Italy in 1935 produced in official London something of a siege mentality, a collective psychology so pessimistic that it often bordered on defeatism. It was no accident that those who were closest to the rearmament programme and privy to the secrets of the defence effort were among the most fervent advocates of those policies that history has lumped together under the opprobrium of 'appeasement'. The relationship between military strategy and diplomacy was direct and profound, and any study of pre-war British foreign policy that ignored the strategic element in appeasement would have to be deemed quite inadequate.

The analysis of British foreign and defence policies in the Eastern Mediterranean[14] from the Abyssinian crisis to the outbreak of the war in Europe in September 1939 provides the political historian with a fascinating study of detailed decision-making — one that, it is hoped, may also offer some important insights into the policy of appeasement. It was in the Mediterranean, above all, that British strategic consider-ations interacted with diplomatic interests and that the oppressive weight of global weakness most frequently impinged upon local events. Thus it is in London's Mediterranean policy that the aforementioned relationship of empire to appeasement must be explored. In an important sense too, it was here that the premises and assumptions, unspoken and explicit, that underlay the entire policy of appeasement were most clearly and consistently in evidence. The internal debate

---

13 E. H. Carr, 'Britain as a Mediterranean power', *The Gust Foundation Lecture*, University College of Nottingham (November 1937).

14 This study is primarily concerned with British policies in the 'Eastern Mediterranean' but occasionally addresses itself as well to the problems of Anglo–Italian relations, Anglo–French relations in the Mediterranean and strategic issues in the central Mediterranean. Greece, Turkey, Palestine and Egypt are thus included, but Spain and Yugoslavia have been excluded, save where they intruded into the above issues. For analytical reasons that have been mentioned, it is not desirable to delineate artificial geographical parameters.

within the British government over the Mediterranean crisis that was touched off by Mussolini's aggression in mid-1935 and resolved only two and a half years later with the resignation of the Foreign Secretary, Anthony Eden, became a broader forum for the articulation of a variety of views about the nature of the global predicament and the proper way to approach it.

At a more theoretical level of explanation, the student of bureaucratic decision-making and foreign policy[15] will find much of interest in a detailed analysis of the formulation of Mediterranean appeasement. How foreign policy decisions were arrived at under the Baldwin and Chamberlain leaderships is a subject at least as relevant as the question of motivations; but the literature of appeasement is seriously deficient in this respect, partly because of the nature of the available sources, but also, one suspects, because of the prevailing association of certain personalities, such as Chamberlain and his personal advisers, with the disastrous course of pre-war policies.

That Neville Chamberlain's unorthodox ideas on external problems often found their way into official thinking is beyond dispute; but his alleged role as the sole initiator of diplomatic strategy and tactics requires careful re-examination. Like any other leader facing difficult choices and dilemmas, Chamberlain sought advice from official and unofficial sources and often acted on such advice, sometimes, indeed without questioning it closely enough. It will be argued in later chapters that his attempts to reach accord with Italy after June 1937 did not amount to a departure from established policy but were consistent with Cabinet decisions taken as early as 1933 and confirmed during and after the Abyssinian crisis.[16] The architects and initiators of Mediterranean policy were in fact those leading bureaucrats and military planners closely associated with the rearmament programme who were able, using a variety of techniques and channels of influence, to implement their ideas. Mediterranean appeasement is best interpreted as a device conceived by planners to mitigate temporary strategic weaknesses and implemented by a Prime Minister whose decision-making role on this issue was decisive primarily in the execution stages.

15 For some theoretical expositions, see Graham Allison, *Essence of decision: explaining the Cuban missile crisis* (Boston, 1971); Morton Halperin, *Bureaucratic politics and foreign policy* (Washington, D.C., 1971). Richard Neustadt, *Alliance politics* (New York, 1970).
16 For a somewhat similar interpretation of the antecedents of Chamberlain's German policy, cf. W. N. Medlicott, 'Britain and Germany: the search for agreement 1930—1937', *The Creighton Lecture in History* (London, 1969).

1. The Heritage: Neglect of Security

When it suddenly became apparent in the summer of 1935 that England and Italy were on a direct collision course because of the former's commitments to the League of Nations and the principle of collective security and because of what Sir Robert Vansittart dubbed Mussolini's mania for fame and sand in the obscure East African country of Abyssinia,[1] the British Government could not have been more surprised or less prepared for a crisis in the Mediterranean. For more than two years the Government's leading military and diplomatic policy-makers had analysed and debated the double menace to British interests posed by Hitler's Germany and an expanding, militaristic Japan. But no thought had been given nor preparations made for a confrontation with Italy. In fact, that power — along with France and the United States of America — had been explicitly excluded from the Empire's strategic list of possible enemies.

The upshot, as one official viewed the opening of the Abyssinian affair, was this: 'The fact is we are properly caught with our trousers down.'[2] When the English Chiefs of Staff convened in early August to discuss the crisis and to order measures to improve the Mediterranean situation, their spokesman, Admiral Sir Ernle Chatfield, First Sea Lord and Chief of the Naval Staff, was shocked by the result. 'I was surprised', he told Vansittart, Permanent Under-secretary of the Foreign Office, 'to find how very unready the other two Services were and how long it would take them before they could offer any effective resistance to Italian action by land or air. The Naval situation is bad enough.' Everything possible should be done to forestall hostilities with Italy, Chatfield went on, at least until the Services were ready for a war in the Mediterranean.[3] Vansittart passed on this warning to his political

---

1 For purposes of consistency 'Abyssinia' is used throughout this study in place of the more familiar modern usage 'Ethiopia'. The former most frequently appears in the pre-war British documents.
2 The official was Colonel Henry Pownall, then serving as an aide to Sir Maurice Hankey in the Cabinet office.
3 Chatfield to Vansittart, 8 August 1935. Cab.21/411.

superior, Foreign Secretary Sir Samuel Hoare, and added his own bleak moral:

> This country has been so weakened of recent years that we are in no position to take a strong line in the Mediterranean – anyhow not for some time. We are in fact experiencing, on of course a far less marked scale, something of the impotence . . . which we experienced without present hope of remedy in the Far East. I have of course for many years past been stressing our weakness to successive Governments and dwelling on its inevitable political consequences.[4]

England's Mediterranean dilemma – which was to have far-reaching 'inevitable political consequences' for its foreign policy between 1935 and 1940 – had existed for some years, but, until Mussolini's rude challenge, in an incipient and latent form. To most Englishmen the Mediterranean was as much an 'all-red route' in the 1920s and early 1930s as it had been before and during the Great War. Britain's hegemony was apparently assured by its control of both major entrances to the sea, at Gibraltar in the west and Suez in the east, through its strategic naval base at Malta in the central Mediterranean, and by the year-round presence of a substantial part of the main English fleet in its waters. Moreover, under the terms of the Lausanne peace treaty Turkey's exclusive control of the Straits had been ended and the Admiralty could show the flag in the Black Sea. In the Middle East Britain had acquired strategic depth and reserve for the defence of the canal through its mandated rule in Palestine, and its regional interests seemed well guarded by the mobility of the Mediterranean fleet and by a network of mutually reinforcing military garrisons and air bases in Iraq, Palestine, Transjordan and Egypt. Britain dominated the eastern shores of the Red Sea through its unrivalled political influence in Arabia and its control of the key base of Aden. No other great power with Mediterranean aspiration could match this grip over the region's commanding heights and its communications system: England was *the* Mediterranean power, an entrenched *status quo* defender *par excellence.*[5]

This post-war hegemony, however, rested on a deceptive foundation

---

4 Vansittart to Hoare, 9 August 1935. *Ibid.*
5 The best general studies of the inter-war Mediterranean are two older works: Elizabeth Monroe, *The Mediterranean in politics* (London, 1938); and Royal Institute of International Affairs, *Political and strategic interests of the United Kingdom* (London, 1939). Less dependable but sometimes useful is M. Boveri, *Minaret and Pipe-line* (London, 1938). Cf. also bibliography to this study.

of strength and was more apparent than real. As is well known, the 1920s and early 1930s were hard, lean years for Britain's fighting Services: peace-time retrenchment, Cabinet and Treasury parsimony, the 'Ten-Year Rule' and the disarmament will-o'-the-wisp all took their toll in this age of domestic appeasement and international illusions. Additionally, the navy were committed to spending every available penny allocated for imperial defence on their giant base at Singapore, strategic hinge of Far Eastern security.[6] In these circumstances Mediterranean defence received very low priority and grave deficiencies were permitted to stand untouched. Malta, Gibraltar, the Mediterranean Fleet, Egypt and every other regional British interest were void of air defences. Most of the warships maintained in the fleet were dated, unmodernized and scarcely fit for war duty. The military and air forces kept in the Middle East were equipped for imperial policing duties rather than for strategic defence. This was not exceptional, however: Britain's world-wide interests and commitments far out-ran its military capacity to defend them. Perhaps Sir Maurice Hankey, Secretary of the Cabinet and Committee of Imperial Defence, had the Mediterranean example in mind when he charged in 1934 that the government had starved the Services for too many years: 'They can stage Navy Weeks, Tatoos [*sic*] and Air Displays, but cannot sustain a major war. We have but a façade of Imperial Defence. The whole structure is unsound.'[7]

Another dimension of Mediterranean insecurity derived from its unique geography and from the changing technological face of warfare. The bottle-necks and narrows of the Mediterranean route made shipping in those waters especially vulnerable to a *guerre de cours* waged by submarines, light surface vessels and aircraft. Enthusiasts of modern air and naval technology argued even in the 1920s that Mediterranean hegemony was an antiquated ideal belonging to the age of sea power. In 1925 the military writer Captain B. H. Liddell Hart postulated what was later to be known as the 'Cape School' strategy:

> When to the proved menace of submarine power is added the potential effect of aircraft attack against shipping in the narrow seas,

---

6 On problems of inter-war defence, see S. W. Roskill, *Naval policy between the wars. I: The period of Anglo–American antagonism 1919–1929* (London, 1968); Basil Collier, *The defence of the United Kingdom* (London, 1957); Robin Higham, *Armed forces in peacetime* (New Brunswick, N.J., 1963); S. W. Roskill, *Hankey, man of secrets*, vol. 2 (London, 1972), and vol. 3 (1974).
7 Hankey, 'Defence Requirements', 22 June 1934. Cab.63/49.

it is time the British people awoke to the fact that, in case of such a war, the Mediterranean would be impassable, and that this important artery would have to be abandoned. Thus, as a strategical asset, the Suez Canal has lost a large part of its value in face of modern naval and air development – for in such a war we should be driven to close the Mediterranean route, and divert our imperial communications round the Cape of Good Hope.[8]

This was a radical and highly pessimistic viewpoint – far *too* pessimistic as events were later to demonstrate – and among official strategists only Air Ministry planners seem to have shared its conclusion. In 1931 the air staff drew the attention of the Service chiefs to 'the magnitude of the threat to our sea communications in the Mediterranean which is implicit in the development of the air power of France and Italy'. Shipping would have to evacuate the Mediterranean, and Malta and Gibraltar would be of dubious utility in the event of war with either of these powers.[9] As early as 1923 the Services had agreed that mercantile shipping should not use the Mediterranean route in wartime, but the air staff's generally bleak prognosis was regarded with scepticism at the Admiralty. Inter-war naval officers – Chatfield prominently among them – still regarded air power as an unknown, unproven factor and in general took a 'confident, even supercilious attitude to the threat from the air'.[10] As Liddell Hart remarked, this complacency was more an act of faith than a reasoned judgement: 'A battleship had long been to an admiral what a cathedral is to a bishop.'[11] The unresolved air–naval debate had its bearing on Mediterranean decisions, for in the absence of actual war observation – first provided by the wars in Spain and China in the latter 1930s – the Chiefs of Staff and their joint planning assistants were able to tell the Government only that they regarded the air threat to sea communications and installations as problematic. To cite but one consequence, the lack of consensus among the Services was one reason why so little was done in the inter-war years to improve the vulnerable defences of England's primary Mediterranean naval base, Malta.

As the fighting Service most dependent on Mediterranean security,

8   B. H. Liddell Hart, *Paris, or the future of war* (London, 1925).
9   Chief of Air Staff, 'The Air Threat to our Sea Communications in the Mediterranean', C.O.S. 274, 7 July 1931. Cab.53/22.
10 Arthur Marder, 'The Royal Navy and the Ethiopian crisis of 1935–36'. *The American Historical Review* (June 1970), 1344.
11 Sir B. H. Liddell Hart, *Memoirs*, vol. 1 (London, 1965), p. 326.

the Royal Navy took a strangely ambivalent attitude to the defence of that imperial artery. On the one hand, the Mediterranean was a valuable training ground for fleet manoeuvres and exercises, an excellent strategic centre for a move either east or west, and a vital short-cut to India and the Far East. Operating on what amounted in practice to a one-power standard, the navy was still responsible for the defence of sea-borne commerce and for the protection of British interests in two hemispheres. The basis of imperial defence under these conditions was the mobility of the main fleet, its capacity to proceed from central waters to an emergency situation and to arrive there in fighting condition. The defence of Singapore and of the vast eastern British Empire to a great degree depended on this mobility, for the Government had ruled that a provision of a permanent fighting fleet in the Far East was beyond its resources. The Mediterranean—Suez—Red Sea route was by far the shortest, fastest and cheapest passage to Singapore; it was, accordingly, a vital interest of British naval strategy.

On the other hand, to borrow Miss Monroe's apt phrase, successive British governments and strategists had long regarded the Mediterranean as a means rather than an end.[12] In inter-war British strategy, at least before the Abyssinian crisis, its primary role was as a training and staging ground for Far Eastern defence. 'In the strategic field the problems involved in the reinforcement of the Eastern Fleet and of passing convoys carrying military reinforcements to Singapore received great attention' in the 1920s. 'Again and again did the naval staff prepare detailed plans to cover such contingencies.'[13] As primary route of passage the Mediterranean naturally figures in these plans; and it also played a role in a series of fleet exercises held within its confines from 1925 onward — the purpose of which was to explore some problem of Far Eastern defence.[14] But the contingency of an actual Mediterranean war was never taken seriously between 1919 and 1935 and the historian will uncover very few references to such a possibility in the records of the C.I.D., Chiefs of Staff and the three Services. In the pre-Abyssinian period the only British war plan dealing with Mediterranean security was the Suez Canal defence scheme — and that envisaged *Japanese*

12 Monroe, *The Mediterranean in politics*, p. 1.
13 Roskill, *Naval policy between the wars*, p. 537.
14 *Ibid*. pp. 537–9. In a letter to the author dated 18 August 1972, Captain Roskill remarks, 'About naval policy in the Mediterranean, I am sure you are right to say that it got very little attention in the 1920's. I was on that station for a good deal of that period and well recall how static naval affairs were.'

sabotage.[15] The Mediterranean figured in imperial defence policy as a subordinate communications system whose role was to enhance British security in areas distant from the taming influence of the main fleet.

There was an underlying economic and political logic beneath this set of strategic priorities. As a source of trade, markets, investment and raw materials the British Empire east of Suez was of vastly greater significance than the undeveloped and apparently unpromising Mediterranean. English businesses, to be sure, had substantial investments in, for instance, Spanish mining, the Greek public debt, Egyptian cotton and the Suez Canal Company, and Middle East oil, but none of these — save possibly the last — had the actual or potential importance of the capital invested in India, Burma, Malaya, the East Indies and the country that Neville Chamberlain once called the world's most promising market — China. The oil wells of Iran and Iraq and their outlets at Haifa and Tripoli were of course of great commercial and strategic value, but in the inter-war years even oil was of greater potential than realized wealth. Britain took about 20 per cent of its total petroleum imports in 1937 from Middle East sources, but over 50 per cent came from Venezuela, the Dutch West Indies and the U.S.A.[16] England imported about 11 per cent of its foodstuffs and raw materials from the countries of the Mediterranean, but this consisted mainly of non-essential and replaceable commodities. The entire Mediterranean bought less from Britain than India alone, and even this market was to contract in the 1930s when Germany took over the economic life of the Balkans. Up to 15 per cent of Britain's total imports — including jute, tin, rubber, tea, oil and rice — passed through the Suez route, but in the last resort these could be diverted to the Cape and Panama traffic.[17]

The priorities of British strategy also reflected the government's commitments to the Far Eastern Dominions, Australia and New Zealand. At the 1923 Imperial Conference, meeting in the aftermath of the signature of the Washington treaties and the abrogation of the Anglo—Japanese alliance, the Admiralty unveiled to the Dominions their plan for the development of Singapore as a repair and fuelling base, the key to their strategy of rapid reinforcement of the Far East. The conference took note of the 'deep interest' of the eastern Dominions in the provision of the Singapore base and of 'the necessity

---

15 The plan is in Adm(iralty) 116/3489.
16 Monroe, *The Mediterranean in politics*, pp. 9—13.
17 *Ibid*. pp. 12—34, 249, 253.

for the maintenance of safe passage along the great route to the East through the Mediterranean and Red Sea'.[18] In early 1924 the Labour Cabinet of Ramsay MacDonald angered the naval staff by abandoning the Singapore scheme on the ground that it contradicted the spirit of Labour's internationalist foreign policy; but the government fell and its successor, the Conservative administration of Stanley Baldwin, lost no time in breathing fresh life into the navy's pet project.[19] From that day forward the development and defence of Singapore was the dominant theme of inter-war naval policy as well as a cardinal link in intra-Commonwealth diplomacy. And when, on a memorable occasion ten years later, the Chancellor of the Exchequer, Neville Chamberlain, tried to have work on the base postponed in order to conserve resources for home defence, he was soundly trounced: not even the British Communist Party had stooped *that* low, the First Lord complained.[20] Shortly before the outbreak of the 1935 Mediterranean war scare Sir Maurice Hankey had toured the Dominions in an effort to elicit from their governments further financial assistance towards the mounting costs of imperial defence. As Hankey had warned his chiefs before his departure, this policy involved a tightening of British obligations to the paying Dominions, particularly to the Australians, for any weakening of resolve on the Singapore base question would undermine Commonwealth co-operation in naval strategy.[21] This − added to the feelings of impotence left by the 1931−2 Far Eastern crisis[22] − explained something of the pre-war determination of the British to hold the situation in the Far East, even if it meant making sacrifices in, for instance, the Mediterranean. Here was a key to the system of priorities that characterized grand strategy from 1935 to early 1939.

In view of Britain's economic, political and strategic interests and commitments east of Suez, its neglect of the security of its communications through the Mediterranean and Middle East is all the harder to comprehend; and the above-mentioned factors do not provide

18 Command 1987, *Imperial Conference 1923, Summary of Proceedings.*
19 Cf. Roskill, *Naval policy between the wars*, pp. 420−2, 432.
20 50th and 51st mtgs. of the ministerial committee on disarmament, 25 and 26 June 1934. Cab.16/110. Chamberlain's proposal was attacked by the Services as 'heartbreaking', as a 'policy of despair and defeatism'; in fact, it was − as events subsequently demonstrated − highly realistic.
21 See Hankey's notes of 3 August 1934. Cab.21/434.
22 Cf. Thorne, 'The Shanghai crisis of 1932: the basis of British policy', *op. cit.* for a persuasive discussion of Britain's interlocking problems and weaknesses and the latent contradictions of its policies in the Far East in the early 1930s.

an entirely satisfactory explanation. It is difficult to avoid the conclusion that a good deal of the neglect was the offspring of complacency
and that that complacency in turn derived from a heritage of virtually
unchallenged Mediterranean supremacy. The last serious threat to this
supremacy had come from pre-war czarist Russia and that country had
been so weakened by war, revolution and civil war that until 1936 its
aspirations to the waters of the East Mediterranean were not taken
seriously in London. The new republic of Turkey was an obvious
candidate for revisionism, but its hold on the Dardanelles had been
loosened and it was in any event preoccupied with internal development.
Greece and Spain were weak and friendly, so only France and Fascist
Italy could be considered potential challengers to the Mediterranean
status quo. In 1933, however, even these two powers were excluded,
with America, from those countries against whom defensive plans and
preparations were to be taken by the new defence requirements subcommittee of the C.I.D.[23] In view of the Government's worries in
Europe and the Far East, the decision to ignore the hypothesis of
Mediterranean war was understandable. But it was also full of risk, for
the political and diplomatic relationships of the Mediterranean powers
were anything but stable. Here it will be advisable to review briefly
some of the dominant themes of Britain's involvement in those relationships in the years preceding the Abyssinian crisis.

In the first place, the British had made a conscious and consistent
attempt to form a good working relationship with Benito Mussolini's
Italy, a policy which incidentally involved a good deal of tacit
acquiescence in the Duce's programme of imperialism. The policy of
Mediterranean appeasement can be traced to the Corfu incident of
1923, when the powers initiated the practice of punishing the victim of
aggression: Mussolini's bombardment of Corfu was tacitly approved as
the other great powers took steps to humiliate Greece.[24] But it was Sir
Austen Chamberlain, Foreign Secretary in Baldwin's 1924—9
Conservative administration, who presided over the real flowering of the
Anglo—Italian *entente*. Chamberlain shared with many English
conservatives a certain fondness for Italian vacations and a

[23] Cf. N. Gibbs, 'British strategic doctrine, 1918—1939', in M. Howard, *The
theory and practice of war* (London, 1965) pp. 203—7; P. Kemp, *Key to
victory* (Boston, 1957), pp. 18—20; W. Hancock and M. Gowing, *Britain's war
economy* (London, 1949), pp. 63—5.
[24] See J. Barros, *The Corfu incident of 1923: Mussolini and the League of
Nations* (Toronto, 1966).

complementary ideological sympathy for Mussolini's style of governing. 'I am confident that he is a patriot and a sincere man; I trust his word when given and I think that we might easily go far before finding an Italian with whom it would be as easy for the British Government to work.'[25] The Duce was a good man to do business with and if his regime restricted personal liberties, it also brought stability and order to the Italian nation.[26] Sir Ronald Graham, British Ambassador to Rome, was another sympathetic observer of the Fascist experiment and his dispatches evidently carried some weight with the Foreign Office and Cabinet.[27] Mussolini's diplomatic support for the 1925 Locarno treaties delighted Chamberlain: Austen, like his half-brother Neville, believed that the key to European peace lay in the establishment of a sound, working arrangement among the four great powers, England, France, Germany and Italy, and Mussolini's diplomatic ideas pointed in the same conservative direction.[28] Implicit in this conception was the idea of spheres of influence and of limited acquiescence in revisionism – though at the expense of the smaller powers. Thus Austen Chamberlain ceded to Italy the Jarabub on the Egyptian–Libyan border, silently accepted all of Mussolini's claims over Albania and negotiated an important agreement in 1927 whereby the two powers agreed to respect the imperial *status quo* in the Red Sea region.[29]

The vital point was that Mussolini's revisionist foreign policy carefully avoided a direct challenge to England's Mediterranean supremacy. Most of his grandiose demands were directed against the French Empire and against France's allies in Eastern Europe, particularly Yugoslavia. Italy's demands for concessions in North Africa, its support for separatism in Yugoslavia, its diplomatic policies in the Adriatic and Balkans and its insistence on full naval parity with France were the touchstones of a Franco–Italian rivalry that constituted the greatest danger to Mediterranean stability in the pre-Abyssinian period.[30] The dispute over naval armaments – the offspring of Italy's theoretical

25 C. Petrie, *The life and letters of Sir Austen Chamberlain* (London, 1940), vol. 2, pp. 295–6.
26 R. Bosworth, 'The British press, the Conservatives, and Mussolini, 1920–34', *The Journal of Contemporary History*, 5:2 (1970).
27 P. Edwards, 'The Foreign Office and Fascism 1924–1929', *ibid.*
28 F. Marzari, *Mare nostrum* (forthcoming), chaps. 2 and 3.
29 *Ibid.* and Sir G. W. Rendel, *The sword and the olive* (London, 1957).
30 E. M. Robertson, 'Mussolini and Ethiopia: the prehistory of the Rome Agreements of January 1935', in *Essays in Diplomatic History, in Memory of D. B. Horn*, M. Anderson and R. Hatton (eds.) (London, 1970).

intransigence and France's security mania — was responsible, along with British caution and American isolation, for the collapse of the naval arms control system established at Washington.[31] The French took the Italian challenge very seriously and by the early 1930s had changed their military plans and strategic dispositions to meet the possibility of a Mediterranean war.[32]

Britain's attitude to this Mediterranean rivalry was one of acute concern; its policy, active mediation without the acceptance of binding commitments. In one of his general memoranda on world affairs Vansittart pointed in May 1931 to Italy as 'leader of the revisionist group' and commented on the heat and polar distance that alternately characterized Franco—Italian relations. The Chief of the Imperial General Staff, in one of the few strategic analyses of Italian power, concluded that Italy's goal was imperial expansion by peaceful or war-like means; Mussolini's policy was 'playing with fire' and this would make him a potential danger to world peace.[33] The British were also fully apprised of the complications inherent in this situation for the French. Shortly after Hitler's advent to power, for instance, the head of the French naval staff, Admiral Durand-Viel, complained to Chatfield of the 'impossible task' he faced in having to prepare for war with Italy as well as Germany. Naval, air and military dispositions had to take into account the Mediterranean as well as Europe, a fact that made Italian demands for parity utterly unreasonable. Were Italy friendly, the predicament of French strategy would be eased; but Mussolini was ambitious and hostile to France. And this was why naval disarmament was out of the question and why — much against English wishes — the French were forced to increase their submarine fleet. Chatfield drew the correct conclusion that the French navy were thinking of one thing only: war against Italy and Germany.[34]

In the early 1930s the British Foreign Office, playing the role of intermediary and message carrier, tried on numerous occasions to bring the two Mediterranean antagonists together. It was open to England, as the leading Mediterranean Great Power, to play a more direct role in the settlement of the dispute, for instance by acting as an external

---

[31] Cf. R. O'Connor, *Perilous equilibrium* (Kansas, 1960).
[32] Robertson, *op. cit.* p. 349.
[33] Vansittart, 'An Aspect of International Relations in 1931', May 1931. C.P.125(31). Cab.24/221; and Milne, 'The Military Tendencies of Italy', 6 February 1931. W(ar) O(ffice) 32/2548.
[34] Chatfield's record of private and unofficial talk with Admiral G. Durand-Viel, 1 April 1933. Chatfield Papers.

guarantor for the region. In 1927 the French and Italians had each suggested that some kind of pact modelled on the Locarno treaties would stabilize the Mediterranean and head off a naval arms race. In 1929 the French hinted that naval disarmament was a lost cause unless a pact of mutual guarantee was negotiated among the Mediterranean powers. Next year at the London Naval Conference they unofficially communicated to the British the text of such a pact, which, it was argued, would ease Franco–Italian tension and facilitate the search for arms control. The Foreign Office did not respond to that initiative, but the question arose once again in late 1931 in connection with London's attitude to the World Disarmament Conference. In a memorandum of 1 January 1932 Sir Robert Vansittart submitted that a 'Mediterranean Locarno' was an 'inducement' Britain might have to give France as a *quid pro quo* for French disarmament and the success of the conference. The Cabinet committee on disarmament agreed that the failure of the conference would be a 'disaster' and a 'catastrophe', but they were nonetheless unwilling to permit the British delegation to put forward or to agree to any 'Mediterranean Locarno' that might involve direct commitments for England. Britain would gain no additional security for its Mediterranean communications; it would face possible entanglement in local disputes in which it had no interest; the Dominions would be unlikely to back London in its role of Mediterranean guarantor and the issue might well split the Commonwealth. In essence, Britain would be accepting a strategic commitment greater than that required to protect its communications because, in the final analysis, it could avoid the Mediterranean entirely.[35]

   This unwillingness to sacrifice strategic freedom to obligations in the Mediterranean was to become a central theme of British policy during and after the Abyssinian affair. The Admiralty argued — with some logic — that the defence of the Far Eastern empire and of New Zealand and Australia was already a supremely difficult proposition; but if the navy was also tossed into the cauldron of Mediterranean politics then it might well prove impossible. Grand strategy therefore constrained England's diplomatic choices in the Mediterranean, and until the principles of strategy were changed — and this occurred only in 1939 —

---

35 Foreign Office, 'Memorandum respecting the Development of the Idea of a Mediterranean Pact', 2 July 1934. R3660/3366/67 (18389); and 'Report of a Cabinet Committee on a Mediterranean Locarno', January 1932. C.P.27(32). Cab.24/227.

18

London's range of decision and margin of flexibility there were sharply constricted.

Despite Britain's cautious isolationism and its disinclination to assume Mediterranean risks, France and Italy initiated diplomatic talks to compose their differences and these eventually culminated in the so-called Rome agreements of 7 January 1935, described by one historian as 'perhaps the last major example of classical imperialism in action in the Middle East'.[36] As is well known, the real author of this Latin *entente* was Adolf Hitler. His advent to German power in 1933 and the violent Nazi menace to Austria the following year convinced the French of the need to secure their southern flank and to draw Mussolini into common diplomatic action; likewise, the Italian dictator, having tentatively decided on expansion in East Africa, also required European security.[37] Negotiations opened in the autumn of 1934 but quickly bogged down on the issues of Austrian integrity and Italo–Yugoslav relations. In December the French Foreign Minister, Pierre Laval, begged his British counterpart, Sir John Simon, to use his good offices with Mussolini to promote agreement. Simon agreed, provided that no obligations were required from Britain, and confided to his diary early in January 1935 that negotiations – 'in which I have had an undisclosed part to the extent of cipher telegrams to Paris and Rome every day for the last week' – were far advanced. He was delighted by the outcome and described the accord as 'a good preparation for a wider European understanding. The two countries have settled their differences in Africa.'[38] In fact, however, Laval and Mussolini had lit a slow fuse to the Mediterranean powder-keg, and when the explosion came half a year later the British – partly because of their own vacillating and timid policies in early 1935 – found themselves in an acute global dilemma.

Mussolini thought (and he had some solid reasons for his assumption) that Laval had – at least tacitly – granted him a free hand in Abyssinia as the price of Italy's friendship and co-operation in Europe. By late January he had begun to sound out British opinion, but

[36] D. C. Watt, 'The secret Laval–Mussolini agreement of 1935 on Ethiopia', *Middle East Journal*, 15 (Winter 1971); reprinted in Robertson, *The origins of the Second World War*, pp. 225–42.

[37] Robertson, 'Mussolini and Ethiopia: the prehistory of the Rome Agreements', *op. cit.*; George W. Baer, *The coming of the Italian–Ethiopian war* (Cambridge, Mass., 1967); Geoffrey Warner, *Pierre Laval and the eclipse of France* (London, 1968); and *Documents diplomatiques français* (D.D.F.), Ière Ser., II, no. 180.

[38] Diaries of Sir John (later Viscount) Simon, 23 December 1934, and 1, 8 and 13 January 1935. By permission of the present Viscount Simon.

the Foreign Office lacked consensus, leadership and policy and made
little response to his initial overtures. Vansittart and Sir Eric
Drummond, Britain's Ambassador in Rome, did caution the Italians on
several occasions, but London's attention in early 1935 was centred on
Berlin and it had no decided policy on Abyssinia. The best and probably
last opportunity to blunt Mussolini's imperial designs was missed in
April when Simon and Ramsay MacDonald, the British Prime Minister,
met with the French and Italian leaders for consultations on Germany's
sensational repudiation of the armament restrictions embodied in the
Treaty of Versailles. The Italians came to the Stresa conference (11—14
April) expecting to discuss the Abyssinian question, but the British
delegation maintained a conspicuous silence, which Mussolini interpreted as acquiescence.[39] Simon, who had recently met with Hitler and
had been deeply impressed by his resolve to rehabilitate the German
people and to rid Europe of the communist plague, came away from
Stresa with no faith at all in the 'united front'. Hitler would go on re-
arming but he had no designs in the West; his fears of Russia were
'perfectly genuine' and no front could or should try to restrain him. If
Germany had to act, 'it is surely better that she act to the East. That
will at worst occupy her energies for a long time . . . '

> I greatly doubt whether the efficiency of the 'united front' is as
> great a controlling force on German policy as it might appear to be.
> Its value is not so much that it diverts and restricts Germany's
> present action as that it is our only security *if* Germany turns nasty.
> But to use it in empty and futile protests (Geneva, Stresa) seems to
> me to *weaken* its utility.[40]

Simon remarked in his diary that the result of Stresa had been to give
a strong *impression* of solidarity, and this provides the clue to Britain's
enigmatic policy. MacDonald warned the C.I.D. on 16 April that his
main impression of the meetings was that British rearmament might
have to be stepped up. The real danger was not German aggression; it
was the possibility that the French and Italians might go off the deep
end and force Hitler into some wild action. Britain was therefore
trying to restrain Paris and Rome.[41]

---

39 Baer, *op. cit.* pp. 118—29; and G. Thompson, *Front-line diplomat* (London,
1959), pp. 96—100.
40 Simon's diary, 11—14 April 1935; and his notes, dated 17 April, written
between Stresa and Geneva.
41 Such was Colonel Pownall's impression of the meeting. The official minutes in
Cab.2 do not convey the same impression, but Pownall's presence at the

The preoccupation of the British leaders in the spring of 1935 was to prevent a disastrous encirclement or preventive action against Germany. This involved reassuring the French and Italians and giving an impression of solidarity, but Simon and MacDonald certainly did not perceive the Stresa front as a device of anti-German politics or as a permanent feature of European diplomacy. Perhaps it was this tentative and highly qualified attitude that underlay British silence on the Abyssinian issue: if Stresa's only value was to give an immediate impression of solidarity and if Britain's real motive was to restrain France and Italy, then it might well seem the wiser and safer course to ignore areas of possible friction in the interest of apparent accord. In any event, the chance was missed and from then on a Mediterranean crisis was probably unavoidable. Through their silence and apparent indifference to Mussolini's designs on Abyssinia the British had merely encouraged Mussolini to adopt a harder, more inflexible line. Shortly after Stresa he 'reached his point of no return. From then on, he moved toward invasion as swiftly as he was able, believing that nothing in Europe would stand in his way.'[42]

This study is primarily concerned with the consequences and implications of the Italo–League crisis of 1935–6 for Britain's long-term strategic and diplomatic situation, particularly in the East Mediterranean. Necessarily, this imposes some severe limitations on the present treatment of the crisis itself. For instance, it is not within the scope of this thesis to discuss the tortuous, zigzag course of British foreign policy during the lengthy war scare. Nor is it necessary to make a study in detail of the British decision-making process at work in the same period, to review the total impact of the crisis on British naval policy, a fascinating subject already given admirable and probably definitive attention by Professor Marder.[43] Interesting and important as these and the other facets of British attitudes to the crisis are, to give them their scholarly due would require another dissertation. In what follows, therefore, two themes of policy which recur again and again in the pages of this study have been given highly selective treatment: first, what was the general attitude of leading British strategists to the crisis with Italy; second, how did they attempt to influence policy decisions?

meeting and his lengthy comment suggest that – as usual – he was being frank and truthful.
[42] Baer, *op. cit.* p. 139.
[43] Marder, *op. cit.*

Britain's Mediterranean policies during and after the Abyssinian affair bear the unmistakable stamp of the strategic thinking of two key individuals, one a naval officer, the other a civil servant: Admiral Sir Ernle Chatfield and Sir Maurice Hankey. Chatfield, First Sea Lord and Chief of Naval Staff from 1933 to 1938, has been called 'the finest officer the Royal Navy produced between the wars'.[44] He had administrative ability, experience, determination and intellectual power. He dominated the thinking of his own department (including the various First Lords he served) and — with Hankey — that of the Chiefs of Staff subcommittee. His views on strategy carried strong weight with the C.I.D. and Cabinet, partly because of the authority of his office (the navy was still the most influential service) but also because of his own high standing with ministers. In an era when the British were singularly unfortunate in their choice of military advisers, Chatfield's global perspective and his willingness to think systematically and logically about difficult questions of strategy were almost unique gifts. He appears to have viewed defence policy and diplomacy as interdependent and inseparable realms and he rarely hesitated to interpose his often controversial opinions into debates of high policy — a practice which more than once roused the ire of the Foreign Office. Chatfield's advice was not without political bias (he was conservative and an imperial isolationist), but in the main it seems to have been shaped by several central ideas about imperial defence.[45]

In the first place, Chatfield always conceived of naval defence in global categories and was virtually incapable of considering action in one theatre without weighing its possible immediate and long-range consequences for all the others. Second, in matters of imperial priority he was — like almost every other inter-war naval man — a committed 'easterner', a supporter of the Admiralty's policy of holding the eastern Empire through the development and defence of Singapore. Third, he believed in the absolute necessity of tying the Dominions into imperial defence, a conviction closely linked to his 'easterner' perspective. Fourth, and most important, he was convinced that Britain's margin of naval strength was too narrow to risk, that battleships took years to build and minutes to destroy, and that the schedule for modernizing and adding to the ageing fleet meant that the coming five or six years

44 *Ibid.* pp. 1336–7; also, Roskill, *Naval policy between the wars*, pp. 48–9.
45 The analysis of Chatfield's ideas is based on a reading of his memoirs, *The Navy and defence*, 2 vols. (London, 1942 and 1947); especially the second volume, *It might happen again*, pp. 65–90.

would be full of danger. Time was the major theme of Chatfield's thinking and advice. He wanted the standard of naval strength increased drastically, but he recognized that even this would take years to accomplish and that the coming period of danger when — as capital ships were docked for lengthy overhauls — Britain would grow progressively *weaker* in naval strength could not be avoided. For these reasons he was a fervent supporter of England's controversial 1935 naval treaty with Hitler and an equally fierce opponent of any policy that appeared likely to stretch Britain's commitments or risk war while rearmament was proceeding.

In his typically frank memoirs Chatfield made no secret of his attitude to the coming of the Abyssinian affair. The navy's 'vast responsibilities' were already stretched and it was quite impossible to fight simultaneously in Europe while holding the Far East unless a neutral or friendly Italy was ensured. The Mediterranean was the navy's main line of communications with India, Australia and New Zealand, and any act that left a hostile nation on that line was directly opposed to naval strategic interests. Chatfield thought that Britain's support for the League and Abyssinia involved an intolerable strain on the navy's resources and carried with it an unacceptable risk of war. He therefore hoped, as he wrote to his Mediterranean commander-in-chief, Admiral Sir W. W. Fisher, that 'the Geneva Pacifists will fail to get unanimity and the League will break up'.[46] Chatfield was making plans and preparations for a war against Italy that he grew daily more determined to avoid. He had no objection to the Italians establishing themselves in Abyssinia:

> I think it would prove to them to be a weakness rather than a strength and make them more anxious to be friends with us than the contrary. Actually it is a disaster that our statesmen have got us into this quarrel with Italy who ought to be our best friend in the future as she has been in the past because her position in the Mediterranean is a dominant one. Once we have made her an enemy the whole of our Imperial responsibilities become greater for obvious reasons. However, this miserable business of collective security has run away

---

[46] Chatfield to Fisher, 25 August 1935. Chatfield Papers. 'The bumptiousness of Italy is so great that it may be worth fighting her now to re-assert our dominance over an inferior race. But against that a hostile Italy is a real menace to our Imperial communications and defence system. We have relied on practically abandoning the Mediterranean if we send the Fleet east. For that reason I do not want to go to extreme measures.'

with all of our traditional interests and policies and we now have to be prepared as far as I can see to fight any nation in the world at any moment. Everybody will hate everybody else, and suspicion and intrigue will be worse than ever.

Meanwhile, I am in the unpleasant position of preparing for war and for a war which we have always been told could never happen . . . we shall have many losses in ships and men, thereby our world position as a naval power will be weakened.[47]

With all of this the Government's second key adviser on strategic questions concurred. Sir Maurice Hankey's reaction to the emergency with Italy and his thinking about imperial defence policy were in many ways identical to Chatfield's. Hankey also viewed with alarm and distaste the government's willingness to risk Mediterranean security for the League. Like his naval friend, he was personally committed to Far Eastern and Commonwealth defence, and there is no doubt that his fears on that score underlay much of his attitude to the crisis with Italy. Neither he nor Chatfield had any doubt that Mussolini must lose a war with England, but 'we are not in a position to take on the job without dangerous reactions elsewhere. We might easily have surprises and losses, particularly from the unknown factor of aircraft attack against ships. We should unquestionably incur heavy damage at Malta. And the financial drain might be serious . . .'[48]

The Times said of Hankey at the time of his death in 1963 that 'he stands out unchallenged as the greatest backroom figure of our political history'.[49] Winston Churchill once remarked: 'He knew everything: he could put his hands on anything: he knew everybody; he said nothing; he gained the confidence of all.'[50] Captain Roskill's fine three-volume biography, *Hankey: man of secrets*, more than confirms those assessments. For some twenty-five years and in spite of several changes of government Hankey presided over the inner machinery of the British Cabinet and Committee of Imperial Defence, wielding the substance of power and influence and eschewing the role of public figure. It is clear from Roskill's account and the documents now available that Hankey's influence remained undiminished until his retirement in 1938; that he supported both rearmament and the policy of appeasement; that he both influenced and drew inspiration from Neville Chamberlain; and

47 Chatfield to Admiral Sir F. Dreyer, 16 September 1935. Chatfield Papers.
48 Hankey to Vansittart, 21 November 1935. Cab.63/50.
49 *The Times*, 28 January 1963.
50 *The Daily Telegraph*, 26 January 1963.

that, in particular, he was actively involved from 1935 to 1938 in the search for friendship with Mussolini and security in the Mediterranean.

The measure of Hankey's influence is hard to take, but at the time of the Abyssinian crisis he held at least the following posts: Secretary of the Cabinet; Secretary of the Committee of Imperial Defence; Secretary of the Defence Policy and Requirements Subcommittee (which functioned as a kind of war cabinet during the crisis and then supervised rearmament); Secretary of the Chiefs of Staff Subcommittee; and Secretary of the all-important Defence Requirements Subcommittee, which was responsible for advising the government on the direction of rearmament and in many ways authored British pre-war strategic doctrine. He and his staff therefore dominated the apparently amorphus but actually tightly centralized 'defence by committee' policy-making process.[51] They controlled the agenda, circulated the documents, called some of the meetings and in general became the indispensable machinery within which most defence policy and many diplomatic decisions were made. Add to this Hankey's incredible energy, memory and knowledge and his mastery of political tactics and strategy, and one begins to fathom the man's justified reputation as perhaps the most powerful bureaucrat of recent Western history.

In the autumn of 1935 the Defence Requirements Subcommittee — chaired by Hankey and attended by the three chiefs of staff, Vansittart and Sir Warren Fisher, the powerful Permanent Under-secretary of the Treasury and head of the Civil Service — was reconstituted and met throughout October and much of November. Its debates set the tone for Britain's subsequent Mediterranean policy and they are analysed in some depth in the next chapter of this study; here it need only be said that the D.R.C. recommendations on the future of imperial defence reflected the ideas of Chatfield and Hankey and pointed out the need for a quick reconciliation with Mussolini. Hankey and his allies within the administration now moved to implement that objective.

During October and November the Foreign Office — exercised by the same fear of a 'mad dog' act by Mussolini which had so alarmed the Cabinet and Admiralty in August — supported mild sanctions and professed full support for the League front while simultaneously

---

51 The nature of this process from 1933 to 1939 awaits its historian, but some information may be gleaned from Franklyn Johnson's *Defence by committee* (London, 1960), and from D. C. Watt's 'Sir Warren Fisher and British rearmament against Germany', in *Personalities and policies*. The best available source is contained in the three volumes of *Hankey: man of secrets*.

pursuing two separate strategies designed to increase British security in the Mediterranean. First, an attempt was being made — largely at the insistence of the Chiefs of Staff — to draw the French into full strategic collaboration. Second, the British were attempting to arrange a *détente* in the Mediterranean with Mussolini. Neither of these attempts succeeded. Laval's reservations and wavering, his intriguing with the Italians and the 'profoundly unsatisfactory' outcome of the staff talks with the French unquestionably had a strong influence on the attitude of British strategists (Chatfield in particular seems to have harboured resentment about French disloyalty long after the event).[52] The policy of *détente* seemed about to succeed in early November, but Hoare — evidently sensing the political dangers in the wind — told the Defence Policy and Requirements Subcommittee that he wanted to postpone any further conciliation of Mussolini until after the election.[53] The upshot was that by the third week in November the Government had won an overwhelming victory at the polls, the Defence Requirements Subcommittee's report was released, France's attitude was still uncertain and the Mediterranean situation was highly insecure. Against this background the British had begun to weigh the risks involved in hardening the sanctions front by placing an embargo on oil shipments to Italy, an action that inevitably impeded its military campaign and that Mussolini had warned would force him to desperate measures.

In an exchange of anxious notes with other members of the Defence Requirements group on 19 and 20 November, Vansittart warned that in his opinion France was unreliable and that the imposition of the oil embargo would put Britain in the danger zone of war with Italy: 'I think the risks of an attack on this country will be appreciably nearer by the beginning of next year.'[54] Hankey took this to heart and quickly went to work on Prime Minister Stanley Baldwin and Hoare. He warned Baldwin in a 'Most Secret' memorandum of 25 November that 'our defence forces and defences are not at present in a state to justify us in running that risk, especially if we have regard to the other risks that we are running in other parts of the world'. England would defeat Italy, but a war might be prolonged and there might be losses of precious

---

52 Cf. Marder, *op. cit.* pp. 1346–50; Vansittart to Hankey, 19 November 1935. J8767/1/1 (19166); and Hankey, 'The reliability of French Co-operation', 11 December 1935. Cab.63/50.
53 D.P.R./13th Mtg., 5 November 1935. Cab.16/136.
54 Vansittart to Hankey and Chatfield, 20 November 1935; Hankey to Vansittart, 20 November 1935 and 21 November 1935. Cab.63/50.

capital ships and cruisers. France was unreliable and might leave England 'in the lurch'. Because of the concentration in the Mediterranean, Britain would be powerless to 'show a tooth' in the Far East where Singapore's defences were still incomplete. Finally, 'we should have embittered for many years the Italian people, whose country lies athwart our main line of communications to the Far East, to say nothing of the possible creation of deplorable relations with France'.[55] As discussions on the proposed oil embargo proceeded, Hankey, Chatfield and their allies kept pressing home this general line of attack. Their campaign peaked on 2 December when the Cabinet convened for a vital debate on future policy. The Service ministers used all of Hankey's and Chatfield's arguments to demonstrate to Hoare that diplomacy had far outstripped military resources, that the situation in the Far East was dangerous, that the air situation was very weak, that the naval staff feared the loss of capital ships and that the French attitude was still unsatisfactory:

> it was represented that our defence forces and defences in the Mediterranean were not in a proper condition for war, and from this point of view it was urged that an effort should be made to obtain peace, holding the threat of the oil sanction over Italy, and that the fixing of the date should not be decided until after a failure of peace discussions.[56]

It was neither whim nor accident that sent Hoare to Paris for his fateful talks with Laval; rather, it was the pressure of strategic advice persistently and convincingly brought to bear upon ministers that lay behind the actions of the Foreign Secretary while in France. To be sure, Hoare's bad tactics were his own and his motives were complex: Vansittart's responsibility and his influence over Hoare were great, and both men were exercised by fears of Germany and of an irreparable split with France. Nevertheless, the strategic element dominated British thinking and policy, and the responsibility for that policy was collective: Hoare was sacrificed but the efforts of Baldwin and his colleagues to dissociate themselves from the Hoare—Laval pact cannot be upheld by the historical evidence. Simon remarked in his diary, 'He [Hoare] greatly puzzled his late colleagues by asserting that he had been

---

55 Hankey, 'Italy and Abyssinia: the Proposed Oil Embargo', Most Secret memorandum for Prime Minister, 25 November 1935. *Ibid.* Hankey's version of a lengthy conversation with Hoare on the 25th is reprinted in S. Roskill, *Hankey: man of secrets*, vol. III (London, 1974), pp. 186–9.
56 Cab. Conclusions, 2 December 1935. Cab.23/82.

"pressed on all sides" to undertake this Paris negotiation. But he is a sick man, who needs a long rest.'[57]

Although this first major essay in Mediterranean appeasement was repudiated by the British public and then by the Government, the debate over future policy had only begun. From the perspective of strategy the events of December 1935 had resolved nothing — though the blow to the League and collective security was welcome — and the arguments for conciliating Mussolini remained as strong as before. Politically, however, the policy was evidently a dangerous one and Hoare's successor as Foreign Secretary, Anthony Eden, was understandably reluctant to become its second victim. Eden was more concerned to restore public faith in the Government, to repair Anglo–French relations and to reconstruct Britain's prestige abroad than to make any new gesture of amity to Italy.[58] Thus a conflict between what seemed strategically necessary and what appeared politically feasible was the major consequence of the Hoare–Laval fiasco for British foreign policy. This conflict, usually latent, sometimes open, was to become a central theme of the debate on the Mediterranean, which — against an ever-worsening global background — had now been joined among policy-makers and was to last for more than two years.

---

57 Simon Diaries, December 1935. There is a key document in the archives of the Dominions Office that effectively puts to rest the lingering myth that Hoare's visit to Laval was unplanned. He is quoted as having told the High Commissioners on 5 December that 'He was going to see M. Laval on Saturday, and if it was possible to reach an agreement with him on joint proposals, and if the Italian Government then showed any disposition to consider them', then it might be wise to postpone the oil embargo. D.O.114/66.
58 The Earl of Avon, *The Eden memoirs: facing the dictators* (London, 1962), pp. 315–30.

2. The Mediterranean and the Global Crisis, 1936-8

1. 'A tranquil Mediterranean without commitments'

The Abyssinian crisis had deeply unsettled the European diplomatic system. The failure of collective security and the League, the near-collapse of the Anglo—French *entente*, the estrangement of Italy and the bitter domestic divisions within the League nations were all to leave a permanent mark on the international order. In the short run Mussolini seemed the only victor, but we know that his imperialist triumph was actually the beginning of the end for Italian fascism. From the diplomatic, strategic and economic viewpoint, Italy lost far more than it gained in East Africa: Abyssinia, Anthony Eden liked to remark, was the greatest sanction of all. The only power that really gained anything from the dislocations of the crisis was Nazi Germany. For not only had Italy weakened its own capacity to influence events in Europe but France also had lost the strategic advantages accruing from the military agreements of May 1935. These factors have since been shown to have influenced Hitler's timing of the remilitarization of the Rhineland;[1] as usual, he displayed a masterly understanding of his opponents' weaknesses and the implications for his own policy. Of course the implications were apparent to others. Sir Eric Phipps, British Ambassador to Berlin, had cautioned the Foreign Office that it would suit Hitler's book to have Italy weakened. This weakness might well bring on German activity, especially against Austria, and France would be unlikely to intervene if Italy stood aside.[2] But if the flimsy 'Stresa' system was moribund so too was collective security. With Hoare—Laval, the so-called dual policy was demonstrated to be a contradiction: Britain and France could not have Stresa and the League at the same time, but they could easily have neither.

If the crisis of 1935—6 was something of a diplomatic revolution, for Britain it was also a strategic revolution. It has been shown how Italy

---

[1] E. M. Robertson, *Hitler's pre-war policy* (London, 1963), chap. 7.
[2] See remarks of Sir R. Vansittart during the Defence Requirements Sub-committee discussions in October 1935. Cab.16/112.

had been deliberately excluded in late 1933 from the provisions of the rearmament programme. The Mediterranean continued to play a vital role in defence policy as a line of communications but the priorities for expenditure and planning were to be found elsewhere, in Europe and the Far East. However, the confrontation between Mussolini and the League had now raised the prospect of a permanently antagonized Italy, and this, it was clear, could severely complicate Britain's global position. Not only would such a development put intolerable demands on its limited resources but it could also undermine its system of priorities and thus have far-reaching consequences in the Far East and nearer home. It has been suggested that these considerations weighed heavily on the Services during the period of tension in the Mediterranean. It was evident that temporary risks might become permanent disabilities unless the concepts of imperial defence were restudied and a consistent policy laid down for the future. An opportunity for this occurred in October 1935 when the Defence Requirements Subcommittee, re-constituted earlier in the year, met to sort out defensive needs and to debate policy recommendations. Whereas the Mediterranean had hardly figured in the 1934 defence debates, the autumn discussions of 1935 centred on the long-term implications of the Italo—League crisis for rearmament, planning and diplomacy. They are consequently an indispensable source for an understanding of Britain's Mediterranean policy in the post-Abyssinia period.

Aside from the issues of French intentions and the overriding German menace the D.R.C. debates[3] contain several recurring and inter-dependent themes relating to imperial defence. In the first place, Chatfield and Hankey, whose ideas dominated the discussions and recommendations, charged that Britain's commitments had far outrun its strength. Both blamed the Government's League policy for this: it had cost the country dearly in the Far East in 1931—2 and now it had antagonized another traditional friend, Italy. 'If we regarded Japan as our chief danger [argued Hankey], then it followed that the safety of our Mediterranean communications was essential, but now, owing to our commitments under the League, we were at loggerheads with Italy. In fact it appeared directly two nations quarrelled we were pushed to the brink of war against one or other of them, with whom we had no essential difference of opinion.' Chatfield thought it impossible to draw

---

3 What follows is based on the minutes of the D.R.C. meetings from 3 October to 5 November 1935. Cab.16/112.

up a programme of naval rearmament if collective security was to be maintained. The League system was based on a 'psychological mistake': people would fight or pay only when their own interests were involved. The heavenly dream of collective security, Chatfield would later remark, was the sailor's nightmare.

A second theme centred on the perception of Italian policy and Britain's future attitude to that power. Hankey and the Service chiefs thought the two empires had no irreconcilable interests — certainly Abyssinia was no British interest — and, but for the League, no conflict need have arisen. Italy's traditional interests lay in a friendly England, and a realistic diplomacy could restore amicable relations in the Mediterranean. Vansittart, however, saw the Abyssinian adventure as a 'stepping stone to greater things', the conquest of the Mediterranean. The British Empire thus did have a very real interest in the crisis and in resisting further Italian expansion. This issue, the interpretation of Italian policy, was not resolved during these discussions and was to remain a major source of conflict between the Services and Foreign Office; though Vansittart did not dissent from the Report which reflected the Services' viewpoint.

A third thread of the D.R.C. debates related to the implications of an insecure Mediterranean for Britain's Far Eastern commitments. British naval power was now considered inadequate for a simultaneous war against Japan and Germany but the same applied to Japan and Italy. In the latter case, Hankey and Chatfield argued, the Mediterranean and Middle East would have to be abandoned; to lose the Far East 'would be the start of the break-up of the Empire'. Chatfield's information suggested that the Japanese would take advantage of British difficulties in Europe and the prospects for an Anglo—Japanese settlement were not regarded as good. Here was the beginning of a system of imperial priorities.

Finally, what was the relationship of naval strength to this global predicament? In any two-front war it was plain that the 1932 naval standard would be heavily strained, particularly until 1939 when the replacement and modernization programmes would be completed. The emergence of a German naval threat, the Mediterranean war scare and the strain in Anglo—French relations all indicated the need for a programme of naval expansion. Hankey outlined his solution to the imperial dilemma, a new two-power naval standard plus a *rapprochement* with Italy:

we ought to have a Navy which could provide a safe defensive in the

Far East and also maintain our position *vis à vis* Germany. Mention had been made . . . of the danger of Italy and our lines of communication. He was inclined to leave out consideration of Italy's strength in assessing the requirements of the Navy as he felt that Italy will be exhausted after the present trouble, and in any case it should be possible for this country to get on comfortable terms with her again . . . No risk could be taken in the Far East. If Japan could defeat us there she could overrun the East and we should be in an impossible position with Australia and New Zealand cut off. The whole security of the Empire and maintenance of our prestige in the world depended on the possession of a defence which without risk could leave us in a strong defensive position in the East in the event of trouble in the West.

In their Report of 21 November 1935 the D.R.C. members noted that the Mediterranean crisis had exposed Britain to probings in Europe and the Far East. The main theme was the German menace and the consequent overwhelming arguments 'for avoiding any further estrangement either of Japan . . . or of any Mediterranean Power which lies athwart our main artery of communication to the East. Least of all could we contemplate without the gravest misgiving an estrangement with Japan and a Mediterranean Power at once.' The D.R.C. stressed that the priorities remained Germany and Japan and recommended the adoption in principle of a new standard of naval strength. but it was materially impossible to make provisions against Italy as well, especially if 'an appropriate policy can be pursued in the international field to counter this'. There was renewed need for an 'ultimate policy of accommodation and neighbourliness with Italy'.[4]

Here in the recommendations of a small group of civil servants and military planners were the essential outlines of British policy in the Mediterranean for the period 1936 to 1940. The Abyssinian crisis was to make no change in global defence policy; diplomacy would somehow have to fill the gap in the Mediterranean. That these recommendations were fully ratified by the Cabinet in early 1936 (although approval for the new naval standard was withheld) is an indication that the Government shared the anxiety of the Services eventually to liquidate their Mediterranean difficulties and return to the *status quo ante* in that region. However, the collapse of the Hoare–Laval scheme meant that

---

4 Third Report of the Defence Requirements Subcommittee (D.R.C. 37) 21 November 1935. C.P. 26(36). Cab.24/259.

Britain was committed for the remainder of the Abyssinian war to some kind of sanctions front. The Cabinet had been deeply shaken by the intense reactions, both at home and abroad, to the events of December and some ministers, including Baldwin, were driven to the conclusion that the Government must support an oil embargo to regain the support of public opinion.[5] England's prestige abroad was in eclipse, particularly in the Eastern Mediterranean and Balkans where the force of Italy's apparent success was most acute. On the other hand, the arguments for an ultimate reconciliation with Italy remained. From the strategic point of view the strains on the unmobilized fleets were becoming intolerable and the naval staff were increasingly vocal, throughout the spring of 1936, in their demands for a relaxation of tension. They drove home the point that the Admiralty could not guarantee Far Eastern security while the Mediterranean concentration continued.[6] British trade was also suffering from sanctions and this too argued against any stiffening of the Geneva front, and it was evident that the French were still anxious to abandon sanctions and conciliate Mussolini, especially after he threatened to denounce the Gamelin—Badoglio military agreements; indications that Germany might be about to move into the Rhineland only reinforced these tendencies.

These conflicts of interest were not resolved and instead produced a paralysis of policy. The Cabinet declined to take a lead at Geneva, ineffective sanctions were retained and Britain's policy fell back on two gambles beyond its own control: first, that Abyssinia would hold until the rains halted the Italian offensive and economic sanctions began to tell; second, that Europe would remain quiet. On both these counts Britain lost. The Rhineland action occurred at a moment when British power was deployed in the Mediterranean and when the reconditioning programme had hardly begun. The defensive position in home waters in early March was 'amazingly bad'[7] with the navy unable to guarantee the defence of England's coasts or shipping. Warships could not be withdrawn from the Mediterranean without jeopardizing the fleet's security there, and because of their commitments in Egypt the army and air force at home were in the 'worst position imaginable'. If there was any danger of war at home, the Chiefs of Staff warned, Britain would have to withdraw from the Mediterranean. Until then it would remain in a

---

5 Cab. Conclusions, 26 February 1936. Cab.23/83.
6 D.P.R./19th mtg., 3 March 1936. Cab.16/136. Cf. also, Marder, *op. cit.*
7 The phrase was Colonel Pownall's, and he was right.

very weak position in Northern Europe.[8] This was the substance of
what was conveyed to the French and Belgians during the 'staff talks' of
mid-April. The Rhineland thus was a vivid demonstration of Italy's
ability to complicate England's general strategic posture and weaken it
vis-à-vis Germany.

By the spring it had also become apparent that a rapid Italian success
in East Africa was inevitable unless drastic action — such as the closure
of the Suez Canal — was taken by the sanctions front. This was proposed by one or two minor officials at the Foreign Office, and for a
time Eden himself did not rule out such a 'solution' of the crisis;[9] but
in the end counsels of moderation prevailed and no attempt was made
to persuade a divided Cabinet to adopt the line of boldness. Chatfield
could tell his Home Fleet commander that, because of the changed
European situation, 'the chances of trouble in the Mediterranean are
now greatly reduced'.[10] By the end of April the Foreign Office were
worrying about a further move by Germany, this time against Austria,
and the French were taking the first steps back to a *rapprochement*
with Rome. Drummond warned the Government that a failure to lift
sanctions at the war's end could produce serious financial and economic
problems in Italy (this was corroborated by Treasury evidence) and that
might drive Mussolini into desperate action.[11] After Rhineland, the
Admiralty's complaints about the strain of the Mediterranean concentration found sympathetic ears among important politicians; Hoare
reportedly refused to end his brief period in the political wilderness by
taking up the post of First Lord unless the Home Fleet was moved back
to England.[12]

Once the decision was finally taken to abandon sanctions — and it
was Eden who so advised the Cabinet, Chamberlain giving the public
lead with his 'midsummer madness' speech — the Foreign Office faced
the immediate problem of liquidating the tense situation in the
Mediterranean region and then moving on to a long-term settlement.
The usual arguments for a conciliatory policy were as strong as ever. On
the other hand, confidence in English diplomacy had been undermined

---

8 Cab. Conclusions, 16 March and 1 April 1936. Cab.23/83. C.I.D./276th mtg.,
   3 April 1936. Cab.2/4.
9 See memorandum by O'Malley, 24 April 1936. R2844/226/22 (20411).
10 Chatfield to Backhouse, 27 March 1936. Chatfield Papers.
11 Drummond to Eden, disp. no. 499, 25 April 1936. R2397/2132/22 (20422).
12 Bingham (London) to Hull, tel. 269, 19 May 1936. *Foreign Relations of the
   United States (F.R.U.S.)*, 1936, I, pp. 304–5.

by the failure of the League. This prestige factor is a difficult variable to measure, but a comment such as Sir Warren Fisher's captures something of the public reaction to the dénouement:

> The English attitude of willingness to wound but fear to strike was not converted into anything more resolute by the evident determination of the French to avoid at all costs any conflict with Italy. In these circumstances no country believes that we ever intended business; and our parade of force in the Eastern Mediterranean, so far from impressing others, has merely made a laughing-stock of ourselves. All that is now needed to complete the opera bouffe is a headline in the newspapers 'Italians Occupy Addis Ababa British Evacuate Eastern Med.'[13]

At the Geneva meetings in May, the representatives of the Balkan *Entente*, nervous about Italy's future intentions, pressed Eden to support a general Mediterranean pact including Italy and guaranteed by France and Britain. The League Secretary General, Joseph Avenol, and the new Prime Minister of France, Léon Blum, had urged the same course to restore confidence in collective security arrangements.[14] Eden, however, had told Avenol that English public opinion would not permit the Government to revoke sanctions and then sit down with Italy to negotiate a pact.[15] The Foreign Office thus ruled out a multilateral pact and suggested, as an alternative to general agreement, a two-stage policy. For the period of transition after sanctions were lifted Britain should unilaterally renew its assurances of military support (originally made in December 1935) to Greece, Turkey and Yugoslavia. In the second stage, as a long-term measure to counter Italian expansion and restore British prestige, it was suggested that the Government consider 'a restricted naval defensive agreement, under League auspices, between Great Britain, Greece and Turkey'. From such an agreement Britain could expect to gain important strategic advantages in the East Mediterranean (use of harbours, air bases and so on), and the assumed commitments were vital interests anyway. However, the inclusion of Yugoslavia in such a treaty would have to be resisted. The political benefits, the Foreign Office reckoned, would be immense: it would

---

[13] Fisher to Vansittart, 21 April 1936. Cab.21/421.
[14] Minute by Rendel, 13 May 1936. C3726/1/17 (19856). Cf. also reports from Gilbert, U.S. Consul to Geneva, in May and June. *F.R.U.S.*, 1936, III, pp. 136–8.
[15] James Barros, *Betrayal from within* (New Haven, 1969), pp. 116–18.

stabilize the Middle East, strengthen the Balkan *Entente*, indirectly reassure Roumania and Yugoslavia and counter German and Soviet, as well as Italian, influence in the region. The 'Mediterranean Locarno' would be postponed for an uncertain future.[16]

The Foreign Office denied that this was an anti-Italian policy, but it would hardly have been interpreted as conciliatory in Rome and it would seem more plausible to describe it as an attempt to extend the Mediterranean sanctions alliance on a permanent basis. This is borne out by Eden's remark that, 'If as a result of her aggression Italy sees closer relations between H.M.G., Greece and Turkey I cannot help feeling that the effect would on the whole be salutory.'[17] The temporary extension of assurance was, according to Vansittart, for home consumption and face-saving,[18] but a defensive naval agreement, whatever its other benefits, did not promise an Anglo—Italian reconciliation. Drummond had cautioned Eden against such a policy, but, more significantly, Sir Percy Loraine, British Ambassador to Ankara, thought that the Turks would also prefer a comprehensive agreement including rather than excluding Mussolini; Turkey wanted 'a settlement which consecrated and did not alter the existing equilibrium of power'.[19] However, this opposition — and Vansittart's on more general grounds — carried little weight with Eden and the proposal was placed before the Cabinet and Services in early June as the recommended post-sanctions policy.

Although it had been at the request of the Chiefs of Staff that mutual support agreements had been negotiated with Turkey, Greece and Yugoslavia at the end of 1935, it had soon emerged that for Britain these involved more liabilities than assets. The granting of naval anchorages and repair facilities was important in view of Britain's unsatisfactory strategic situation, but the material contribution that the three nations could or would make to a war against Italy was very slight. Greece, for instance, was weak in coastal defence and exposed to air attack. Yugoslavia was in a similar position, and the Prince Regent made embarassingly large requests for military and financial aid. Turkey was

---

16 Memorandum by Eden, 'Problems Facing H.M.G. in the Mediterranean as a Result of the Italo-League Dispute', 11 June 1936. C.P.165(36). Cab.24/262.
17 Minute by Eden, 8 June 1936. R3182/2132/22. (20422).
18 Minute by Vansittart, November 1936. R6149/294/67. (20383).
19 Minute by Sir P. Loraine, 9 June 1936. R3325/294/67. (20381). Also Drummond's letter to Eden, 30 May, commenting on the latter's conversation with Avenol. R3182/2132/22. (20422).

in much better military shape and its control of the Dardanelles made it an ally worth having, but its policy had only one end: to seize the Dodecanese islands from Italy.[20] For the most part, then, Britain's East Mediterranean allies resembled welfare dependents more than healthy coequals. Once more the gulf between the theory and the practice of collective security was an education in realism rather than idealism.

These considerations did not augur well for Eden's plan to turn the temporary Mediterranean agreements into a permanent system. Asked to comment on stage one of the policy, the extension of assurances, the Chiefs of Staff argued that this would further burden the Services with commitments in the Mediterranean at a time when they were anxious to return to normal conditions in all theatres. If Britain was adequately to defend its global interests, it would have to return to friendly relations with Italy. The entire rearmament programme was based on this assumption: 'In the contrary event, a complete revision of the whole strategical situation and of the needs of the Services would become necessary.'[21] This report reached the Foreign Office too late, however, and Eden announced an extension of assurances in the House of Commons on 18 June when he declared sanctions at an end.[22] Chatfield complained privately that this entailed a 'very unreasonable commitment', and the Service ministers insisted at the next Cabinet that 'no further commitments could be undertaken in the Mediterranean'.[23] The Chiefs of Staff were also clear that a defensive alliance would burden Britain with obligations it might have to break, especially if the fleet moved to the Far East. Chatfield thought Eden's policy was being determined by immediate expediency and Hankey noted that it was in conflict with the objective posited by the Defence Requirements Sub-committee: 'a tranquil Mediterranean situation without commitments'.[24]

In a lengthy analysis of the alliance proposal, the Joint Planning Subcommittee concluded that a military understanding with Greece would burden England with liabilities and give little return gain. The Greeks were rated poor fighters, the country would be hard to defend

---

[20] A good summary of the mutual support agreements and the follow-up staff talks, conducted by the attachés, is in J3991/1/15. (20161). Text of the agreements may be found in Command Paper 5072 of 1936.
[21] Chiefs of Staff report, 18 June 1936. C.P.174 (36). Cab.24/263.
[22] Parl. Deb., H. of C., vol. 313, col. 1206.
[23] Chatfield to Hankey, 24 June 1936. Cab.21/436. Cab. Conclusion, 23 June 1936. Cab.23/84.
[24] C.O.S./179th mtg., 25 June 1936. Cab.53/6.

and there was a risk of becoming involved in local Balkan disputes. By contrast, an alliance with Turkey would bring valuable military advantages in a war against either Italy or Soviet Russia, and the joint planners wanted to give Turkey a guarantee to avoid the possibility of its falling under a Soviet guarantee: Communist Russia would always be a potential enemy of the British Empire. The Service chiefs agreed with the analysis but rejected this proposal on the grounds that it would alienate Italy. From the strategic point of view the first need was a secure Mediterranean and this involved an Anglo–Italian reconciliation.[25]

The Foreign Office's proposal to establish a system of guarantees in the Eastern Mediterranean, which would have resembled that created in 1939, was in sharp conflict with those criteria and priorities with which Britain's strategists screened alternatives for that region. The Services viewed the Mediterranean as an aspect of the wider global predicament and their sights were set on the larger question. As the Abyssinian affair drew to a close, Hankey penned his own thoughts on 'Foreign Policy and Imperial Defence'. The main issue for England was Germany. Japan was preoccupied, though a definite menace, and although Italy was well placed to secure its imperial interests it also lived in dread of a German march through Austria and the Tyrol. Britain should avoid simultaneous crises; disentangle itself from its obligations in the Mediterranean so that the fleet could proceed, if called, to defend the circumference of the Empire in the east; and curtail where possible other commitments, especially any relating to the League. A war in the Mediterranean, Hankey argued with that hyperbole he reserved for his favourite prejudices, would be lengthy and would risk the entire Empire as well as 'Western civilization'. Therefore, 'We should grasp the hand held out by Signor Mussolini, however repugnant it may be, and do our utmost to get back to cordial relations with Italy . . . We cannot afford to fight, so we may as well make friends quickly.'[26]

For his part, Chatfield had concluded from the Mediterranean war scare that the Empire was 'disjointed, disconnected and highly vulnerable. It is even open to debate whether it is in reality strategically defensible.' He wanted to settle with Japan, secure the Mediterranean and stand against territorial change in Western Europe: 'beyond that

25 Chiefs of Staff report, 'Eastern Mediterranean: Understanding with Turkey and Greece' (C.O.S. 506), 29 July 1936. C.P. 211 (36). Cab.24/263.
26 Memorandum by Hankey, 8 June 1936. Cab.63/51.

commit ourselves to nothing of a military nature. We have been quixotic once.'[27] He and Hankey both supported the idea of a drastic reform of the League, the latter arguing the need to drop automatic sanctions and 'to make it clear that in the present state of world disorganization our people will undertake no commitments whatsoever under Articles 10 and 16'. Writing in the first shadows of civil war and revolution in Spain, Hankey thought that Britain must detach itself from European entanglements and eschew Locarno-type treaties or alliances: 'In the present state of Europe, with France and Spain menaced by Bolshevism, it is not inconceivable that before long it might pay us to throw in our lot with Germany and Italy.'[28] Here, in the spectre of revolution, was common ground for at least a *rapprochement*, if not a holy crusade, with fascism.

Hankey and Chatfield did not outline how the 'repugnant' hand of Mussolini was to be grasped but they presumably approved of the formula worked out in London and Rome in July whereby Italy gave assurances to the smaller Mediterranean nations and Britain withdrew its guarantee. These were mainly tension-reducing exchanges, however, and it was felt at the Foreign Office, after the demise of Eden's Mediterranean policy, that no firm approaches could be made to Italy until opinion cooled and a new atmosphere prevailed. The French formally proposed in a note of 22 July their scheme for a general Mediterranean pact and asked that it be given urgent consideration,[29] but the Foreign Office did not deliberate their strategy until October. European questions had precedence and few officials of that office in any case shared the sanguine image of future Italian policy propounded by Drummond from Rome and the English conservative press. That image, aptly coined 'the python theory', saw Italy losing its appetite for foreign adventures and busy digesting its new colonial morsel. Mussolini

---

[27] Chatfield paper on League reform, August 1936. Chatfield Papers. The Foreign Office wished to avoid the obloquy of reforming the Covenant and simply put its controversial clauses into cold storage. Sir Orme Sargent thought the Covenant could stand in the same relation to international law as the New Testament stood to Christianity, 'as an ideal for mankind to aspire to even if it cannot at present apply it in practice', 'A whiff of Mr Mackenzie King', remarked Vansittart in jocular agreement.

[28] Hankey, 'The Future of the League of Nations', 20 July 1936. W11340/79/98. (20475). He also supported a settlement with Hitler on the grounds that an Anglo–German war would be so exhausting to both 'that we should probably become a prey to Bolshevism – the very thing Hitler most fears'. Hankey to Sir Eric Phipps, 9 October 1936. Cab.21/540.

[29] *D.D.F.*, 2e Serie, Tome II, No. 461.

would revert to his former role of 'good European', a stabilizing factor in world politics. This image found many adherents on the right of British politics and also in the Government's military advisers, but Eden and Vansittart agreed with a contrasting and prescient analysis of Italian policy written by Mr Lambert of the Southern Department of the Foreign Office. Lambert, a long-time student of fascism, thought that Mussolini faced a severe domestic crisis because of Italy's worsening economic and financial situation, that Abyssinia had postponed but also aggravated this crisis and that he would be driven into fresh adventures and also into Hitler's open arms:

> The conviction is that Italy has now reached a point at which not only Fascist principles . . . but also the necessity of distracting the attention of the Italian public from an ever worsening internal economic situation, will compel her to undertake fresh military adventures. That, in fact, Italy is like a man whose income is vanishing, but who is prepared to risk what he has left in a gamble because he knows the stakes are very high.[30]

Spain tended to bear out that forecast and so too did much other intelligence received from the regions where the British and Italian empires rubbed shoulders. A lengthy memorandum of August 1936, to which several Foreign Office departments contributed information, suggested that Italian imperialism was working from Spain to the Red Sea systematically to undermine British influence. The patterns of this policy were everywhere apparent: in Morocco, where an elaborate espionage campaign was directed against Gibraltar; in Malta, where anti-British Italians had been expelled; in Yugoslavia, where Italy encouraged Macedonian and Croat separatism; in the Near East, where subsidized anti-British propaganda flourished in Egypt and Palestine; and in the rest of Arabia, where Italy sponsored reactionary nationalist movements or hostile figures such as the Imam of Yemen. A system was at work and the Abyssinian crisis was not the root cause, for some of its manifestations had been in evidence since the early 1930s.[31] Italy might wish to maintain the European system generally intact, but in the Mediterranean it seemed bent on a collision course with the traditionally paramount empires. It followed from this image of Italy's objectives that a policy designed to conciliate it should be adopted only from a strong bargaining position and taken with a healthy dose of scepticism.

30 Minute by Lambert, 27 April 1936. R3335/226/22. (20411).
31 Foreign Office memorandum, August 1936. R5839/226/22. (20411).

There was thus a lack of consensus among the English policy-making élite on the vital issue of whether a reconciliation with Mussolini was likely or even desirable. Political interests and strategic needs seemed out of step and the debate on Mediterranean policy continued unresolved throughout the summer of 1936. Meanwhile other problems, beyond the resumption of a dialogue with Italy, attended Britain in the same region of the Empire. The Anglo—Egyptian treaty negotiations, the crisis in Palestine and the Montreux conference on the Straits all saw vital British imperial interests at work and these are discussed elsewhere in this study. Foremost among all other questions of international import, however, was the outbreak of civil war in Spain in late July and, far worse, the intervention of outside powers. This introduced a fresh destabilizing factor into the great power relationships of Europe and the Mediterranean. In part, it was an ideological class conflict spread beyond national borders into the international arena, but there were also vital political and strategic interests at stake in the Spanish battleground. 'Ever since the long range gun was invented', the First Lord would later write, 'our whole position in the Mediterranean has been dependent on a weak or friendly Spain'.[32] For Britain the Mediterranean crisis had passed into a new phase, one which would be at times as dangerous as any period of the earlier crisis over Abyssinia. Although this study does not attempt to trace in any detail the tortuous and complex diplomatic history of the Civil War, nevertheless it played such a vital role in Anglo—Italian and Franco—Italian relations from 1936 to 1939 that there will be occasion to return to the Spanish issue from time to time. Here the attitude of British decision-makers to the early stages of the conflict will be summarized briefly.

From the outset, Eden and his advisers at the Foreign Office were clear in their minds that British interests lay, first, in the defeat of both extreme factions in the Civil War and the emergence of a compromise, middle-of-the-road Spain still amenable to British diplomacy. Second, for the duration of the war it was vital to contain it within national boundaries and keep it from widening into a general European conflict. Non-intervention was a complicated policy whereby England tacitly acquiesced in intervention by 'volunteers' but used its influence to shape the contours of the conflict according to these two principal and overriding interests. That, at least, was how the Foreign Office saw their policy. It was always open to Britain to play a far more energetic role in

[32] Lord Stanhope to Halifax, 19 May 1939. Premier 1/409.

Spain because it enjoyed naval superiority in the Western Mediterranean — and indeed Eden proposed this on several occasions in 1937 — but this involved the agreement of the Admiralty. The naval staff had firmly defined their own attitude to the Spanish conflict in early August, when two officers from the French Ministry of Marine, one of them Admiral François Darlan, called on Chatfield 'at a moment's notice' to express their anxieties about Spain and its implications for French naval communications. It seemed to the French naval staff that Spain would be exhausted by a long war and would be unable to resist predatory action by Italy or Germany. Already it looked as though Italy might seize the Balearic islands, and France was consequently anxious for its North African lines of communication. France would not, however, take unilateral action but would only follow Britain in what it did, especially as regards naval dispositions. Chatfield had made it very plain that the Admiralty was not about to give a lead, especially as Darlan insisted (incorrectly) that he was not representing the French Government, only the Ministry of Marine, and that he was also highly sceptical of any ideas of outside mediation in the war. He fobbed off Darlan's request to see Hankey, and the French officers returned to Paris, not for the last time, empty-handed.

Informing the Foreign Office of this strange visitation, Hoare, now First Lord, thought that the French Ministry of Marine was in a panic — 'What other reason can be assigned for this curious visit of two Admirals in plain clothes, at a moment's notice and apparently without the knowledge of the Quai d'Orsay?' — and underlined that no action could be taken on such information. Britain should continue its policy of neutrality; Hoare would be 'astonished' if Germany or Italy contemplated predatory action:

> When I speak of 'neutrality' I mean strict neutrality, that is to say a situation in which the Russians neither officially or unofficially give help to the Communists. On no account must we do anything to bolster up Communism in Spain, particularly when it is remembered that Communism in Portugal, to which it would probably spread and particularly in Lisbon, would be a grave danger to the British Empire.[33]

33 Hoare to Foreign Office, 5 August 1936, covering minute by Chatfield of the same date. W7781/62/41 (20527). The official French account of the Darlan visit is in *D.D.F.*, II, No. 87. These agree that Chatfield and Hoare were told that the mission was merely one of information and that the French Ministry of Marine alone had taken the initiative. In post-war testimony Léon Blum said

Hoare's remarks must be seen in the context of the debate over whether or not to supply arms to the legitimate Spanish Government, a government he referred to in public as a 'faction'. The inference was that a fascist victory in Spain would not bring equivalent dangers. In an appreciation of the conflict written a few weeks after the Darlan visit, the Chiefs of Staff warned the Foreign Office that, following the lessons of Abyssinia, England should take no action that might simply alienate Italy and fail to achieve the real objectives. A neutral Spain was vital to Britain and it was equally important to bolster Spanish independence, but the Chiefs of Staff thought that the best way to achieve this was through non-interference.[34]

Public and private naval papers bear out that Britain's professional naval officers shared Hoare's concern over the Communist menace posed by the Spanish war and deprecated the dangers of a fascist victory in Spain. As we have seen, Hankey had alluded to the dangers of Bolshevism in Europe in late July and held out the possibility of Britain 'throwing her lot' in with Germany and Italy at some future date. Chatfield and his staff undoubtedly had had the same idea and there is evidence that Admiral Roger Backhouse, commander of the Home Fleet and Chatfield's successor as First Sea Lord, proposed in late 1936 that Britain associate itself with Germany and Italy in crushing revolution in Spain.[35] Chatfield and Hoare also led the unsuccessful attempt to accord belligerent rights to the Spanish 'factions', a measure that all knew would aid, possibly decisively, Franco's forces. (It must be said,

---

that he and Daladier had sent Darlan to impress Chatfield and Hankey with the need to oppose fascism in Spain. The mission was a failure, said Blum, and this had considerably influenced the final decision of his government to support non-intervention. *Les Evenèments Survenus, Rapport*, vol. I, témoignage de L. Blum, 23 July 1947, p. 218. This may be so, but the British certainly did not get the impression of a high-level initiative. The conflicting evidence is assessed in D. Carlton, 'Eden, Blum and the origins of non-intervention', *The Journal of Contemporary History*, 6:3, (1971).

34 Chiefs of Staff, 'West Mediterranean: Situation Arising from the Spanish Civil War,' C.O.S. 509, 24 August 1936. C.P. 234(36). Cab.24/264.

35 Vansittart to Chatfield, 16 February 1937. Chatfield Papers. The British consul in Barcelona, Norman King, had denounced 'Red Spain' and impressed Backhouse with the need to crush the revolution; Chatfield had passed on Backhouse's comments to the Foreign Office but Vansittart defended the British line: 'No Government could possibly . . . have taken the line to which Backhouse alludes of association with Germany and Italy . . . ' In a letter to Backhouse of 16 February Chatfield remarked, 'I do not see how Franco can help winning, because one feels that he has a much nobler cause than the Reds.'

however, that Chatfield had some strong technical arguments to support his case.) For the most part British naval officers were content to follow the Foreign Office lead and support non-intervention, but their denying influence over policy came into play on at least three occasions in 1937 when Eden tried to use the fleet to support policies which the Admiralty deemed provocative. If the navy's willingness to enter into intimate relations with Franco's naval officers appeared a little unseemly to some Cabinet members,[36] it was nonetheless the Cabinet, not the Admiralty, who made Britain's Spanish policy and naval considerations were only one element in a very long list of English interests supposedly covered by the umbrella of non-intervention.

The hopes of both the Cabinet and navy for a quick end to the Spanish conflict were high in early November 1936 when the city of Madrid seemed about to fall, and it may not have been entirely co-incidental that the Services and Foreign Office concluded that the time was at hand for a reconciliation with Franco's benefactor, Benito Mussolini. Eden's advisers had worked through the French *démarche* for a Mediterranean pact. This called for a mutual guarantee treaty embracing Britain, France, Spain, Italy, Greece, Turkey, Yugoslavia and possibly Black Sea countries. The pact was to operate with the Locarno distinctions between 'flagrant' and 'non-flagrant' violations, would guarantee freedom of communications in the Mediterranean and would also be invoked in cases of air or sea attack directed against frontiers or possessions; finally, it contained no proposals for naval limitations.[37] This resembled the scheme suggested in the Foreign Office in 1931–2 as a possible way of averting a collapse of the disarmament conference. That proposal, it will be recalled, had been rejected by a Cabinet committee on mainly strategic grounds: Britain could not accept further commitments, especially in a region that it might wish to abandon in wartime, and the Dominions would not regard the agreement as binding on them.[38] The strategic objections still applied, perhaps with extra force, in 1936, but Sir Robert Craigie, resident naval expert at the Foreign Office, had weighed in in favour of a general Mediterranean pact as part of a wider system of regional agreements within a reformed League, an idea much in the air after Abyssinia and one incidentally

36 Simon Diaries, 5 February 1938.
37 Cf. note 29 above.
38 Report of a Cabinet Committee on a Mediterranean Locarno, 14 January 1932. C.P.27(32). Cab.24/227. Also C.P.17(32).

favoured by the Chancellor of the Exchequer, Neville Chamberlain.[39] But it was too ambitious for Craigie's superiors, who were already involved in complicated negotiations for a new western pact. Eden and Vansittart did not dispute the need for a settlement with Italy, however, particularly in view of the developing relationship between that power and Nazi Germany. What argued decisively against the French multi-lateral scheme was the time factor: 'time', wrote Vansittart, 'is the essence of the thing. At present we are simply drifting, and letting Italy slip beyond recall.' The Foreign Office therefore agreed in early November to press for immediate bilateral soundings in Rome.[40]

Britain's strategists had reached a similar conclusion for a different set of reasons. Inevitably, Italy's successful defiance of the League gave rise to much public speculation about Britain's future in the Mediterranean. Among enthusiasts of air power the theory was current that the Italian challenge and technological developments had rendered the route and British bases along it too insecure for planning, and they urged the government to concentrate resources in South Africa for an alternative line of imperial communications. These amateur strategists, the so-called Cape School, were challenged by other writers and speakers closer to official naval policy. These, the 'Mediterranean School', argued that to abandon the Mediterranean, or even to discuss it, would undermine British prestige in the Middle East and its other political positions. The latter school found powerful government support when the First Lord himself joined the debate to silence it. There was no intention, Hoare affirmed, of 'abdicating our position in that sea, or of scuttling from Malta. It is simply a question of adapting ourselves to the new conditions, and of making the fullest use of our own air power.'[41] To reinforce this view the navy embarked upon an intensive public relations campaign in the summer of 1936 to 'show the

---

[39] Chamberlain's ideas on League reform and regional pacts are in W11340/79/98. (20475).

[40] Memorandum by Sir R. Craigie, 'Mediterranean Pact', 14 October 1936. R6149/294/67. (20383). Cf. also, The Earl of Avon, *The Eden memoirs: facing the dictators* (London, 1962), p. 428.

[41] Hoare's remarks cited and questioned in B. H. Liddell Hart, *Europe in Arms* (London, 1939), p. 112. Also, *The Times*, 23 September 1936. On the debate over strategy see E. Monroe, *The Mediterranean in politics*, chap. 1; C. V. Usborne, 'British links through the Mediterranean', *Great Britain and the East*, 19 August 1937; an important essay was Wing Cmdr R. A. Cochrane's 'The Effect of the Development of Air Power on British Interests in the Mediterranean', *Journal of the Royal United Services Institute* (May, 1936). Also articles by H. C. Bywater and Admiral H. Richmond.

flag' in the Mediterranean. Hoare and the King both made well-publicized cruises with the fleet, naval visits were exchanged with the Greeks and the navy's 'humanitarian' activities on the outbreak of war in Spain were played up to the hilt.

This show of official resolve effectively disguised the fact that the Chiefs of Staff had very little in the cupboard for Mediterranean rearmament and that their private plans closely resembled the calculations of the Cape School. Italy's exclusion from the list of enemies meant that Britain was as weak in the region after the Abyssinian crisis as it had been before it and all of the planning studies demonstrated that 'adapting' to the new conditions would be an expensive proposition. The use of Alexandria during the period of tension, Chatfield later admitted, had been 'strategically unsound' and the naval staff questioned whether they would ever again be justified in concentrating a fleet in the Eastern Mediterranean. The joint planners had concluded that a new naval repair and operations base at Cyprus would be required if England wished to regain its former position of supremacy in the Mediterranean, but this could cost £25 million and take up to ten years to complete.[42] Opposition to any such expenditure, rather surprisingly, was strongest in the Chiefs of Staff Subcommittee. Mediterranean rearmament, increasingly popular with the Foreign and Colonial Offices, was resisted by Hankey and the Service chiefs on the grounds that the money could be spent on higher priorities. The Chiefs of Staff refused to pass on the planners' recommendations for Cyprus, considering the scale 'far too generous'. Instead they determined to question the Foreign Office about their intentions towards Italy and to underline that the alternative to an accommodation would be a 'terrific expenditure'. The War Office did not want another heavy base to defend, and in the worst case the navy could always retire to the Cape route for their Far Eastern communications.[43] It was a conclusion remarkably similar to that reached by the Cape School of strategy and which Hoare had taken such pains loudly to refute.

As a result of this discussion the defence ministers, led by Sir Thomas Inskip, Minister for Co-ordination of Defence, reminded Eden in the Cabinet in early November of the importance attached by the Services to a *rapprochement* with Italy. The Mediterranean presented great difficulties and badly complicated planning for imperial defence;

42 C.I.D./294th mtg., 17 June 1937. Cab.2/6.
43 C.O.S./187th mtg., 20 October 1936. Cab.51/6.

better relations with Mussolini would 'solve at a stroke' a number of
vexing problems. Eden thought that such an attitude could be mistaken
for 'flabbiness' and he was pessimistic about the prospects but he
admitted the force of the strategic arguments.[44] Next day (5 November)
he used the House of Commons to make a public gesture of conciliation
to Italy and on the same day Mussolini broached the idea of a
'gentleman's agreement' with England in a *Daily Mail* interview. In the
ensuing talks it emerged that both sides deprecated a general, multi-
lateral Mediterranean pact. Italy favoured a *détente*, to be followed by
the settlement of outstanding issues. There was no mention of Italian
demands, first raised in the autumn of 1935, for a limitation of English
warship using the Mediterranean passage.

The naval staff were especially interested in Mussolini's new proposal
as it seemed to involve neither diplomatic commitments nor arms
limitations, and it was on these two grounds that the navy had long
opposed participation in Mediterranean pacts. What the sea lords
wanted was 'some form of exchange of mutual assurances that we do
not intend to interfere with one another while avoiding the acceptance
of new commitments'. They wished too to divide Italy from Germany
and thus lessen the risks of a general anti-British combination. On 21
November the Admiralty addressed the Foreign Office in this sense,
stressing the strategic importance of improved relations with Italy. The
letter noted Italy's new military reputation and warned that naval
limitations proposals would be 'totally unacceptable'. It was equally
important to avoid fresh commitments in the region:

> such commitments would be a serious danger from the military point
> of view. Although it may be admitted that our position in the Near
> East is of great importance, it does not follow that we should be
> obliged or in a position to fight in that area in the event of war.
> Under certain conditions, it would be necessary to divert our com-
> munications now passing through the Mediterranean for the duration
> of the war, and to depend upon a successful outcome of the war for
> the restoration of our position in the Near East. An obligation to
> undertake operations in the Mediterranean would be a restriction on
> our strategic freedom which might have far reaching effects upon the
> upshot of the war.[45]

---

[44] Cab. Conclusions, 4 November 1936. Cab.23/86.
[45] Adm. 116/3302. Chatfield was evidently dissatisfied with the Foreign Office's
attitude to Italy. He doubted whether 'the F.O. are seized with the military
importance of an agreement – or whether they will really get one, because

These desiderata, which formed part of the Foreign Office's instructions to Drummond on the type of settlement sought by London, reflect a grand strategy very different from the concentrated naval policy eventually adopted in 1939. Hankey referred to it as 'sterilizing' the Mediterranean: if Britain became involved in difficulties in the Far East, that sea would be evacuated regardless of Italy's attitude. If it came to war with Mussolini while the fleet was away, an attempt would be made, with French aid, to hold Gibraltar and the Middle East, but severe losses were anticipated. It was a question of 'balancing risks' and weighing priorities. The naval staff insisted that these risks had to be vitiated through diplomacy but they set strict limits to the form of any settlement with Mussolini. Obligations to wage war in the Mediterranean would be avoided until the spring of 1939 when the Admiralty, revising the principles of strategy, developed the conception of an early offensive against Italy.

Within months, this system of post-Abyssinian defence priorities was turned into a categorical political commitment to the Dominions, and before the year 1937 was over Britain's global predicament had intensified to such an extent that strategic policy was in a state of paralysis.

2. Balancing risks: a system of imperial priorities

Developments in the Mediterranean and British policy in that region in the critical year 1937 must be seen against a background of overall imperial commitments simultaneously straining limited resources. The failure of the 'gentleman's agreement' in January meant that hopes of reducing liabilities 'at a stroke' and securing the Mediterranean had been at best premature. The latent tension between British capabilities and its interdependent obligations in the Empire thus remained unresolved. The Committee of Imperial Defence reluctantly acknowledged this in the next month by striking Italy from England's already tiny list of friends. Italy had not yet been counted a probable enemy, but that was a compromise formula which reflected Britain's rearmament capacity rather than the actual state of Anglo–Italian relations. These relations are discussed in detail in the next chapter; here it may simply be noted

> there seem to be so many things we are to ask for and so little is our liking diplomatically to sacrifices . . . I doubt if F.O. appreciates what a much more efficient and stronger force Italy is now than she used to be'. *Ibid.* Chatfield appears to have subsequently revised his own appreciation of Italy's prowess.

that they deteriorated so rapidly that Anthony Eden was convinced by April 1937 that Mussolini was the most immediate danger and that war, if it came early, would probably break out in the Mediterranean.[46] England's military planners were extremely unhappy about this turn of events: the menace posed to imperial communications remained acute at a moment when the Chiefs of Staff were working out an analysis of the strategic situation for the forthcoming Imperial Conference and the tactics to be followed in dealing with the Dominions. Grand strategy was on the horns of a major dilemma. Should the gravity of the Services' predicament be disclosed and the naval guarantee to the anti-podean Dominions modified; or did the political risks in such a policy outweigh those inherent in a continuation of the *status quo*? In other words, how would the Mediterranean crisis affect political and strategic relationships within the Commonwealth?

Whatever their influence on diplomacy, and the forms that influence took, that the Dominions loomed large in British strategy in the late 1930s is incontestable. The aim of the British Services was to encourage rearmament programmes that would complement their own imperial policy and to discourage autonomous programmes of local defence. This would ease Britain's own defence burden while at the same time tying the Dominions to London in a practical way. The naval staff took a special interest in the direction of planning in Australia and New Zealand because of their guarantee, rendered after the Washington conference, to defend them from aggression in the Far East. The old dream of a single imperial navy had long since been abandoned, but in the 1930s, as before, the Admiralty 'did their utmost to instil the Dominion Governments with the idea that naval defence could not be treated in a fragmented manner, but had to be regarded as a world-wide issue on which the security and prosperity of all the scattered territories largely depended'.[47] This tradition was carried on with enthusiasm by Chatfield and by Hankey, who supplemented official contacts with his network of correspondents and confidants built up over his career and especially during his tour of the Dominions in 1934–5. Contacts, how-ever, were not enough. What kept the Dominions close to the Common-wealth was their dependence upon Britain for economic prosperity and external security; the latter need varied tremendously from country to

---

[46] Defence Plans (Policy) Subcommittee [D.P.(P.)]/1st mtg., 19 April 1937. Cab.16/181.
[47] Roskill, *Naval policy between the wars*, I, p. 409.

country: Australia considered itself in a highly vulnerable position and largely dependent upon Singapore and the British fleet, but Canada, by contrast, looked to Washington rather than London for its security. As this factor varied, so too did the amenability of the various Dominions to the Admiralty's advice.

In their preliminary discussions on the Imperial Conference of 1937, Stanley Baldwin and his colleagues determined to use the forum to re-assert the general principles of Commonwealth co-operation and unity. Previous conferences had stressed the constitutional sovereignty of the individual members of the Commonwealth and, it was agreed, it was time to establish a balance. This conference was to be the first in a series planned by the National government to this end.[48] That general political aim complemented the Admiralty's intention to use the conference to persuade the Dominions to make a larger contribution to global defence, an objective that sprang from the image of imperial weakness pervading most of the naval staff's appreciations and advice. A year previous, the Cabinet, in an effort to avert an enormous expenditure, had reserved approval of the Defence Requirements Subcommittee's recommended new two-power standard of naval strength, the so-called D.R.C. fleet. Even this programme, which would have doubled the cost of naval rearmament, did not take into account possible Italian hostility. It must be noted too that, whatever the schedule of construction on paper, naval capabilities *had* to diminish before they could increase. The naval replacement and modernization programme was unique in that the fleet had to pass through an extended period of weakness before rearmament was complete and naval strength could be felt. The worst period, the most dangerous phase, would begin in 1938 and end in September 1939, when war was anticipated; during this transitional stage — which could be shortened, but not eliminated, by faster rearmament — Britain's number of capital ships would decrease dramatically from twelve or thirteen in late 1937 to as few as nine, and no new ships would appear before 1940. If England was weak overseas in 1937, it would be weaker in 1938 and weaker still in 1939. Thus, to anticipate, the Munich crisis was to occur at the worst possible moment from the naval viewpoint. But in 1937 the coming period of danger was already a major con-sideration in naval planning and in Chatfield's determination to force the Government to reduce liabilities through diplomatic action.

Oppressed by the strains of commitments and a sense of declining

---

48 Cf. Eden's remarks in Cab. Conclusions, 17 June 1937. Cab.23/88.

strength, the sea lords began to campaign in the spring of 1937 for ministerial approval of the new naval standard. At an important debate on defence policy in early May, Hoare circulated an appreciation of the 'very grave naval dangers' of the world situation. This demonstrated that, on the existing standard of naval strength, once the capital ships being built in Europe were completed Britain would be unable to safeguard the empire in the Far East if already engaged with Germany, even if the latter's fleet were still limited to 35 per cent of England's navy. Hoare pointed out that political repercussions of this weakness were already being felt in the Dominions where doubts about Britain's ability to defend Singapore were widespread. The naval staff thought it vital to re-establish confidence in the system of imperial defence. The 'keys to the situation' were New Zealand and Australia. The Admiralty wanted the former to abandon local defence in favour of naval co-operation and the latter to build a battle-cruiser. Hoare and Hankey both had private information that there was a real danger of Australia 'retiring into her shell' as local defence was growing as a political issue there. With an election pending, the Australian delegation were anxious to have a very frank statement of the position; should they be given 'a fright'? Hoare sketched the line the naval staff proposed to take at the Imperial Conference to deal with this tendency:

> In his view, it was of first importance that we should not adopt a negative attitude, i.e., we should not say that it was impossible for the Navy to implement our naval policy in the Far East, since that would almost inevitably lead to the Dominions abandoning the idea of Imperial Defence and concentrating on local defence measures. It would be equally wrong to let the Dominions think that there was no question of our ability to defend our interests in the Far East, irrespective of their co-operation, since that would also lead to their contenting themselves with local defence measures. In fact, our policy should be, to some extent, to leave them guessing.[49]

Chatfield, recalling the Admiralty's position at this time, would later remark that the naval staff wished the Dominions to 'go wider' and contribute to imperial defence. Unless they were given very firm assurances, it was feared that they might look to the United States for their security. Britain had had to assume a heavy commitment and that

---

[49] D.P.(P.)/2d mtg., 11 May 1937. Cab.16/181. First Lord, 'A New Standard of Naval Strength', 29 April 1937. Cab.16/182. Also Hoare's notes for this meeting in Templewood Papers, IX, 2, University College, Cambridge.

was why the Chiefs of Staff had emphasized the grave implications of fighting three powers at once.[50]

All of this had a strong bearing on the question of the Mediterranean and its place in any system of defence priorities. Australia was known to be vitally concerned with the status of imperial communications and, like the British Chiefs of Staff, its leaders considered every pre-war Mediterranean issue from that angle. Australia had taken a consistent anti-sanctions line during the Abyssinian crisis, had urged the early lifting of sanctions and now sought 'a restoration of traditionally friendly Anglo–Italian relations' and a general pacification of the Mediterranean.[51] Along with South Africa, it had intervened in April 1936 during preliminary discussions on the Anglo–Egyptian treaty with a forceful and successful plea that this question, so crucial to Far Eastern lines of communication, be entirely dissociated from the League of Nations.[52] The Lyons government was the only Dominion represented at the Montreux conference on the Straits; Australia consistently supported British policy in Spain; it urged in 1938 the early implementation of the Anglo–Italian Agreement; in 1939, as will be seen, it pressed London to mediate between France and Italy; and it supported a pro-Arab solution to the Palestine issue. During the 1937 Imperial Conference, Prime Minister Lyons, as well as making a much-publicized (and apparently politically motivated) call for a Pacific pact, brought a personal message of friendship from Mussolini to the British Government.[53] This attitude, which sprang from Australia's concern for that fragile short line of imperial communications, was well known in London. In order to keep Australia to a wider pattern of imperial defence it was clear that it would have to be reassured about Britain's intentions in the Far East *and* the Mediterranean.

In their 'Review of Imperial Defence', circulated to the Dominion delegations, the Chiefs of Staff painted a grim picture of global politics, noting that the Empire faced three potential first-class enemies. They saw Italy as an expansionist power in decline and they were frankly pessimistic about the chances of regaining its friendship; but they saw that as the only alternative to a major rearmament effort in the

50 Minutes of Strategical Appreciation Subcommittee, 2d mtg., 13 March 1939. Cab.16/209.
51 N. Mansergh, *Survey of Commonwealth affairs: problems of external policy 1931–1939* (London, 1952), pp. 154–65.
52 C.I.D./227th mtg., 27 April 1936. Cab.2/6A. Pownall Diaries, 27 April 1936.
53 Imperial Conference, 10th meeting of principal delegates, 1 June 1937. Cab.32/128.

Mediterranean and Middle East. Nonetheless, risks and weakness in that area would not be nearly so serious as the surrender of imperial sea power in the Far East. Singapore's security was a primary priority, rated only below British home defence and above Mediterranean defence.[54] Eden echoed these sentiments in his *tour d'horizon* of the world situation at the Imperial Conference on 19 and 21 May. Although he noted that the Foreign Office considered Italy a more immediate danger than Germany, he admitted that Britain might have to abandon its Mediterranean positions temporarily; but, he added, Britain would eventually regain its paramountcy there.[55] Although he, Inskip and Hoare were all reassuring about the intention to defend Singapore, there were indications that something more explicit and categorical would be required. The Australians arrived at the conference armed with a series of detailed questionnaires for the Chiefs of Staff. These ranged over the entire breadth of defence policy but returned to the vital point on which (for them) all else depended: could the British navy, in view of their heavy commitments nearer home, guarantee the security of Singapore? In particular, what would the Admiralty do in a Far Eastern crisis in the event of (*a*) Soviet, (*b*) Italian intervention?

The Chiefs of Staff, with their backs to the wall, replied with an unqualified promise that these eventualities would not affect their dispositions. Soviet policy would be unlikely to influence these in any case, but:

The intervention of Italy against us would at once impose conflicting demands on our fleet.

In this situation our policy must be governed by the principle that no anxiety or risks connected with our interests in the Mediterranean can be allowed to interfere with the despatch of a fleet to the Far East.

British battleship strength would be at low ebb in 1939 but 'at no time up to 1940 will we be unable to send a Fleet to the Far East'. Even if Britain was already at war with Germany, the Admiralty would establish a strong fleet at Singapore soon after the outbreak of hostilities with Japan. Chatfield repeated these assurances at a meeting with Australian, New Zealand and Indian delegations. Whatever Britain's losses in the Mediterranean, and they might be substantial, its position there could

---

54 Chiefs of Staff, 'Review of Imperial Defence', 22 February 1937. C.P. 73(37). Cab.24/268.
55 Imperial Conference, 1st and 2d mtgs., principal delegates, 19 and 21 May 1937. Cab.32/128.

be regained; but the Pacific might never be recovered.[56]

Hoare's strategy to 'leave them guessing' had apparently been abandoned in the face of Australia's pointed inquisition. It is true that the general commitment was nothing new; since 1923 it had formed the very basis of imperial defence policy and had been reiterated on many occasions. Equally, it is true that, quite apart from these assurances to the Dominions, there were very powerful inducements to Britain to retain its sea power in the Far East at all costs. As Hankey put it, 'The security of India, Straits Settlements and Hong Kong and our vast trade in the Far East depended upon the Fleet's ability to go to Singapore.' On the other hand, the tensions between commitments and capabilities had never been so great and the Admiralty had not had to face a Mediterranean crisis before 1935. At the very least it may be said that the assurances of May–June 1937 were not only out of keeping with the Admiralty's private appreciations but they constituted a widening of a traditional guarantee in the Far East at a moment when problems nearer home were also expanding and naval strength was in decline. Whether, in view of the embarrassment that this new commitment created in 1939, the game was worth the candle is another question. Measured against the criteria of the Cabinet and naval staff — especially the need to elicit better Dominion co-operation in imperial defence — it may well have been. But it involved the sacrifice of naval flexibility and, as will be seen, reduced Britain's diplomatic options in the Mediterranean.

It is probably true that the naval guarantees given so freely to the Dominions would not have been so unequivocal but for the fact that during the Imperial Conference the Far Eastern situation seemed brighter than for some time. Eden and Neville Chamberlain, now Prime Minister, told the conference of their hopes that the new Japanese government would prove reasonable and they both professed support for Australia's project for a Pacific pact. At the same time they underlined the difficulties. Japanese economic competition was a great obstacle, and to associate with Tokyo would offend not only the United States but also China, 'whose goodwill is necessary for successful trade'. Chamberlain bemoaned the fact that Britain's once unrivalled position

---

56 Chiefs of Staff, 'Questions Submitted by the Australian Delegation', C.O.S. 590, 31 May 1937. Cab.53/31. And C.O.S./209th mtg., 1 June 1937. Cab.53/7. A more comprehensive version of Far Eastern strategy, the so-called 'Far East Appreciation', Paper D.P.(P.)5, was also shown to certain of the Dominions. Cab.16/182.

in China was being sliced away. The Government, he revealed, was under pressure from British business interests to maintain the *status quo* in the Far East. He personally regarded China as one of the world's greatest potential markets and thought that increased trade could provide valuable employment for Britain after rearmament.[57]

In the event, the optimism expressed about Anglo–Japanese accord proved grossly mistaken. In July the 'China incident' quickly developed into full-scale war and Western interests inevitably came under attack. Within weeks fighting spread to the imperial strongholds of Shanghai and the International Settlement. British shipping was interfered with and London's Ambassador to China, Sir Hughe Knatchbull-Huggessen, was severely wounded in an incident in August. When the Cabinet met in early September to discuss this deteriorating situation, however, they faced an equally grave challenge in the Mediterranean, where the 'piracy crisis' had dashed hopes of an early settlement with Italy. In fact, the question of a naval movement to the Far East was first raised (by Chamberlain) on the very eve of the Nyon conference.[58] Already it was plain that insecurity in the Mediterranean could be a grave handicap in dealing with the China crisis. For Britain the Mediterranean and Far East were intimately linked, not because of Axis collusion but simply from the exigencies that followed from its own capacity to deal with simultaneous emergencies in two hemispheres. Eden, fully aware of the pull of European problems, had tried to fill the vacuum in the Far East through some kind of co-operative action with the United States, but the Roosevelt Administration maintained an independent line. Anglo–American relations were not without friction, particularly where the Far East was involved, and the autumn saw some memorable examples on both sides of good intentions misinterpreted. The upshot of this was that by November, when the Brussels conference closed, a dismal failure, the war in China was worse than ever and the Western powers were still unable to overcome their mutual suspicions to agree on 'joint' or even 'parallel' action against Japan.

Despite the apparent futility of his past efforts Eden determined in the aftermath of Brussels to draw America into a joint naval demonstration in the Far East. Chamberlain, although not objecting to the policy, doubted that it would be successful, and he emphasized that

---

[57] Imperial Conference, 11th and 15th mtgs., principal delegates, 2 and 8 June 1937. Cab.32/128. Also notes for Eden statement in F3597/597/61 (21205).
[58] Cab. Conclusions, 8 September 1937. Cab.23/88.

Britain could not effectively coerce Japan without Roosevelt's aid.[59] That was, indeed, the harsh truth, for the global situation was so unsettled in late 1937 and British naval power so inadequate to meet concurrent threats that England was already heavily dependent upon American decisions in the Pacific. The Nyon conference had been only a temporary success and by October the Mediterranean crisis was again distracting London's decision-makers. A storm had blown up over Britain's willingness to maintain its military and political position in Egypt, and the Chiefs of Staff had revealed just how remarkably bare the cupboard still was. It was clear that the Mediterranean Fleet was about all that was available for a major action against Italy; but what would happen if the fleet was withdrawn? Here was the crux of the global dilemma.

The Admiralty had firmly decided against any general division of the main battle fleet. It would be unsound to send to Singapore mere 'reinforcements', such as two capital ships, and such a small force would not deter, and might even tempt, the powerful Japanese navy. The naval staff's policy would be to send a fleet large enough to engage the entire Japanese fleet under normal conditions.[60] Should Britain act, either with or without U.S. co-operation, the fleet must be composed of eight or nine capital ships and a strong accompanying force. A few ships could be spared for home waters but the Mediterranean would be completely denuded of commissioned warships. Could Britain, Chatfield worried, risk a 'stab in the back' from Mussolini? At best the Admiralty must depend upon the French navy to deter Italy for operations against Egypt and Suez, but a threat to Mediterranean communications while the fleet was in the Far East would be a grave complication.[61] The Government would be risking everything in the Near East, the First Sea Lord warned, if it sent a fleet east to Singapore; Italy would strike at the British Empire only if it was preoccupied elsewhere and its local superiority gave it the chance of an early success.

Chatfield's anxiety about Italian opportunism was based on more than an over-active imagination. Admiral Sir Dudley Pound, the Mediterranean Commander-in-chief, privately cautioned his superior that:

Only today the Press people here . . . brought me a telegram which

59 Cab. Conclusions, 24 November 1937. Cab.23/90.
60 Note by First Lord, 'Reinforcement of British Naval Forces in the Far East', 23 September 1937. Cab.27/634.
61 Chatfield to Hankey, 7 December 1937. Cab.21/579.

showed that Italy is watching our reaction to the Eastern situation very closely (as one naturally imagined they would be) and it pointed out (for what it is worth) that any weakening of the Fleet in the Mediterranean would be seized upon by Italy to . . . stiffen Germany up.[62]

Pound, who shared Chatfield's misgivings about any eastward naval moves, summed up the Admiralty's predicament in a later letter:

Our German and Italian friends would be delighted to see the Fleet the other side of the Canal. To send out reinforcements only and not the Main Fleet would simply be playing into the hands of the Japanese.[63]

For these reasons Chatfield and his advisers remained averse to sending the main fleet and adamantly opposed dispatching anything less. The First Sea Lord's general attitude was based on strategic judgement, but it also reflected his strong emotional distrust of American policy; as recently as October, at the time of Roosevelt's 'quarantine' speech, Chatfield had vented his feelings in strong terms, and even after the *Panay* attack of 12 December when the President, in talks with Sir Ronald Lindsay, agreed to staff talks and alluded to a naval blockade of Japan, he held to his view that 'one can never be sure what they [the Americans] will do'.[64] However, naval preparations were set in motion and Pound was warned that he might have to take the main fleet to Singapore in January.

The documents relating to the Far Eastern crisis of November 1937–January 1938 demonstrate conclusively that Eden was the main force within the Government pressing for naval action against Japan. He wished to promote Anglo–American co-operation and to re-establish 'white race authority' in the Far East. To do this and to 'retain our position as a world power' Eden advocated on several occasions the dispatch of the main fleet to Singapore, and took the lead as well in urging strong action to anyone with influence in Washington.[65] When Captain Royal Ingersoll, U.S.N., Roosevelt's appointee to the naval staff talks, arrived in London Eden immediately questioned him about

---

[62] Pound to Chatfield, 22 December 1937. Chatfield Papers.
[63] Same to same, 7 February 1938. *Ibid.*
[64] Chatfield to Pound, 30 December 1937. *Ibid.* Also, Chatfield to Backhouse, 8 October 1937. *Ibid.*
[65] Eden to Chamberlain, 9 January 1938. Premier 1/276. Same to same, 31 December 1937. Premier 1/314. Eden to Sir A. Cadogan, 9 January 1938. F407/84/10. (22106).

Roosevelt's intentions. He may have pressed too hard, for Ingersoll got the impression that the Foreign Secretary was more interested in immediate gestures than in long-term strategic planning.[66] Eden believed in an Anglo–American hegemony, based on a monopoly of the world's sea power, raw materials and commerce, and thought that, after England had resolved its differences with Germany, peace based on the *status quo* could be imposed in the Far East and Mediterranean, if necessary by an overwhelming show of force. His concern to hold Britain's imperial position in the Far East was shared by Chamberlain, Hankey and the Service chiefs, but unlike them he was relatively calm about the Mediterranean. He was, he told Chamberlain in a letter bitterly critical of the Chiefs of Staff, apprised of the naval dangers, but he thought that Italy's reaction to a fleet move would be influenced by German policy; and Hitler was unlikely to be dragged into war by Italy. In any case, he argued, the Chiefs of Staff overrated Italy and under-rated France, and he was angry about their refusal to have staff talks on the Mediterranean with the latter power,[67] yet another facet of the widening split between Britain's strategists and diplomats.

By early January the optimal moment for achieving agreement on Anglo–American naval action had passed. Japan handled the *Panay* crisis shrewdly, accepting the notes of protest with profuse apologies and thus obviating the chance of an overwhelming Anglo–American combination. Lindsay recognized this from his Washington vantage-point, and he warned the Foreign Office that the Americans 'greatly prefer to act independently of us and to avoid any appearance of collusion or of joint action'.[68] Despite this, London decided to resolve the matter, and Lindsay was told on 7 January that British naval preparations were in their most advanced state short of actual mobilization: was the President likely to declare 'a state of emergency' or would he agree to parallel steps, such as sending an advance naval force to Hawaii?[69] Roosevelt's decisions were taken at a conference with his advisers on the tenth, and Lindsay was informed that (*a*) it would be announced, as previously arranged, that three American

---

66 Ingersoll memorandum for Admiral Leahy on discussions in London. Office of Naval History. Washington, D.C. Copy in Adm. 1/9822. Eden's account in, Eden to Lindsay, disp. No. 23, 1 January 1938. F95/84/10. (22106).
67 Eden to Chamberlain, 31 January 1938. Premier 1/276. Also, J. Harvey (ed.), *The diplomatic diaries of Oliver Harvey, 1937–1940* (London, 1970), p. 81.
68 Lindsay to Foreign Office, tel. No. 5, 3 January 1938. F96/84/10. (22106).
69 Cadogan to Lindsay, tel. No. 19, 7 January 1938. *Ibid.*

cruisers would visit Singapore; (*b*) if — but only if — Britain announced preparations, then within a few days it would be announced that vessels of the U.S. Pacific fleet were to have their bottoms scraped, namely, prepared for action; (*c*) after that, an announcement would be made that the U.S. Pacific manoeuvres were being advanced to early February.[70] This effectively put the ball back in the British court and on 11 January the Foreign Office (Eden was in France), Chatfield and Chamberlain reviewed the situation. They agreed that Britain was getting dangerously close to mobilization, and it was feared that an announcement would set in motion an automatic sequence of actions and reactions. Chatfield, Cadogan told the Prime Minister, was especially worried about the Mediterranean:

> He has, as you know, some misgivings on the score of the Italian situation, and it certainly has to be remembered that if the fleet were to sail in three or four weeks, that might be just at the time when we are trying to come to terms with Mussolini, who might choose to think that he was in a stronger position for dealing with us if the fleet were removed from home waters and the Mediterranean.

Chamberlain agreed that it was 'a most unfortunate moment to send the fleet away and I would therefore take no immediate action which would involve us in having to do so'. It was decided instead to protest in Tokyo and play for time.[71] As it turned out these were the final important exchanges in this episode, as the absence of further incidents in the Far East and the appearance of Roosevelt's celebrated initiative in the realm of international law defused the emergency.

London's 'misgivings' about the Mediterranean, which crippled initiative in the Far East at the one moment in the pre-war period when decisive Anglo—American co-operation seemed possible, were frankly admitted during the naval talks between Ingersoll and the naval staff. The agreed 'Record of Conversations' of 13 January 1938 is an important historical document because it reflected the reality of Britain's strategic dilemma far more accurately than did the soothing appreciations circulated to the Dominions six months earlier. After outlining the size of Britain's Far Eastern fleet and the plans for its passage to Singapore, the document returned to possible European contingencies, what Chatfield called his 'back door'. If the fleet had moved east and Germany became hostile, 'a most serious problem

---

[70] Lindsay to Cadogan, tel. No. 29, 10 January 1938. F407/84/10. (22106).
[71] Minutes by Chatfield, Cadogan and Chamberlain. *Ibid.*

would arise'. The Admiralty were not anxious about submarines but they were 'seriously apprehensive of British trade routes in the Atlantic', should the Germans use their three pocket battleships and the two new 27,000-ton ships as commerce raiders:

> An even more dangerous situation would arise should hostilities with Italy also supervene after the greater part of the British Fleet had proceeded to the Far East. It would be necessary for the Admiralty to rely entirely on the alternative route to the East via the Cape of Good Hope. In these circumstances the main problem in the Mediterranean would be to hold the Suez Canal and Egypt. The Admiralty would have to depend on the French Navy to hold the Western Mediterranean and some of her Naval forces would have to be based on Gibraltar to secure the Western entrance . . .
>
> In the event of such a general European war it would almost certainly be necessary to effect a considerable reduction in the British strength in the Far East.[72]

All of this made Chatfield's warnings during the Abyssinian crisis seem prophetic indeed. Insecurity in the Mediterranean at a time of naval weakness had exposed, as he predicted, the eastern circumference of the Empire to Japan; and *ipso facto* it also increased Britain's dependence upon decisions made in Washington. Had the fleet been sent, England's interests in the Mediterranean and Middle East would have become hostages to fortune and the whims of Mussolini. But there was another overriding incentive to keep the fleet in European waters. Chamberlain had decided, and the Cabinet and the Chiefs of Staff were strongly in favour, that a fresh and comprehensive attempt at European appeasement must be made in early 1938. This would involve bilateral approaches to both Italy and Germany. For these to be successful Britain would require a strong bargaining posture; it would, as the Prime Minister wrote, be a 'most unfortunate moment to send the fleet away'. The time for dealing with Japan would come when naval re-armament was complete and, it would be hoped, stability had been achieved in Europe.

England's global predicament had entered a new phase. London's defence policy-makers drew two important conclusions from their analysis of the threatening, concurrent difficulties in two hemispheres.

---

72 'Record of Conversations', 13 January 1938. Adm. 116/3922. The author has discussed the Far Eastern crisis and the Ingersoll mission in, 'The Anglo–American naval conversations on the Far East of January 1938', *International Affairs* (October 1971).

In the first place, they were forced to re-assess the measure of risk that was acceptable in the Mediterranean in light of a potential Far Eastern crisis. Whereas they had for several months refused to allocate even marginal defence resources to that theatre, by February 1938 they had concluded that British forces in the Middle East should be brought up to a degree of self-sufficiency in case the fleet moved east. 'The greater the tension in the Far East', they admitted, 'the more important becomes the necessity for security in the Mediterranean.'[73] The imperial defence system was interdependent.

The Services now also determined to have liabilities reduced through decisive action on the international front. Faster rearmament was essential, but a more immediate need was a diplomatic effort to reduce the number of England's enemies. 'Realizing', Chatfield told Inskip, 'that a long period must elapse before we can be reasonably secure, we have urged . . . the reduction of our enemies.' The greatest weakness lay not in Europe but in the Empire:

> Imperially we are exceedingly weak because we are so vulnerable. If at the present time, and for many years to come, we had to send a Fleet to the Far East, even in conjunction with the United States, we should be left so weak in Europe that we should be liable to blackmail or worse.[74]

Britain's half-armed imperialism could not yet hope to cope with a dual attack from Germany and Japan, and the loss of its traditional security in the Mediterranean had so complicated its general strategic posture that security would have to be sought in the diplomatic market-place. The global dilemma was thus the forcing-house of appeasement.

But appeasement of whom? A general settlement with Hitler was the *sine qua non* of imperial safety and a policy that was advocated by all of Britain's top policy-makers and fervently supported by their military advisers. Agreement with Japan, which would inevitably involve recognition of that power's position in China, was a far more difficult proposition because of England's growing dependence on the United States. Not even Chamberlain was willing to assume the risks inherent in such a policy. On the other hand, appeasement of Italy would strengthen Britain's position in Europe and the Far East and the sacrifice of prestige would be tolerable. It was evident that risks in the

[73] Chiefs of Staff, 'Defence of Egypt'. C.O.S.686, 14 February 1938. Enclosure in C.P. 41(38). Cab.24/275.
[74] Chatfield to Inskip, 25 January 1938. Chatfield Papers.

Mediterranean could not be so easily dismissed in practice as in theory, and this in turn suggested that British grand strategy was grounded in illusions. Unless Italy could somehow be eliminated from the complications of overlapping and conflicting commitments, the whole system of imperial defence priorities would have to be recast. From the strategic point of view, at least, all the indicators pointed in the direction of a Mediterranean appeasement.

3. Strategy, Diplomacy and Mediterranean Appeasment

The policy debate on Mediterranean questions touched off among Britain's decision-makers by the Abyssinian affair had, as outlined above, outlasted that crisis and was expressed in its aftermath in the search for fresh policies that would serve both strategic and diplomatic interests. The Foreign Office had come under steady pressure from the fighting Services to conciliate Italy despite the fact that England's general position throughout the Mediterranean seemed to be under constant attack from that power. By November 1936 Anthony Eden, influenced by this advice and having digested the bitter pill of the League's failure, had given the green light to conversations in Rome between Sir Eric Drummond and Count Galeazzo Ciano, the Italian Foreign Minister. The talks bore the fruit of the 'gentleman's agreement' of 2 January 1937, an instrument dedicated to the consecration of the *status quo* in the Mediterranean. The pact was rendered void of meaning within days and the Mediterranean crisis passed into its most dangerous phase of the pre-war period, a phase characterized by relentless antagonism between Italy and Britain and Italy and France and by a series of emergencies and war scares arising from the war in Spain. Against a rapidly deteriorating global background London's decision-makers weighed and debated alternative policies: should England lead an anti-Italian coalition in the Mediterranean; plan war and divert its own rearmament programme into the Mediterranean; isolate Italy by settling with Germany; or come to a bilateral understanding with Mussolini — and at what cost? The options were not clear-cut and the priorities of defence, diplomacy and finance strongly exerted themselves to circumscribe freedom of choice and action. But there was nothing inevitable about the decision finally reached to appease Italy; rather, it reflected the outcome of a long-standing dispute among leading ministers and officials over an appropriate role for England at a time of grave international crisis.

The 'gentleman's agreement' had attempted to resolve little and accomplished nothing. Both sides acknowledged the right of free passage through the Mediterranean and agreed to observe the regional *status quo*, but the outstanding conflicts dividing the two competing empires were untouched and left to fester. It was not an effort in 'appeasement', for no concessions were made on either side; 'we had yielded nothing to get this Agreement', Lord Avon recalled,[1] but on the other hand, nothing was gained. No mention was made of Italy's desire for *de jure* diplomatic recognition of its Abyssinian conquest, Britain's position in the Middle East remained vulnerable to propaganda and Rome's assurances on the integrity of Spain were rendered meaningless within days. In all, it was an unimaginative approach to a complex set of problems and that it failed to bring about an Anglo–Italian reconciliation or to pacify the Mediterranean can have surprised neither party. For Britain it above all failed to bring security.

Shortly after the signing of the 'gentleman's agreement', the Foreign Office learned that an additional, large expeditionary force of Italian troops had landed in nationalist Spain. The news, Eden wired Drummond, 'has seriously disquieted and disappointed me'.[2] It must also have embarrassed him as it appeared that Mussolini had used the negotiations with London as a cover for his military moves and that the Foreign Office had, whether unwittingly or not, thereby aided the fascist cause in Spain. War Office intelligence sources working inside Italy gave the British a detailed picture of that power's role in the first weeks of 1937 when a major Axis intervention into the Civil War was carried out. Between December and February, they estimated, a minimum of 50,000 blackshirts complete with arms, equipment and transport had entered Spain,[3] more than fulfilling what Vansittart called the unholy bargain among fascists. Eden, who had earlier agreed to friendly approaches to Italy, now concluded 'that there was no value in negotiating with Mussolini again, unless he first carried out the engagements he had already entered into'.[4]

The Foreign Secretary was also facing setbacks at home on

1 The Earl of Avon, *The Eden memoirs: facing the dictators* (London, 1962), p. 433.
2 Eden to Drummond, tel. No. 13, 7 January 1937. W457/7/41. (21318).
3 See War Office letters and intelligence summaries in W1698/W2548/W3038/ 7/41. (21321–21323). The War Office described their 'anti-Fascist' sources as 'most secret sources of unimpeachable authority' and later surmised that Russia had access to 'the same excellent Italian sources that we have ourselves'. Their Italian information was better, they claimed, than their intelligence in France! Later, however, at the time of the Munich and Albanian crises there seems to have been a dearth of reliable intelligence from Italy on military matters.
4 Avon, *Facing the dictators*, p. 433.

Mediterranean issues. He had urged the Cabinet in early January to approve a vigorous role for the navy off the coasts of Spain in an effort to reduce intervention and also, it seems certain, to defuse domestic criticism of Britain's ineffective role. His policy was not to end the Civil War but to gain time by prolonging it, thus denying Hitler and Mussolini and their radical advisers another early success. The Foreign Office plan for a unilateral British naval blockage foundered, however, on the Admiralty's entrenched opposition. Hoare worried that the plan would aid Bolshevism in Spain and other ministers raised the prospect of major incidents at sea. Hoare and the naval staff had mustered an impressive list of technical arguments in support of their do-nothing policy and Eden, after a two-day discussion, abandoned the scheme. The Cabinet agreed to continue the existing so-called control plan, and Hoare wrote off the incident as just another instance of Foreign Office irresponsibility.[5] It was an important victory for Hoare and his colleagues on the Right and adds credence to the argument that in fact they tacitly agreed with the Italo—German intervention in Spain and used their considerable influence to block any action that might forestall the success of that policy or contribute to the republican-Soviet cause.

England's short-lived reconciliation with Mussolini was followed by an abrupt deterioration of Anglo—Italian relations at all levels in the early months of 1937. By mid-April Eden had to tell his military colleagues that Italy seemed a greater danger to peace than Germany and that 'at the present moment trouble was more likely to arise in the Mediterranean than elsewhere in Europe'.[6] The friction and tension, much aggravated by the *Deutschland—Leipzig* crisis, continued to grow until early July when the developing atmosphere of a war scare galvanized the British Government into new approaches to Mussolini. Spain had touched this off and it remained an important element in the volatile Great Power politics of the Mediterranean; but there were other far-removed sources of Anglo—Italian antagonism that saw the two imperialisms competing for mastery of the Mediterranean and for political advantage from the Balkans to the Red Sea.

To begin with European questions: London had watched with

---

5   Memorandum by Eden, 8 January 1937. C.P.6 (37). Cab.24/267; Cab. Conclusions, 8 and 9 January 1937. Cab.23/87. Avon, *Facing the dictators*, pp. 433—6. Hoare's comment in Templewood Papers: listing this as one item of Foreign Office irresponsibility, Hoare added, 'I destroyed it.'

6   D.P.(P.)/1st mtg., 19 April. Cab.16/181.

growing dismay as Hitler and Mussolini began to compose their differences and, reacting to events, especially the war in Spain, drew closer together. By December 1936 Vansittart, who had predicted such a development during the Abyssinian crisis, warned that it now dominated 'the whole situation along the Danube' and called for a policy to divide Rome and Berlin. There were historic conflicts of interest between them, especially in Austria, and these could best be cultivated if Britain was strong enough to be an attractive alternative.[7] Vansittart, like many other British policy-makers, including Chamberlain, Halifax and Hankey, never departed from the conviction that the Italo—German friendship was a forced and totally unnatural alliance which ran against historical tradition and was bound to result in Italy's exclusion from the affairs of Central Europe and ultimately turn it into a German satellite. It followed that Italy should welcome a return to friendly relations with the leading Mediterranean power; moreover, it was in Britain's interest to offer this. To appease Italy might divide the Axis and isolate Germany, or at least Mussolini could be used as a 'Trojan horse' to gain access to the Axis camp and indirectly influence Hitler. The whole analysis suffered from a distorted mirror-image logic by assuming that Italian interests were calculated in Rome by the same criteria as those employed in Whitehall; certainly it underestimated the role of personality and ideological factors in the formation of Italian diplomacy. In any event, Vansittart was correct when he warned the Chiefs of Staff that the Axis had been strengthened in early 1937, and that 'Whether or not this axis will endure is a speculation which is not at present to the point. What we have to deal with is the fact that it is there now.'[8]

The danger signals were thus up in Europe but also in the Middle East, where the British and Italian empires jostled each other with an uncommon amount of friction. Italy's clumsy attempts to form links with pan-Arab nationalists opposed to the existing imperial order were seen in London as sinister and potentially dangerous, with Palestine in rebellion and British prestige in eclipse because of the Abyssinian fiasco. The Foreign Office closely monitored Bari radio broadcasts in Arabic attacking the Palestine administration, the British army in the Middle East and English imperial policy in Arabia and India. In the Middle East

7 Vansittart, 'The World Situation and British Rearmament', 31 December 1936. W18355/18355/50. (20467).
8 Vansittart to Colonel Ismay, 15 February 1937. App. 2 to C.O.S./198th mtg., 18 February 1937. Cab.53/7.

itself, Italian propaganda was quite well organized around 'cultural centres' and 'tourist agencies' and particularly flourished among the large Italian community in Egypt. The British saw Italian finance linked to several radical newspapers and of course to organizations such as the 'green shirts' of Egypt, which were modelled on Fascist style. Mussolini gave the campaign a personal and pretentious boost during his visit to Libya in March 1937 when he proclaimed himself 'Protector of Islam', a title not without a gruesome irony considering Italy's colonial policies.

These and other symptoms of Italian intrigue were carefully studied at the seat of British influence in the Near East, the Residency (now Embassy) in Cairo, since 1934 administered by Sir Miles Lampson (later Lord Killearn), England's formidable Ambassador to Egypt. Lampson, whose role and policies in the Middle East will be examined later, was already known in London to be highly alarmed about Italian expansionism and convinced that a trial of strength between the two empires was inevitable. By the end of 1937 he was to launch, with Vansittart's support, an impressive campaign for British rearmament in the Middle East; shortly after the failure of the 'gentleman's agreement' — a failure he had confidently predicted — he began to strengthen his own propaganda network and to work an anti-Italian theme into that portion of the Egyptian press subsidized by British funds. He believed, with Eden, that Italy's ambitions stopped short of nothing less than the rebirth of the Roman Empire and this clearly meant a struggle with England for Mediterranean supremacy. The way to deal with Mussolini, he advised his superior, was to come to terms with Germany; Italy would thereby be isolated and Britain stronger in the Mediterranean to force a showdown on its own terms.[9]

Lampson and the Foreign Office were also deeply suspicious of Italian aspirations on the Arabian shores of the Red Sea, where England and Italy supposedly refrained from forward policies under the terms of the Rome Understanding of 1927. They accused Italian political agents of fomenting intrigue in the Yemen, which was 'very unstable', and the Foreign Office wanted to issue a public declaration of interest in the region. They were, however, blocked by the Admiralty's insistence that

---

9   Sir M. Lampson (Cairo) to Eden, tel. No. 52, 22 May 1937. R3795/1/22.
(21159). Cf. R3160/1/22. (21158), for a selection of reports from Bari radio
and other organs of Italian propaganda. Also, S. Arsenian, 'War time
propaganda in the Middle East', *Middle East Journal* (1951).

nothing was more important than Anglo–Italian amity;[10] the naval staff seem to have been strangely indifferent to the fate of their communications through the Red Sea before 1939. Lampson, however, had the strategic view much in mind and viewed Italian activity in Arabia with 'extreme gravity'. He was frankly sceptical of the value of conciliating Italy 'in her present mood of cocksuredness': 'I have long felt convinced that we are approaching the parting of the ways with Italy, who, having annexed Abyssinia was certain sooner or later . . . to try and do the same thing across the Red Sea in the Yemen.'[11] In lieu of a settlement of these differences, the Foreign Office resolved in early 1937 to extend their own influence in the Aden Protectorate and also, if possible, to penetrate the Yemen. Thus they served notice that they would not passively acquiesce in a challenge to England's traditional paramountcy in the Red Sea and Persian Gulf region.

In the Balkans, Britain was actively working to keep Italy divided from the lesser powers of the Eastern Mediterranean. In a memorandum of 1 April Eden set down his personal suspicions of Italian motives and betrayed his disappointment at the conclusion of the Italo–Yugoslav treaty of 25 March 1937. England had worked to thwart an agreement to prevent Yugoslavia being dragged into the Italian camp or becoming a neutral in any future Mediterranean war. Italy's menace to British interests in the Balkans was 'limited only by her material weakness' and he disagreed with a *Times* article advocating a Turkish–Italian understanding. The Embassy in Ankara was warned that London did not want the Turks to repeat the Yugoslavs' essay in diplomacy, the Rome–Belgrade talks had been viewed with 'much misgiving' at the Foreign Office.[12] Eden's sentiments on these points, including his description of Italian policy as 'vindictive', were passed on to British missions in the Balkans and also to Drummond in Rome, where they apparently fell into the hands of the Italian intelligence service during one of its regular burglaries of the British Embassy safe. This information, according to Professor Toscano, was in part responsible for the vicious personal campaign against Eden waged by the controlled Italian press in this period.[13]

10 Middle East (official) Subcommittee [M.E.(O.)]/51st mtg., 8 June 1937. Cab.51/4.
11 Lampson to Eden, 18 December 1936. E2979/872/91. (10780).
12 Minute by Eden, 1 April 1937. R2258/1/22. (21158). Eden to Sir P. Loraine (Ankara), tel. No. 56, 5 April 1937. *Ibid. The Times*, 1 April 1937. J. Harvey (ed.), *The Diplomatic Diaries of Oliver Harvey* (London, 1970), pp. 24–6.
13 M. Toscano, 'Problemi Particolari della Storia della Seconda Guerra Mondiale', in *Pagine di storia diplomatica contemporanea* (Milan, 1963), II. Cf. D.C.

The pace and direction of Italian rearmament constituted another issue of contention between the two empires. In early March 1937, after several weeks of regime-inspired polemics on the British rearmament programme, the Fascist Grand Council announced their intention to increase military expenditure and to attain a high degree of autarchy 'because only thereby could a poorer people resist possible aggression by those richer in money and possessors of greater natural resources'. The southward thrust of Italian rearmament, with the development of aerial bases in south Italy, Sicily and Pantelleria, was remarked publicly by General Valle, head of the Italian air force, while Admiral Gavagnari proclaimed a programme of naval expansion. In Africa Italy had announced an expansion of its native army in Abyssinia, thus horrifying South Africa and most white imperialists; it had instituted a North African High Command, raised the establishment of the Libyan garrison and opened a coastal road in that colony that pointed ominously at the Suez Canal.[14] These decisions and their extravagant picture of Italy's true military capacity received much comment in the House of Commons and in the English press.[15] An ongoing press feud between the two countries peaked in late March when several British journals, which had previously carried reports of the massacres of Abyssinians in February, gleefully headlined Italy's humiliation by Spanish republican forces at Guadalajara – 'The Italian Skedaddle', wrote Lloyd George; 'a second Caporetto', reported the B.B.C. – and had to be restrained by the news department of the Foreign Office.[16] From Rome an unhappy Drummond did what he could to allay suspicions, pointing out that Italy had its own suspicions about Britain's rearmament: Italians feared that England might use its strength 'to brow-beat in the ancient Jingo style, even if the ships and the men and the money are trumpeted forth in the name of collective security'.[17]

Thus the Anglo–Italian interaction, with its intensive competition

---

Watt's remarks on Italy's penetration of British security, both in London and Rome, in his introduction to D. Irving (ed.), *Breach of Security* (London, 1968).

[14] Drummond to Eden, tel. No. 113, 2 March 1937. R1579/1/22. (21157).

[15] See, for example, *The Economist*, 6 March 1937; *The Scotsman*, 3 March 1937; *The New Statesman*, 6 March 1937; *News Chronicle*, 3 March 1937; *Sunday Times*, 7 March 1937.

[16] Harvey, *The diplomatic diaries of Oliver Harvey*, p. 34. On several occasions Harvey noted how the House of Commons was 'almost bellicose' about Italy.

[17] Drummond to Eden, disp. No. 263, 25 March 1937. R183/1/22. (21157).

and conflict, mutual suspicions and popular outcries, was beginning to resemble the early stages of the classic arms race. Eden was on several occasions urged by his advisers — Vansittart and Drummond in particular — to break the increasingly bitter Mediterranean deadlock by acting on *de jure* recognition of Italy's conquest of Abyssinia, but the Foreign Secretary was cool to this proposal and he did not give a strong lead at the May assembly at Geneva to have this done.[18] On this issue Eden agreed with the oft-repeated remark that one could call a corpse a corpse without condoning murder, but he clearly preferred a less conspicuous role than undertaker. 'I can imagine', he later minuted, 'nothing more gratifying to [Mussolini] than the picture of a British Foreign Secretary "touting" for signatures to secure the expulsion of Abyssinia in order that conversations may begin with Italy.'[19]

The fundamental obstacle to a new conciliatory approach was political. It must be recalled that by early 1937 Italy, far more than Germany, had become anathema to a broad and influential section of British opinion, and not just of the Left. If Mussolini's style of Fascist law and order had once been the object of admiration for the English middle class, that had been largely dissipated by his flaunting of the League and by his invasion and brutal repression of Abyssinia. To the Opposition — that is, the Labour Party, trade unions and Left press — as well as liberal opinion, Italy seemed the arch-villain in Spain, flagrantly mocking 'non-intervention' in a far more conspicuous manner than Germany. But Italy was also unpopular on the Right. Here Italy looked no more reprehensible for its conduct in Spain than Soviet Russia,[20] but Mussolini's actions in the Eastern Mediterranean, England's traditional preserve, were harder to justify; there he seemed to be in deliberate opposition to Britain's own imperial-maritime aspirations. In 1937, before the *Anschluss* and Munich, many enthusiastically supported the idea of agreement with Nazi Germany, a rising nation considered by a powerful body of English opinion to have legitimate grievances; but far fewer advocated the appeasement of Italy, whose ambitions, apparently unlike Germany's, directly

18 Cab. Conclusions, 2 June 1937. Cab.23/88.
19 Minute by Eden, 26 August 1937. R5617/64/22. (21167).
20 On British attitudes to the Spanish Civil War, see K. Watkins, *Britain divided* (London, 1963). Italian colonial policy in Abyssinia is traced in Angelo del Boca, *The Ethiopian war 1935–1941* (Milan, 1965). In early 1937 the English press closely followed the savage reprisals that attended the unsuccessful assassination attempt against Italy's Viceroy in Abyssinia, Marshal Graziani, of whom it was said that his policy was to create 'an Ethiopia without Ethiopians'.

interlocked and clashed with England's and seemed in any case to spring from Mussolini's personal quest for glory rather than from past injustices.

London's military advisers were nevertheless determined to have their understanding with Rome. At the first meeting of the new Defence Plans (Policy) Subcommittee in mid-April they reacted to Eden's criticisms of their planning assumptions by demanding a renewed diplomatic effort to clarify the Mediterranean situation. Hoare thought the atmosphere as bad as it had been during the Abyssinian crisis and Chatfield, Hankey and Duff Cooper, Secretary of State for War, pressed Eden, to no avail, to conciliate Italy. Whenever such an approach was made, Eden glumly reported, an outburst from the House of Commons undid all the good.[21] Strategic and political interests were in conflict and the Foreign Secretary was caught in the middle, as Sir Orme Sargent's minute indicated:

> When at our conversation yesterday the Secretary of State said that the Foreign Office were suspect on account of their 'pro-Italian' policy, I pointed out that the policy of re-establishing friendly relations with Italy was not a Foreign Office invention but was the result of the very strong representations which had been repeatedly made by the Chiefs of Staff, and more particularly by the Admiralty during the last year.[22]

Eden, reflecting popular antipathy to Italy, had in fact shelved conciliation as a strategy for dealing with that power and was preparing to play two alternative cards, both designed to strengthen England's negotiating and war-making posture in the Mediterranean. First, by settling with Germany, Britain could split the Axis and isolate Italy while reducing the strain on home defence; second, this would free the Services to plan and rearm in the Mediterranean and Middle East for a diplomatic showdown or test of strength with Italy, the challenging empire.

Eden was in firm agreement with Sir Miles Lampson that Britain should isolate Mussolini by coming to terms with Germany; this was one reason, he wrote in reference to the planned talks with the German

---

[21] D.P. (P.)/1st mtg., 19 April 1937. Cab.16/181.
[22] Minute by Sargent, 1 April 1937. R2261/5/67. (21136). Sargent suggested the political opposition could be defused if party leaders were confidentially informed of 'the real reasons which make it essential to place our relations with Italy on as friendly a footing as possible'. There is no evidence that this was done.

Foreign Minister, why 'I am anxious for Herr von Neurath's visit'.[23] Insecurity in the Empire was an important incentive to settle in Europe with Hitler. During the Imperial Conference British spokesmen had come under strong pressure from several of the Dominions to seek an understanding with Berlin, and Neville Chamberlain, who succeeded Baldwin as Prime Minister during the conference, had spoken of his own Government's wish for a general settlement with Germany, 'the great hope of emerging from the vicious circle'. Eden had looked forward to a general easing of the international situation and, barely a month after the Guernica atrocity — which the Foreign Office knew had been carried out by German aircraft — he told the prime ministers of the Commonwealth how Germany, unlike Italy, had co-operated 'loyally, efficiently and zealously' at the non-intervention committee. He was clear that Italy was at present a greater danger to European peace than Germany.[24]

An opportunity to seize the diplomatic initiative occurred at the end of May when the capitals of Europe were given a severe fright by the *Deutschland* incident. Eden was not exaggerating when he told the Imperial Conference that the situation was 'critical'. In his memoirs he suggests that the attack on the German pocket battleship *Deutschland* by Spanish republican aircraft was 'apparently a desperate act of indiscipline', but this was not his opinion at the time. With other British policy-makers, Eden believed that the republicans, acting on Soviet orders, had deliberately tried to provoke Germany into declaring war on the Valencia government; that this would bring about a general war, Valencia's only hope of stopping Franco, and serve Moscow's interest in embroiling the capitalist powers of Europe. He told the American Ambassador three days after the incident that 'it looked as if the Soviet Government wanted the British to pull its chestnuts out of the fire and would not be disturbed if Germany was at war with England and France leaving Russia with a comparatively free hand on the other side'.[25] If the intention was indeed to provoke a world war — and evidence from Spanish sources suggests that Stalin and his agents in

---

23 Minute by Eden in R3795/1/22. (21159).
24 Cab.32/128.
25 Bingham to Hull, 1 June 1937. *Foreign Relations of the United States (F.R.U.S.)*, 1937, I, 317–18. Avon, *Facing the dictators*, p. 446. Admiral Pound reported that 'There appears to be no doubt but that the bombing of the *Deutschland* was deliberate and the explanation generally put forward is that the Reds wanted to bring the Germans in against them and make that an

Valencia in fact played a decisive *restraining* role after the German reprisal shelling of Almeria when such a strategy was really being considered[26] — it very nearly succeeded. The German Foreign Minister, Baron von Neurath, told the French Ambassador to Berlin, André François-Poncet, how the decisions to bombard Almeria and withdraw from non-intervention and the naval patrol were moderated versions of Hitler's original intentions:

> Au reçu de la nouvelle concernant l'incident, la première impulsion du chancelier Hitler, transporté d'indignation et de colère, avait été, en effet, de déclarer la guerre au gouvernement de Valence. Il n'aurait pas fallu moins de six heures de débat et d'argumentation pour l'amener à se contenter de sanctions moins graves.[27]

Eden quickly moved to secure the early return of Germany and Italy to non-intervention and the naval patrol scheme and, after a series of exchanges, temporarily succeeded. But his first priority, as he told the Cabinet, 'was to get into direct communication with Berlin, and to bring about Anglo—German co-operation on the Spanish question'.[28] With Chamberlain's approval, the Foreign Office invited von Neurath to London for discussions on this and other outstanding issues; it was to be the first important step towards that general settlement with Germany that Chamberlain had described at the Imperial Conference, a step all the more necessary after the *Deutschland* incident had been interpreted as sinister proof of a conspiracy against such a settlement. No parallel moves in the direction of an Anglo—Italian understanding were planned, however, because an objective of the approach to von Neurath was to isolate Italy, a fact that did not escape a much-alarmed Mussolini.[29]

In the event, the Duce's fears proved unjustified. Hitler, in another

---

excuse for packing up — however, I am not much impressed with that suggestion but there is I believe a growing feeling amongst the Reds that they cannot win . . . ' Pound to Chatfield, 18 June 1937. Chatfield Papers.

[26] Hugh Thomas, *The Spanish Civil War* (London, 1965), citing Spanish memoirs, points out that Stalin, when informed of a proposal to bomb the entire German fleet in the Mediterranean after the Almeria shelling, replied that Moscow had no desire for a world war and that the scheme should at all costs be defeated, even if its backers had to be murdered. The idea was turned down by the Valencia cabinet and without such drastic action. pp. 565—6. It seems therefore unlikely that Moscow was behind the original *Deutschland* attack, but the incident remains something of a mystery.

[27] François-Poncet à Delbos, 31 May 1937, *D.D.F.*, 2, V, No. 476.

[28] Cab. Conclusions, 2 June 1937. Cab.23/88.

[29] *Documents on German Foreign Policy*, D, III, Nos. 320, 328.

fit of temper about alleged submarine attacks against the German cruiser *Leipzig*, cancelled the Neurath visit, left the patrol scheme for good and presented demands for a joint naval demonstration off Valencia. For this show of restraint he was praised in the House of Commons by Chamberlain, but Vansittart told Hugh Dalton of the Labour Party of the Foreign Office's fears that Germany and Italy might blockade the coast of republican Spain and touch off a war. Hitler had never been so ' "hot under the collar", so hysterical and dangerous to the peace of Europe' as after the two naval incidents.[30] Dalton was not told that the Foreign Office apparently believed the German allegations, despite the fact that they were supported by extremely flimsy evidence, that the *Leipzig* had been attacked by Valencia submarines; moreover, the British again believed that they were witnessing a fresh attempt by Leftists to embroil Europe.[31] The explanation was rooted not in sound information but in an ideological image: in January Eden and Vansittart had expressed their agreement with Sargent's opinion that it was the 'consistent and natural policy of the Soviet Government to foster disagreement and discord between the capitalist Powers of Europe and especially between Germany and Great Britain' and that this policy was particularly at work in Spain.[32] Here was a powerful incentive to exclude Russia from the Mediterranean and to eschew ideological blocks involving that power's co-operation.

Although the prospects for isolating Italy through an Anglo–German agreement seemed diminished after von Neurath's visit was dropped, Eden and Chamberlain, as will be seen, had by no means abandoned this card. Meanwhile Eden had a second strategy, which was to bring him into opposition with the Prime Minister. He was determined to have Italy placed on the list of potential enemies so that war plans for the Mediterranean could be drawn up and a regional programme of re-armament begun. This would involve a direct challenge to the system of

---

30 Hugh Dalton Diaries, entry of 24 June 1937. British Library of Economics and Political Science. London School of Economics, Hereafter, Dalton Diaries.

31 Harvey memorandum for Eden, 20 June 1937. In Harvey, *The Diplomatic diaries of Oliver Harvey*, app. E, 409–11. Eden and Chatfield vented their suspicions at the Foreign Policy Committee on 28 June. F.P. (36)/15th mtg., Cab.27/622.

32 W1271/3/41. (21320). A year later Chamberlain mentioned in his diary how the Russians were 'stealthily and cunningly pulling all the strings to get us involved in war with Germany (our Secret Service doesn't spend all its time looking out of the window) ... ' Feiling, *The life of Neville Chamberlain*, p. 347.

defence priorities and a major intervention into the policy-making process. The Foreign Office, charged with maintaining Britain's prestige, were convinced that the risks being taken in the Middle East were unacceptable and they knew, if Mussolini did not, that their own military expansion in that area existed only on paper and that since the lifting of sanctions there had been no Mediterranean rearmament whatsoever. If guns were better than butter, remarked Vansittart, they were also better than Mussolini's word, sentiments echoed by Ambassador Drummond, another 'pro-Italian' official. Drummond felt that, although Italy was not necessarily vindictive, 'her policy is opportunism, based on force, and to deal with her satisfactorily it is essential to be sufficiently strong and if necessary to convey the impression that we should not hesitate to use our strength.'[33] With this Eden certainly agreed; translating conviction into policy, however, was always another matter.

When the formula governing rearmament was reconsidered by the C.I.D. in February 1937 the Foreign Office argued that the operating assumption of Italian friendship was outdated. The Admiralty too thought it folly to exclude the contingency of a Mediterranean war, but it was pointed out that some of the proposals — such as a Cyprus naval base — involved prohibitive expenditure. Chamberlain, then Chancellor of the Exchequer, took the line that it would be unfortunate to follow up the 'gentleman's agreement' by installing 15-inch guns in the Mediterranean, a view that carried the debate. The formula was slightly revised, but Italy was still not to be counted a probable enemy and a stricture was included against large expenditure on Mediterranean ports.[34] Thus policy remained quite unchanged and over the next few months the new formula effectively blocked any major rearmament schemes for the Mediterranean—Middle East—Red Sea region. In April, for instance, the Joint Overseas and Home Defence Subcommittee decided that although the theoretical defence requirements of Gibraltar and Malta included heavy (13·5 inch or above) counter-bombardment guns, in view of the ruling against heavy expense, lighter guns had to be accepted as sufficient deterrent.

The Foreign Office returned to the attack shortly after the Imperial Conference. Eden and his advisers, considering defence policy dangerously out of step with the real world, put their case for Mediterranean

---

[33] Drummond to O. O'Malley, 21 April 1937. R2868/1/22. (21158).
[34] C.I.D. minutes, 11 February 1937. C.P. 65(37). Cab.24/268.

rearmament in a Cabinet and C.I.D. paper of 15 June 1937. The memorandum ranged over the whole panoply of Anglo—Italian relations and concluded that the evidence belied Mussolini's claim that Italy was a 'satisfied Power'. There was 'definite ill will in the whole trend of Italy's present foreign policy', and this could not be sufficiently explained by domestic or psychological factors. Eden had described the Mediterranean as an 'arterial road' the previous November, adding that freedom of entry, transit and exit was a vital British interest, but it now seemed that Italy's expansionist tendencies were irreconcilable with England's control of that road. Italy would probably not start a single-handed war with Britain that it could never win, but there was a far greater danger that if England came into conflict with Germany or Japan, or became involved with an Arab revolt (the Peel Commission had just recommended partition of Palestine), an opportunistic Mussolini might exploit weakness through blackmail or force. A deterrent was required to make British interests less vulnerable to Italian pressure. And there was an even more important reason for being stronger in the Mediterranean theatre. Hitler was not yet ready for a trial by force in Europe, but if Britain and France became entangled in a Mediterranean crisis he might seize the moment to 'embark on adventures likely to precipitate a general conflict'.

> It is surely in just such a conjunction of circumstances that the danger of war with Germany is most readily found; and if this be so, it is manifest that adequate preparation to resist pressure from Italy and consequently to prevent that pressure from being recklessly exercised, is an important if indirect means of preventing a conflict between this country and Germany from breaking out.

The Foreign Office concluded that Italy must be counted a probable enemy and provisions made on the basis of that formula.[35]

This was no academic proposal. The implications of the Foreign Office policy were that Britain must make preparations, and plan, for war on three fronts. It promised diversion of money and resources from home and Far Eastern defence to the Mediterranean and delays and dislocations in existing programmes. In fact it looked like a challenge to the whole 'limited liability' philosophy around which Britain's system of defence priorities had been constructed, and, as such, it seemed to question the policies of those directing the rearmament effort. On all of

35 Eden, 'The Probability of War with Italy', 15 June 1937. C.P. 183 (37). Cab.24/270.

these grounds Eden's proposal could expect entrenched opposition from that centralized group of bureaucrats, ministers and Service planners who effectively controlled the defence policy-making process, especially from the new and very defence-minded Prime Minister. In the last weeks of his period at the Treasury, Chamberlain had launched a study of the defence programme with a view to bringing it under his control. The findings were alarming: departmental feuding among the Services, estimates far in excess of those suggested by the defence requirements studies, 'an indefinite series of new and very costly demands coming forward as soon as they happen to be prepared without correlation with each other'. The immediate risk was that Cabinet and Treasury control might vanish; the ultimate prospect, intolerable taxation or bankruptcy. The only answer was to 'insist on correlating the rising burden of Defence liabilities to the whole of our available resources'.[36] Inskip was set to work, with Treasury and supply experts, on a far-reaching review of the Services' requirements: priorities were to be assessed, resources measured and an overall co-ordination of the rearmament programme finally arrived at. In other words, Inskip's 'review' was already prejudiced by its terms of reference. Chamberlain's initiative went to the heart of rearmament and grand strategy in an attempt to reassert the 'Treasury' view of defence: rearmament tied to rigidly defined priorities and within normal economic and financial conditions with the objective of exploiting the Empire's greatest resource, its commercial and financial staying power. Defence spending would go on, but only within the constraints of fiscal orthodoxy, the stability of the pound and a solvent capitalist economy free from government intervention.[37] These were objectives dear to the collective heart of a Cabinet still on the rebound from the trauma of 1931, and their psychological influence on key policy-makers in debates on diplomacy and strategy cannot be over-emphasized.

36 Sir J. Simon, 'Defence Expenditure', 25 June 1937. C.P. 165(37). Cab.24/270. The author of the memorandum, as Simon noted, was actually Chamberlain.
37 Cf. D. C. Watt, 'Sir Warren Fisher and the rearmament of Great Britain', in *Personalities and policies* (London, 1965). It must be borne in mind that Inskip's review of defence policy, with its emphasis on correlating finance, supply and defensive commitments, was in progress throughout the last half of 1937 at a moment when England's global dilemma was worsening. Unquestionably, this influenced the Chiefs of Staff, Hankey, Chamberlain and other key Cabinet members in their growing dispute with Eden and the Foreign Office. I am grateful to Mr John Lippincott for advice concerning the 1937 defence review and its implications for policy.

Coming as it did within days of this initiative, Eden's proposal to widen British commitments to active defence against three enemies got a predictably frosty reception. The Services were quick to point out that the effect must be to dissipate limited resources and weaken Britain at home and in the Far East; unless revision of the political formula was followed by a drastic acceleration of the rearmament programme – something Eden did not request – no real improvement in Britain's strategic position in the Mediterranean could be made for years. But at the C.I.D. in early July the Foreign Secretary found himself supported by the India Office and Colonial Office, both of whom were upset by Italy's policies in the Middle East and Red Sea region, and by Hoare, now Home Secretary, who wanted more strength to counter the impression that Britain was 'quitting' the Mediterranean. So it was left to Chamberlain, with all his relentless logic, to put the case for financial and diplomatic priorities. Italy, the Prime Minister began, would attack Britain only if it were sure of German support:

> If Germany were contemplating hostile action or became engaged in hostilities against us, there was little doubt that Italy would join in and take the opportunity to fish in troubled waters. The ideal, no doubt, was to be prepared to fight Germany or Italy or Japan, either separately or in combination. That, however, was a counsel of perfection which it was impossible to follow. There were limits to our resources, both physical and financial, and it was vain to contemplate fighting single-handed the three strongest Powers in combination. He did not leave out of account the fact that we should probably have allies in such a war, notably France, but
> France at the present time was not in a very strong position to give us much help.

Defence and foreign policy had to be correlated, Chamberlain went on, because each influenced the other. Britain's policy should be directed towards a settlement with Germany; if this was done Italy would be unlikely to attack. At any rate, 'we should regard Germany as our greatest potential danger and should give first priority to defensive preparations against that country'. These arguments were strongly supported by the Air Ministry and War Office and the compromise result reflected the division of opinion at the meeting. Italy was henceforth to be regarded as an enemy and war plans would be ordered, but the priority of the German menace and a ruling against 'very heavy expenditure' were included in the new formulation.[38]

38 C.I.D./296th mtg., 5 July 1937. Cab.2/6. Also, 295th mtg., 1 July. *Ibid.*

Chamberlain had not even mentioned the idea of a new diplomatic accommodation with Mussolini. Instead he wanted to settle with Germany and detach Hitler from the Axis, a policy designed to isolate rather than conciliate Italy. 'If only we could get on terms with the Germans', he wrote privately, 'I would not care a rap for Musso.'[39] A man in search of priorities, Chamberlain's foremost concerns in diplomacy lay in improving Anglo—German relations and holding the situation in the Far East; during the Abyssinia crisis he had switched from a strong pro-sanctions to a strong anti-sanctions position, but his few interventions on Mediterranean questions after July 1936 suggest that his sole aim was to block any diversion of arms from the home sector, where he had been trying since 1934 to concentrate rearmament against Germany. On Anglo—Italian relations he seems, until the middle of July 1937, to have been relatively indifferent and the evidence certainly does not credit the theory that he came to the premiership determined to settle with Rome and sought the first opportunity to bring this about. Chamberlain was a man who would have to be persuaded to appease Mussolini.

The storm of the *Deutschland—Leipzig* crisis had barely subsided when information from Rome and the Mediterranean Fleet sharpened anxieties over Italian intentions. Sir Eric Drummond secretly warned Vansittart in the first week of July of a possible 'act of folly' by Mussolini. The atmosphere reminded the Ambassador of the 1935 scare, with war rumours circulating and the press bitterly hostile. There was a chance, Drummond thought, that Italy would strike while Russia and France were internally weak (France was in the midst of a serious political crisis) and British rearmament in its early stages.[40] Chatfield, who had had a similar message from Pound, was alarmed and complained that he was being warned by the Foreign Office and soothed by the Prime Minister at the same time.[41] Drummond's letter was read to the Cabinet on 7 July, but Chamberlain persuaded ministers that little could be done to improve matters; the real counter to Italy was to seek terms with Germany.[42] But Chatfield was not satisfied and warned his Home Fleet commander that the international situation 'is now very dangerous':

I have a further anxiety in the Mediterranean generally. We have very

[39] Feiling, *The life of Neville Chamberlain* (London, 1946), p. 329.
[40] Drummond to Vansittart, 2 July 1937. R4766/1/22. (21159).
[41] Chatfield to Hankey, 7 July 1937. *Ibid.*
[42] Cab. Conclusions, 7 July 1937. Cab.23/88.

conflicting reports about the state of affairs in Italy, and the mentality of Mussolini, particularly if this Non-Intervention Committee breaks down. I do not think we are likely to have to go to war with Italy alone, and I think that Germany is a steadying factor rather than the reverse. But things happen so suddenly nowadays that I am making full preparations in case some untoward event happens in the near future.[43]

Eden was of the same mind and returned to the Cabinet on the fourteenth calling for a 'display of strength' to stabilize the Mediterranean.[44] This was discussed at a special meeting of advisers next day. Chatfield disclosed that the naval situation was 'extremely weak'; England was weaker by a full three destroyer flotillas than it had been in the Mediterranean in 1935. He wanted to hold three cruisers at Gibraltar, reinforce the destroyer strength and put the Mediterranean Fleet at a week's notice. But the War Office and Air Ministry were unwilling to divert resources from home sectors to the Middle East, and the general conclusion was that, aside from naval movements, no measures could be taken that 'would not have the effect of proportionately weakening our position at home *vis-à-vis* Germany'.[45]

The interdependence of Britain's predicaments in Europe and the Mediterranean was such that the Foreign Office's advice on defence was ruled impracticable. But the Eden—Chamberlain policy — to make friends with Hitler — was equally no solution to the immediate Mediterranean crisis of nerves, especially after von Neurath declined his London invitation; and by mid-July there were new and ominous developments in the Far East that gave Britain's dilemma global dimensions. It was at this point that Eden, not Chamberlain, first suggested a fresh conciliatory approach to Italy. After consulting Lord Halifax and Sir Ronald Graham, ex-ambassador to Rome, Eden told Chamberlain on 16 July that it would be well to bypass the anti-British Ciano and therefore, he, Eden, was doing to draft 'a personal letter to Mussolini. Such a course is perhaps excusable in that I have met Mussolini and that he has written to me direct — not lately, but in the early stages of the Abyssinian dispute.'[46] He told the Prime Minister that he was also going to make a conciliatory speech; he was as good as

---

43 Chatfield to Backhouse, 12 July 1937. Chatfield Papers.
44 Cab. Conclusions, 13 July 1937. Cab.23/89.
45 Inskip to Chamberlain, 16 July 1937. Premier 1/276.
46 Eden to Chamberlain, 16 July 1937. Premier 1/276. This letter is not mentioned in Lord Avon's otherwise detailed account of these events.

his word, for his ice-breaking remarks in the House of Commons on the nineteenth — 'The word "vendetta" has no English equivalent' — prompted Count Grandi to seek the interview with Chamberlain that led to the correspondence with the Duce.[47]

The ubiquitous Hankey also played an important role in persuading the Prime Minister to abandon his earlier indifference to the Italian question. In a strong note of 19 July he warned Chamberlain that Britain required a full two years of stable peace to complete its re-armament. From the point of view of imperial security its foreign relations were 'very unsatisfactory', for the situation was fast developing where England had potential enemies in the west and east athwart its main line of communications. France, its only friend, was 'very weak'. A policy of rearmament in the Mediterranean would only weaken home defence and dislocate the defence effort generally. Yet the present insecurity was intolerable, for if war broke out Britain would have to expect severe losses at the outset; these could only be made good at the risk of uncovering other vital interests and tempting a general war, for which 'we are totally unprepared'. Thus, better relations with Italy were a necessity, if only for the period of rearmament. Hankey, like Eden, wanted to use an abnormal channel because Mussolini rarely saw ambassadors: 'some eminently commonsense and well-informed person should see Mussolini and discuss all these matters on the dead level and draw him back from his alleged paranoia.' He did not suggest names but it was probably no coincidence that he himself was shortly leaving for a holiday in Italy. Hankey passed on his memorandum to Eden, urging him to take advantage of this 'tremendous opportunity'. He assured the Foreign Secretary that Italy was 'genuinely nervous of us': its intelligence was bad and it really believed that England planned revenge. It was 'quite impossible' for Mussolini to attack in the face of possible French hostility and his own weak strategic position.[48]

While Britain's policy-makers explored their Mediterranean options, the Italian Ambassador was at work to create new friends and point the debate in the right direction. Count Dino Grandi had always been deeply opposed to his masters' Axis policy and his whole political life, as Vansittart told Chamberlain, 'has been founded on the policy of

47 Avon, *Facing the dictators*, pp. 499–500.
48 Memorandum by Hankey, 19 July 1937. Premier 1/276. Hankey to Eden, 23 July 1937. Cab.21/558. Cf. also, Roskill, *Hankey: man of secrets*, III, pp. 266–71.

intimate relations with this country'.[49] Like the Soviet Ambassador,
Ivan Maiskii, Grandi was an astute politician with a developed awareness
of public relations techniques and moved easily in influential English
circles. Vansittart called him 'a very close personal friend' and this
certainly applied as well to several other friends of Italy among the
British policy-making élite. He was a man, again like Maiskii, who knew
how to use his friends and the press to apply pressure on the Cabinet
and Foreign Office, and he was not above a little surreptitious diplomacy designed to isolate those who stood in his way. His most
controversial intervention occurred in February 1938 when, apparently
with the assistance of Conservative Party headquarters and certainly the
Prime Minister's office, he became involved in a quarrel between
Chamberlain and Eden that ended in the latter's resignation.[50] But it
was by no means his only direct intervention. In July 1937 he played a
leading role in creating the new Anglo—Italian *détente* and then used
his press contacts to give it publicity. He made his move after Eden's
friendly speech, telling the Foreign Secretary of a message of goodwill
from Mussolini and requesting a similar gesture from Chamberlain.

Evidently aware of the strong opinions of the Services, Grandi then
sought out Leslie Hore-Belisha, Secretary of State for War, and told him
of Mussolini's fears of Britain. Italy's military moves in the
Mediterranean and North Africa, Grandi insisted, were only reactions to
the British rearmament programme. But tension there certainly was. He
thought this could result in an understanding rather than war, however,
and went on to make the remarkable suggestion that the English and
Italian military staffs should enter into confidential relations. This
would save London money, allow his own nation to escape from what
he called the 'Germanic menace' and might even lead to the rebirth of
the Stresa front. He urged Hore-Belisha to go to Rome to see Mussolini
for himself.[51] Although the War Office and Hankey agreed with
Grandi's analysis of the situation, which he repeated to Chamberlain at
their first interview, the Ambassador's clumsy initiative proved counter-
productive. Eden and Vansittart immediately suspected a 'plant' and
warned of an attempt to lull the victim; which prompted Hankey to

49 Vansittart to Chamberlain, 5 August 1937. Premier 1/276.
50 Cf. Avon, *Facing the dictators*, chaps., 13 and 14; Lord Templewood, *Nine
 Troubled Years* (London, 1954); Iain Macleod, *Neville Chamberlain* (London,
 1961); M. Muggeridge (ed.), *Ciano's diplomatic papers* (London, 1948).
51 J. R. Minney (ed.), *The private papers of Hore-Belisha* (London, 1960), pp.
 101—3; Hore-Belisha to Hankey, 28 July 1937. Cab.21/558.

accuse Vansittart of having a suspicious mind.[52] Despite this mis-step, the Italian Embassy continued to smooth the way: Grandi courted Chamberlain on 27 July and extracted from him a friendly greeting to Mussolini. The chat went so well that the Ambassador told Vansittart that 'England and Italy have been divorced for two years, and might now be remarried', a remark which prompted the Permanent Under-secretary to wonder 'whether he regards Germany as Best Man or Correspondent'; 'we might not get beyond concatenated bigamy', he cautioned Chamberlain.[53] After delivering Mussolini's reply to the Prime Minister's note and working the London press to get the maximum publicity for the *détente*, Grandi departed for Rome on leave in early August. In all, it was an impressive performance.

Neville Chamberlain's role in these exchanges was not especially active and certainly not sinister. He did not initiate the first approach to Rome nor was it he who suggested the use of an abnormal channel such as a letter to Mussolini. He was reacting to the strong advice of his principal advisers on defence and foreign policy and his own actions must be seen within a framework of collective decision-making. At the Defence Plans (Policy) Subcommittee on 23 July, after two weeks of debate and discussion during which his only concern seems to have been the priority of German issues and home defence, he remarked that in view of the tense situation he had agreed to see Grandi. Once more he resisted pressure from Eden and the naval staff for an immediate strengthening of the fleet; the object was to avoid a series of dangerous movements and counter-movements.[54] It is true that Chamberlain quickly seized on the prospect of an Anglo–Italian agreement, but his fervour was that of the convert rather than the true believer. The real circumstances of the Chamberlain–Mussolini correspondence demonstrate conclusively that the policy of 'appeasing' Italy was no invention of one individual, not an aberration in diplomacy attributable

---

52 Hankey to Vansittart, 26 July 1937. Cab.21/558. 'I see nothing in anything they have done which is inconsistent with a defensive attitude and a doctrine of a deterrent.'
53 Vansittart to Chamberlain, 28 July 1937. Premier 1/276.
54 D.P.(P.)/4th mtg., 23 July 1937. Cab.16/181. If there was one distinct trademark of Eden's approach to diplomacy, it was his willingness to use shows of force, often without considering the possible implications. He seems to have indulged this predilection to the end of his political career, as witness his behaviour during the Suez invasion in 1956. Chamberlain by contrast, argued consistently that one must refrain from threats, displays of force, etc., unless one was prepared to back them up to the hilt.

to a single misguided personality. All of the arguments for and against such a policy had existed long before Chamberlain's premiership and it may be said that his first approaches to Fascist Italy therefore marked not a departure but a continuation in British foreign policy in the post-Abyssinia period.

The prospect of further conversations with Rome brought up the issue of British interests. Because the security problem seemed especially acute, there seemed every reason to make it the basis of an understanding. The military dilemma, which will later be discussed at length, consisted of two separate but related problems. First, the preponderance of local Italian power in the East Mediterranean heavily outweighed Britain's standing forces. The decision to raise a mechanized army corps in Libya meant that Italy was building a striking force there of some 60,000 troops (20,000 of them native conscripts) to threaten the British force in Egypt of 10,000 ill-equipped men. Italian regional air power surpassed the British in the ratio of six to one and there was a complete absence of air defence in Egypt and the Middle East in general. England had the margin at sea, but only just, and sea power was in any case notoriously slow to draw blood. The growing danger was obviously that of a sudden attack by land forces from Libya supported by air power in favour of a rapid decision in Egypt. This seemed acute because of the second dimension of the military problem, that of reinforcement. The Mediterranean was, in the words of Admiral Pound, 'the most distant station' in the Empire on a peace-time footing. It would be dangerous, perhaps impossible, to move convoys through the Mediterranean under war conditions, so reinforcements might have to go round the Cape or come from India. The upshot of this, Chatfield wrote to Pound, was that, 'If we have trouble with Italy the Navy can win the war slowly, but the Army and Air Force can lose it in Egypt rapidly, and therefore it is the defence of Egypt that will be our main preoccupation.'[55]

The knowledge that Italy itself was a regional power only and suffering from several glaring strategic weaknesses at that — shortages of vital raw materials, chronic financial and industrial problems, vulner-ability to maritime pressure — was not wholly comforting, for it was clear that precisely these factors contributed to the instability in its foreign policy. Italy was in decline and therefore dangerous. As the margin of superiority in the Mediterranean slowly and inevitably passed

55 Chatfield to Pound, 5 August 1937. Chatfield Papers.

to Britain, who could say with certainty that Mussolini, hard-pressed by domestic difficulties and facing a gloomy future in a rearmed and divided Europe, might not gamble on an early war? It would not necessarily be a 'mad dog' act either, because Italy's weaknesses would bring it down only over the long haul and Britain could not necessarily count on a quiescent Germany.

All of this argued in favour of using the talks with Rome to ease military insecurity. Vansittart, still suspicious of Mussolini's sudden goodwill and Grandi's explanations, put up a strong minute on the Libyan striking force for Chamberlain to use in his first interview with the Italian Ambassador. But Sir Horace Wilson, the Prime Minister's adviser, had quashed this with the remark that it was 'hardly the basis for a genial conversation', and drafted an alternative message that made Chamberlain sound like a Birmingham businessman-cum-tourist playing diplomacy, the exact image of his critics.[56] Undoubtedly it was his decision to use Wilson's rather than Vansittart's approach that prompted him to send his effusive message to the Duce before showing it to Eden.[57] Wilson's diplomatic *début* was not exactly a promising beginning, but Chamberlain, in any case, had no intention of merely parroting assurances. He wanted a comprehensive Mediterranean settlement with Italy and for that he would offer a price. In his opinion conversations would have to aim at a resolution of Britain's security problem in the Mediterranean, an aspect of its overall dilemma. The primary object, he told Halifax, was to get back to the pre-1935 position where Italy had been safely excluded from the list of enemies. Conversations would have to cover all of the difficult political and military questions, including Spain.[58] For this the Prime Minister would be willing to give a lead in having Abyssinia expelled from the League, thus opening the way for *de jure* recognition, but this would be in the 'common interest' as it would increase the chances of a general European settlement.[59] An 'immensely important' secondary objective of talks would be to weaken Italo–German relations, which he felt were 'extremely artificial'. It was thus to be an ambitious programme of negotiations aimed at a permanent settlement of the vexing Mediterranean question. Chamberlain's unpublished notes, written on

[56] Minutes by Vansittart and Wilson, 26 July 1937. Premier 1/276.
[57] Avon, *Facing the dictators*, pp. 452–3.
[58] Chamberlain to Halifax, 7 August 1937. Premier 1/276.
[59] Chamberlain's amendments to a Foreign Office draft on Anglo–Italian conversations. n.d. *Ibid.*

holiday in August 1937, reveal his preoccupation with the inter-relationship of the European and Mediterranean menaces, his conviction that an Anglo—Italian war could not stop at the two nations, and his awareness that the Chiefs of Staff were 'gravely alarmed' and 'most emphatic that better relations essential especially during period of rearmament'.[60] The effort might come to nothing he admitted:

> But in view of the enormous interests involved, including the safety of this country and its communications with the Far East and the frightful cost of rearmament the burden of which has not by any means been fully felt as yet, we should be gravely wanting in our duty if we failed to make every effort to reach a favourable understanding.[61]

Taking his lead from Chamberlain, Halifax (Eden was on vacation) presided over a meeting with senior Foreign Office advisers and Drummond (now Lord Perth) on 10 August. It was agreed to follow up the policy of *détente* by taking the initiative at the coming session of the League to have Abyssinia ejected; after this nasty matter was cleared away London and Rome would get down to serious talks, hopefully by late September.[62] The time-table was of cardinal importance, for if nothing was done at the September League meeting, England would have to wait until 1938 for the next opportunity to appease the Duce's demand for formal recognition of his empire. The holidaying Eden was not happy about the planned procedure, however, and Halifax found him 'very sensitive' about the Abyssinian question and worried that England would get no real return value for its gesture. 'He recognized, however, that having reached the point at which we now stood it was not possible to stand still, but it was in his view of the first importance so to proceed as to protect ourselves against the mischief, moral and political, that he feared.'[63] Eden's objections to appeasing Italy were over procedure, not principle. He hated the idea of recognizing Mussolini's conquest at a moment when Italian 'pacification' was creating an Abyssinian resistance, and he hated even more associating himself with a highly unpopular policy. But he was not an anti-fascist, in principle opposed to concessions to a particularly noxious type of state. Eden's Italophobia was not rooted in any belief about — as he put it — 'forms of government', dictatorships versus democracies, for he

60 Chamberlain, 'Notes on Anglo—Italian Discussions', n.d. *Ibid.*
61 Amendments to F.O. draft. *op. cit.*
62 Minutes of a departmental meeting, 10 August 1937. R5532/1/22 (21161).
63 Halifax to Chamberlain, 19 August 1937. Premier 1/276.

remained to the day of his resignation an opponent of ideological blocs and an advocate of agreement with Hitler, objectively a far greater menace to European democracy than the Führer's Italian friend. Eden's antipathy to Mussolini, like his rather xenophobic attitude to Japan at the end of the year, was forged in a resentment against upstart have-not imperialisms poaching on traditionally English or 'white race' preserves and challenging Britain's historic control of the world's sea lanes. Reduced to its essentials, Eden's dispute with Italy was not: 'Shall fascism or democracy prevail?' Rather it was 'Who shall rule the Mediterranean?'

The Services naturally applauded the prospect of improved relations with Italy at a moment when England's global security problem seemed especially acute. A much-relieved Chatfield told Pound of his hopes that the Mussolini–Chamberlain correspondence would keep the Mediterranean quiet for at least two months, and the Service chiefs gave the *détente* their official blessing.[64] But they were less enthusiastic about discussing matters of strategy with the Italians. The Foreign Office felt that the military subjects should include (*a*) a reduction of the Libyan garrison to 1934 establishment; (*b*) an assurance that all Italian 'volunteers' would eventually leave Spain; and (*c*) an actual withdrawal from the Balearic islands. It was also thought that the Italians might revive the idea of a limitation agreement in the Mediterranean based on parity of naval forces. The Chiefs of Staff predicably vetoed any negotiations on arms control but they also advised against introducing any military subjects into talks: Italy would only make reciprocal demands if the Libyan garrison was on the agenda; there were 'no strong strategical reasons' for ousting Italian forces from the Balearics (this opinion the Chiefs of Staff had often given); further, the whole question of Italy's intervention in Spain was so 'highly controversial' that introduction of the subject was unlikely to improve the diplomatic atmosphere.[65] The Services wanted political appeasement without the discussion of military problems; England should give *de jure* recognition as a spontaneous gesture of goodwill. The Foreign Office took a dim view of this line of least resistance and it was also, as already seen, far from Chamberlain's comprehensive approach. So, for once, the Chiefs of Staff were wisely ignored and, when conversations

---

[64] Chatfield to Pound, 5 August 1937. Chatfield Papers; also, Chiefs of Staff, 'Anglo–Italian Relations', 12 August 1937.
[65] Chiefs of Staff, 'Anglo–Italian Relations', 21 September 1937.

with Italy finally got under way in the spring of 1938, military subjects
— notably the Libyan garrison — were placed on the agenda in spite of
their advice.

The new Anglo—Italian 'honeymoon', as Count Grandi called it, was
not followed after all by a permanent reconciliation. Instead, the brief
courtship ended in another bitter separation and the Mediterranean
settlement had once more to be postponed. It is still unclear why
Mussolini agreed in August 1937 to Franco's extraordinary request for
the intervention of the Italian fleet against shipping bound for
republican Spain; for the risks inherent in such a policy certainly ran
against the logic of a settlement with England.[66] The violent turnings in
Italian policy sometimes are as inexplicable to the historian as they
were to the Duce's puzzled contemporaries. One possible explanation is
that he had gambled heavily on early and decisive results in Spain, to be
followed by a settlement with Britain. If so he lost, for the blatant
attacks on merchant shipping, coupled with Mussolini's boastful speech
on the Santander offensive, completely dissipated the atmosphere, and
Italian suggestions that perhaps the sinister Russians and their friends
had been out sinking their own ships to create a new crisis sounded a
little contrived, even to London's sympathetic ears. There now followed
a series of intensive negotiations on the Mediterranean crisis, ostensibly
on the technical issue of 'piracy' but actually bringing into play all the
political and strategic factors at work among the great powers of the
region. Here was laid out in detail the basis of Britain's Mediterranean
policy.

The submarines responsible for the attacks on shipping were
definitely known in London to be Italian, a fact that makes Eden's
initial reaction to the piracy affair the harder to understand. According
to Admiralty documents, at the end of August, after several incidents
involving British ships, culminating in a submarine attack on H.M.S.
Havock, Eden proposed a policy of drastic reprisal against Franco's
fleet (alternatively, a strong warning to be followed by reprisal if
incidents recurred). He specifically advocated that the British navy
should seek out and sink the largest ship in the nationalists' navy, the
cruiser *Canarias*. The sea lords had seen this kind of impulsive suggestion
earlier in the year when Eden brought before the Cabinet the idea —
first broached by the chairman of the Rio Tinto Company, Sir Auckland
Geddes — that the navy should forcibly intercept on the high seas

66 *D.G.F.P.*, D, III, No. 407.

sequestered Rio Tinto ore bound for Axis ports. The naval staff had
pointed out how such action would be in violation of international law
and might lead to dangerous incidents, even war, and a rather horrified
Cabinet had turned the proposal down.[67] On this occasion too the
Admiralty were violently opposed to a policy that might necessitate
a general concentration in the West Mediterranean, end in another
Anglo—Italian confrontation and anyway smacked of 'Hun-like'
tactics.[68] Chatfield's later dispute with the Foreign Office's style of
diplomacy is probably best understood against the background of
continual disagreements throughout 1937 over the uses to which the
Mediterranean Fleet should be put. Eden did, however, win the Prime
Minister's support for the French proposal for a conference on
Mediterranean piracy,[69] and on 2 September it was agreed to reinforce
the fleet in the West Mediterranean.

In his memoirs Lord Avon has singled out the Nyon conference of
September 1937 as a particularly striking example of his, as opposed to
Chamberlain's, approach to the 'dictators'. By using their 'overwhelming
sea power' Britain and France were able to counter-attack on behalf of
the democracies and call the Italian bluff. It was proof that there was
an alternative to 'retreat', to craven appeasement.[70] Leaving aside the
point that sixty destroyers patrolling for submarines hardly constituted
'overwhelming' naval power, there is no disputing the fact that Nyon
was a diplomatic victory of some force for Eden and for Britain's
battered prestige and that it also brought immediate practical results in
stopping the attacks on shipping. On the other hand, it is necessary to
be very exact about what was arranged at Nyon and what the British
delegation — Eden, Vansittart and Chatfield — were really trying to do
at the conference. What emerges from the politics of Nyon is an
interesting model of Mediterranean policy, though not the same one
conveyed by Lord Avon's recollections.

At the Cabinet on 8 September, against the backdrop of crisis in the
Far East, Eden told his colleagues how he had clashed with the French
on the issue of invitations to the Mediterranean conference. The French
Foreign Minister, Yvon Delbos, had insisted on Soviet attendance —
otherwise the French Government would lose the support of the

[67] Cab. Conclusions, 3 March 1937. Cab.23/87.
[68] Cf. Admiralty minutes of 31 August and 1 September 1937. Adm. 116/3522.
[69] Note by Eden of telephone conversation with Chamberlain, 1 September
1937. Premier 1/276.
[70] Avon, *Facing the dictators*, pp. 459—76.

socialists and fall – and Eden had grudgingly acquiesced, provided that Germany was also invited, and only after making it clear that if Russia 'torpedoed' the conference the responsibility would be France's alone. Surprisingly, the Soviets also figured in Chatfield's scheme for joint naval patrols: the Russian fleet was to aid the Turks, Greeks and Yugoslavs in covering the Aegean Sea. Chamberlain and other ministers objected to these arrangements in the strongest terms, arguing the need to keep the Russians out of the Mediterranean and to avoid siding with them and the French in any ideological coalition against the Italians and Germans. Then for the first time Chamberlain and Eden openly clashed over future policy towards Italy. Eden wanted to peg the issue of Anglo–Italian relations on some improvement of the general situation in Spain and the Mediterranean, and his memorandum argued against making *de jure* recognition part of a 'nefarious bargain' with Rome. Chamberlain warned Eden that France inspired much Italian animosity against England and used Grandi's argument that Mussolini's actions in Libya were connected with Hoare's earlier visit to Cyprus. The Prime Minister wanted early action on the Abyssinia question: the important thing was to 'strive for a change of heart and attitude with Italy'. But he could not budge his Foreign Secretary. The wrangle, which seems to have lasted most of the day, ended when it was agreed to send a conciliatory telegram to Rome urging Italy to attend the conference. But the initiative was no longer in British hands, as the Duce and Ciano took great umbrage at the publication of a sharp Soviet protest against Italian piracy and stayed home, with Germany, in a fit of pique. Chamberlain's last-minute attempt to have the question pigeon-holed by referring it to the non-intervention committee came too late and the conference went ahead as planned.[71]

Leaving technical matters aside, all that happened at the very brief conference of 10–11 September 1937 was that the original Admiralty

---

[71] Cab. Conclusions, 8 September 1937. Cab.23/89. Also, C.P. 210(37). and C.P. 213(37). Cab.24/271. Sir G. Mounsey told Hugh Lloyd Thomas (Paris) how Eden and Delbos had clashed twice on the telephone over the issue of Soviet attendance. Delbos finally said that 'if we insisted on excluding Russia, he, Delbos, would have to resign and we should be responsible for a Ministerial crisis in France! Eventually, when the Secretary of State did agree to Russia's inclusion, he impressed upon Delbos that if things went wrong and Russia tried to torpedo the Conference, it would be the French Government's responsibility.' W16957/16618/41. (21405). The French Ambassador told Eden that France felt Russia would be less trouble inside than outside a conference. W16874, *Ibid.*

scheme for destroyer patrols of the Mediterranean — which envisaged Russian participation in the north Aegean — was modified to give England and France entire responsibility for the patrols. Eden has correctly explained that the change was necessitated at the insistence of the Eastern Mediterranean nations, including Turkey, all of whom objected to co-operation with the Soviet fleet. What he omitted to say, however, was that this fitted perfectly his own policy; for Eden had gone to Nyon determined that the conference should not have an anti-fascist complexion and that Russia should be excluded from as much of its practical work as possible. He wrote to Chamberlain at the close of the meeting proclaiming the result a success: piracy had been ended 'and perhaps most important of all we managed to keep the Russians out of the Mediterranean'. It was fortunate, he went on, that the minor powers had objected to Soviet co-operation and that Maxim Litvinov, the Russian Foreign Minister, had proved amenable to the new scheme:

> It was more than time that the democracies should make themselves felt in Europe. That we were able in this instance while excluding Russia adds all the more significance to the event. My chief anxiety in coming to Nyon, and I think yours also, was lest we should appear to create an Anglo—French—Soviet bloc on an ideological basis. That event even the German and Italian press admit that we have avoided.[72]

Back in London Eden received the plaudits of his colleagues for having achieved the agreed objective, 'which was that the Conference should not have an anti-Fascist tendency, but the technical object of dealing with piracy in the Mediterranean'.[73]

If Russia was to be excluded from the Great Power arrangements of Europe, that applied with even greater force to the Mediterranean, where it could threaten Britain's imperial interests. Not only was Moscow a 'merchant of dangerous thoughts' but it had age-old aspirations, which England had traditionally opposed, in the direction of the Black Sea and the Mediterranean. Britain, as will later be demonstrated, had opposed those ambitions at the Montreux conference on the Straits in 1936, and in early 1937 the Admiralty had refused to ask France for port facilities in the Mediterranean 'as we are

---

[72] Eden to Chamberlain, 14 September 1937. Premier 1/360. Chamberlain thought the British delegation had done 'extremely well' (*ibid.*) although he later claimed that Nyon had been achieved at the expense of Anglo—Italian friendship. Feiling, *op. cit.* p. 331.

[73] Cab. Conclusions, 29 September 1937. Cab.23/89.

anxious to avoid Russian request for facilities at Gibraltar'. Eden and Vansittart had brought strong pressure to bear on the French in April and May 1937 to keep Paris from giving the Franco—Soviet pact any strategic significance whatsoever,[74] and their suspicions of Soviet policy in Spain and the Mediterranean had been aggravated by the *Deutschland* affair. In the pre-Nyon negotiating, as during the conference itself, these suspicions, rather than anti-Italian motives, had dominated British policy and this revealed another important constraint in London's image of the international system. To align England with France in cold-war hostility to either Axis power would be unthinkable, for such a strategy would put them on the side of both Stalin and 'Red' Spain and, the British felt, divide Europe into irreconcilable blocs. If Nyon had the appearance of such a coalition it was only temporary, for Italy was hastily invited to join the patrols in search of its own submarines and this time the strong objections of the smaller Mediterranean powers made no impression at all on British intentions.

The piracy affair and Nyon put an end to hopes of an early bilateral agreement with Rome, for the all-important time-table had been abandoned and no move made at Geneva on *de jure* recognition. The Turks had briefly revived that perennial alternative, a Mediterranean Locarno, but the Foreign Office thought this an unlikely foundation in the 'present swamp of Mediterranean troubles'. Eden and his advisers were sure that Spain was now the crux of the matter and that until that diplomatic tangle improved no further gestures could be made to Italy, especially as the French were threatening to abandon non-intervention. Lord Perth's pleas on Rome's behalf were coldly received in London and Vansittart concluded that, as it was likely that Mussolini had

---

[74] Admiralty instructions in W3722/7/41. (21324). In April and May the French privately told Vansittart and Eden that they intended to enter into limited military conversations, at the attaché level only, with the Soviets. It would be a gesture of good faith, as Russia had been strongly pressing the French; Paris feared that unless it agreed Moscow would begin to open the door to a reconciliation with Hitler. In any case, talks were needed as Soviet air assistance would be required for the defence of Czechoslovakia: 'Nous ne lâcherons pas la Tchécoslovaquie. Nous ne le pouvons pas sans disparaître de la carte de l'Europe.' Eden told Delbos how much he regretted this decision which would have 'most serious psychological effects'; he urged the French to postpone any military collaboration with Moscow. Two weeks later the French Ambassador told Vansittart that in light of Eden's views his government had decided not only to abandon the idea of exchanging military information but to reduce 'to the smallest possible compass' any further developments of the Franco—Soviet pact. C3910/3620/3685/532/62/ (20702).

bargained Austria along with his soul during his recent visit to Berlin, only strength could modify his attitude.[75] Limited conversations were offered to the Italians in early October but *de jure* recognition was omitted from the agenda and the talks were pegged to a joint Anglo–French note on tripartite conversations on Spain. The elusive Mediterranean settlement seemed as far off as ever.

When diplomacy was in deadlock Britain's strategic position in the Mediterranean became uneasy. The Nyon patrols did nothing to alleviate concern over the security of Egypt and Suez, and in October the Italian Government officially admitted to having 40,000 regular troops attached to the Libyan garrison, that barometer of Anglo–Italian tension. In that same month the regional British commanders met in Cairo to discuss planning for the defence of Egypt and forwarded to the Chiefs of Staff in London a series of requests for immediate reinforcements, especially for air defences. Admiral Pound thought his superiors were holding back vital equipment for fear of offending the Italians; a 'Fascist regime naturally respects strength and despises weakness, and the more we pander to them the more they will be inclined to bully or bluff us'. Mediterranean rearmament might prove costly 'but we cannot maintain an Empire on the cheap'.[76] The Chiefs of Staff, however, saw the matter from a broader perspective. The dispatch of the requested anti-aircraft brigade would reduce the number of guns available for home defence by a full 10 per cent (24 out of a total of 212), a fair commentary on the pace of the British rearmament programme, and they ruled out any action 'which would result in a diversion of our limited resources from our main objective which is the security of this country against German aggression'.[77] Some reassurance was taken from industrial intelligence reports of Italy's shortage of vital raw materials, fuels in particular, and from the fact that its forces in Libya could not yet mount an all-out attack across the desert.[78]

This only postponed the issue, however, for Sir Miles Lampson, backed in London by Vansittart, now launched a powerful campaign to have Egypt reinforced. He questioned the complacency of the Chiefs of Staff, described their reliance upon wartime reinforcements through the

75 Minute by Vansittart. R6700/2/22. (21162).
76 Pound, 'Expenditure on Defences of Mediterranean Ports', 12 October 1937. In Pound's Brief Diary of Important Events. Cf. bibliographical notes. Pound to Admiralty, tel. No. 0003/17, 16 October 1937. Cab.21/578.
77 Chiefs of Staff, 'Situation in the Mediterranean and Middle East', 19 October 1937. C.P. 259. Cab.24/272.
78 Hankey to Vansittart, 19 November 1937. Cab.21/578.

Mediterranean as 'suicidal' and warned that the Egyptians were beginning to question the value of their alliance with England.[79] Vansittart
moved to reverse the ruling of the Chiefs of Staff but ran headlong into
the formidable opposition of Sir Maurice Hankey. Hankey's role in the
formation of Mediterranean strategy and diplomacy in these weeks
deserves separate attention, for it illustrates in some detail how he
could use his special position of power to influence the policy-making
process at all its vital stages.

Hankey, as already seen, had made an important plea to the Prime
Minister in mid-July for better relations with Rome on strategic grounds,
and it seems very likely that Chamberlain's ideas on a Mediterranean
settlement were shaped by this advice. In August Hankey left for one of
his periodic vacations in Italy and, as usual, he mixed pleasure with the
business of observation. He came home more than ever convinced of the
benefits of Fascism in Italy, particularly in the morale and efficiency of
the people. There was poverty, it was true, but he had been 'more
impressed by the extent to which the benefits of Fascism have been
maintained than by such signs as I saw of backsliding'. He had found
the Italians still friendly to England and he was sure they would warmly
welcome an improvement in relations; Italy certainly had a great
interest in avoiding an exhausting struggle with a leading sea power. The
key to present-day Italy lay in Mussolini's assertion that the world had
not yet come to know 'this young, resolute and very powerful' nation;
it was this demand for recognition that led the people to follow the
Duce into Abyssinia and Spain. Hankey thought that the Italians had
accomplished great things: 'What Cavour and Garibaldi began' Mussolini
had completed. In the Fascist experiment 'the nation has found itself'.[80]

Thus fortified by his first-hand experience of Mussolini's state,
Hankey returned to London to begin his campaign for an Anglo—Italian
understanding. He was sure that the Foreign Office, especially the news
department, were responsible for much anti-Italian information in the
British press and he began to check into Eden's sources, remarkable
behaviour by an appointed official; but then Hankey was no ordinary
bureaucrat. In early October he complained to Chamberlain and Wilson
about 'F.O. gullibility about stories of Italian reinforcements, etc. to

---

79 Lampson to Eden, tel. No. 653, 12 November 1937. *Ibid.*
80 Hankey, 'Italy, Some Notes of a Holiday Visit', 27 September 1937.
   Cab.21/563. This, like most of his memoranda, was circulated to various
   ministers, including Chamberlain, Service people, officials such as Sir Warren
   Fisher and also to Lord Perth, with whom he corresponded.

Spain' and charged that Eden had used unchecked journalistic information at the Cabinet. Later he told Wilson of the need to stop press officials at the Foreign Office from turning out propaganda against Italy.[81] During an October visit to Paris, Hankey looked up Alexis Léger, Secretary General of the traditionally anti-Italian Quai d'Orsay, and put the argument for a friendlier attitude to Rome. The advantages for England and France, 'especially in view of developments in the far east', were obvious; but there would be gains for Italy too:

> Mussolini, for example, on a long view, can hardly forget the German speaking, Austrophile population of Trentino, nor the ultimate attractions to an expanded Germany of Trieste as a Mediterranean port. Whatever immediate assurances Germany might give as to disinterestedness in these populations and territories, the Anschluss would soon revive 'minority' movements and ambitions which even now are only partially dormant. Mussolini must realize all this. On a shorter view also Mussolini must be concerned about the economic situation in Abyssinia, which requires many years and much capital to develop. Would he not be glad, from this point of view, to secure his communications through the Mediterranean by an arrangement with the Sea-Powers?

But Léger, Hankey sadly recorded, was unmoved; he regarded Italy as a 'parasite' whose policy was now tied to Germany's. 'He had inherited the traditional mistrust and dislike of the Quai d'Orsay for everything Italian.'[82] Perhaps Léger reflected that if Hankey, rather than Mussolini, made Italian diplomacy relations with Rome would certainly be easier.

Back in England Hankey sided with the Chiefs of Staff over arms for Egypt and defended their concern for home defence. The dilemma, he bluntly told Vansittart, was that 'unless the Foreign Office can tell us that we are safe from the risk of a war with Germany for a year or two (which I am sure you cannot) it seems unavoidable to take horrible risks in Egypt'. It followed that 'we should make friends with Italy'.[83] Hankey, who had been asked by Chamberlain 'to do anything I could with the Foreign Office' on the Italian issue,[84] argued that London and Rome had a mutual interest in secure communications. In the political sphere 'a certain amount of eating of our words' would be involved, but

---

81 Hankey to Wilson and Chamberlain, 6 October 1937. Premier 1/360; Hankey to Wilson, 4 January 1938. Cab.21/558.
82 Note by Hankey, 11 October 1937. Cab.63/52.
83 Hankey to Vansittart, 2 November 1937. Cab.21/578.
84 Hankey to Wilson, 4 and 5 November 1937. Cab.21/558.

even if the decision meant sneers from the Left and the loss of one or two by-elections the result would be worth the sacrifice. Patient work in the lobbies and with the press would smooth the way; anyway, he added with the bureaucrat's respect for opposition, 'we take far too much notice of the yapping of the little dogs'. He begged Vansittart to push Eden in this direction: it was vital to the existence of the Empire.[85] As yet another salvo in his campaign Hankey circulated to finance-minded ministers a strongly worded memorandum on the 'Cost of Defence Requirements', the main burden of which was that England could not afford three enemies, that any drain of supplies to the Middle East would weaken England at home and that 'nothing but national interests of the greatest importance should be allowed to stand in the way of a whole-hearted effort to secure better relations with Italy'.[86] Vansittart had managed to get C.I.D. approval for dispatching certain equipment and forces to Egypt on the grounds that they were vital to Britain's prestige in that country, but his tenacity won him a sharp rebuke from Hankey. England could not afford a foreign policy that 'has far out-run the means behind it' or had it at loggerheads with the armed nations and tied down to the 'crocks'. It would end by bringing England down altogether.[87]

Hankey was a relentless and formidable advocate and on this issue he certainly used every opening to press his influence. By virtue of his unique office, his grasp of the information and advice of the Services, his accessibility to Chamberlain and other key ministers, and his net-work of friends and allies throughout the administration, Hankey was able to intervene at almost any stage of the decision-making process to shape policy. On the Italian issue he was strongly motivated by a fear that war would break out in the Mediterranean before Britain was rearmed and, perhaps with an eye to 1914, drag all of the Great Powers into another exhausting conflict. Strategic considerations dominated his thinking, and his emotional approval of Fascism fortified his com-mitment. He was no neutral in the dispute between Eden and Chamberlain, rather he was wholly with the Prime Minister and seems to have been the latter's source of information and ideas on Mediterranean policy. His pressure was not lost on Vansittart either; he 'quite agreed' with Hankey's analysis, but Mussolini had been

85 Hankey to Vansittart, 3 November 1937. *Ibid.*
86 Hankey, 'Cost of Defence Requirements', 23 November 1937. Cab.21/531.
87 Hankey to Vansittart, 15 November 1937. Cab.21/578.

'provocative beyond belief' and had upset all the plans to put the Abyssinian question at Geneva — 'and you know how hard I have striven for that'.[88]

Hankey's arguments seemed the more urgent when on 6 November — the day Italy joined the anti-Comitern pact — Count Grandi made another timely appeal for English friendship. He told Rex Leeper of the Foreign Office how his nation was succumbing to German pressure, and mainly from fears of isolation. Nyon had made a profound impression in Rome. 'It revived in an acute form all the apprehensions felt at the time of sanctions and was at once exploited by Germany in order to put further pressure on Rome.' The price of Italo–German agreement would surely be the loss of Austrian independence, something that could be arrested only by an Anglo–Italian settlement. Leeper and Vansittart had professed to be much impressed by this,[89] although why is not exactly clear. Grandi's was a familiar tune and just two days earlier Vansittart had told Hugh Dalton how Mussolini had lost his valuable independence and literally sold Austria to Hitler.[90] In any case, Vansittart had swung back to his old line and tried to persuade Eden to permit talks with Italy; but the latter, although supporting new approaches to Hitler, was 'opposed to doing anything more with Italy until Spain cleared up'.[91] It was a measure of Vansittart's declining influence that he was unable to budge his superior an inch; Eden wanted to settle with Germany at Italy's expense, but his chief adviser wanted to do precisely the opposite. Here was one reason for Vansittart's fall from his powerful position a month later.

A glance at the agenda of the Committee of Imperial Defence over the last six months of 1937 is sufficient to demonstrate that valuable time, energy and resources were being spent on the problems of the Mediterranean and Middle East when the Far Eastern crisis was worsening and settlement with Germany seemed no nearer. London's defence planners saw themselves approaching a turning point. On the one hand, any respect once held for Italy as a military power had diminished as reports came in of Italy's chronic financial troubles, its shortages of vital resources and its inability to crush the guerrilla resistance in Abyssinia. 'Italy, if I read the signs aright', wrote Inskip, 'may before long be going downhill.' But the priorities of global defence

88 Vansittart to Hankey, 3 November 1937. Cab.21/578.
89 Minute by Leeper, 6 November 1937. R7419/1/22. (21162).
90 Dalton Diaries, entry of 4 November 1937.
91 Harvey, *The diplomatic diaries of Oliver Harvey*, pp. 58–9.

and Britain's temporary predicament of weakness argued for a gradual approach to better relations with Mussolini.[92] Chatfield, smarting a little from Pound's criticisms, told his Mediterranean commander that although there was sympathy for the view that the Italians needed to be taught a lesson, the larger strategic picture and the need for a system of priorities during a period of unreadiness 'dominated the thought of the C.I.D.'[93]

The Chiefs of Staff feared that they were witnessing the beginning of a concerted global campaign against British interests on three fronts; the instrument of orchestration, they felt, was the anti-Comintern pact, apparently only a statement of shared ideology but in fact the foundation of an understanding among revisionist powers. In a gloomy year's-end review, the Service chiefs again warned that commitments and capabilities were badly out of step. Although England could handle a war in the Mediterranean or Far East, it was not ready to meet Germany, and there was an increasing likelihood that a war begun in one of the three areas would spread to the others. It could not even be foreseen when Britain would be strong enough to fight three powers simultaneously. They therefore called for political and international action 'to reduce the numbers of our potential enemies and to gain the support of potential allies'.[94] It was a very frank appeal for appeasement.

The Foreign Office, rising to the challenge, defended their policy in a rather defiant counter-memorandum. Britain would seek to remove the causes of friction but to bribe the aggressive nations would risk opening the floodgates of territorial change. It would be safer, and more honourable, to tolerate the present state of 'armed truce', building on the French and American friendships, and hope that a kind of equilibrium would emerge. Britain's policy should be the unheroic one of 'cunctation', a wait-and-see strategy, plus rearmament.[95] This paper, with its negative tone and its appeal back to the old balance-of-power tradition, came under strong attack at the C.I.D. in early December and Chamberlain had to step in to defend Eden. The Prime Minister too 'could see no prospect of success by methods which would shame

[92] Inskip memorandum, 19 November 1937. C.P. 283 (37). Cab.24/273.
[93] Chatfield to Pound, 23 November 1937. Chatfield Papers.
[94] Chiefs of Staff, 'Comparison of the Strength of Great Britain with that of certain other Nations as at January 1938', 12 November 1937. C.P. 296 (37). Cab.24/273.
[95] Foreign Office, memorandum of 26 November 1937. In F.O. 371/20702.

us in the eyes of the world, alienate the United States of America and ultimately land us in worse difficulties than those which confront us at the present time'.[96] It could have been Vansittart speaking. Hankey later told Chamberlain that he, Inskip and the Chiefs of Staff were un-happy about Eden's statement and he urged the Prime Minister to repeat his defence of diplomacy at the Cabinet; Hankey had not circulated the Foreign Office paper to that body, however, as it 'might easily raise controversy'.[97] So Chamberlain reiterated his warnings against a policy of 'concessions which would involve humiliations and disadvantages to this country'. Britain would not pursue a policy of bribery but would try to prevent a war against three powers.[98]

The conflict among British policy-makers in the months before Eden's resignation was not simply a clash of personalities or a dispute over a single issue. Rather, it reflected an intense debate, usually submerged but sometimes surfacing at the C.I.D. and Cabinet, over the true nature of England's global predicament and the correct response required from strategy and diplomacy. Certain of London's decision-makers increasingly saw themselves fighting a losing struggle with limited resources, a full two years short of rearmament with weak or unreliable friends and facing a dangerous 'coalition' of predatory enemies in two hemispheres. This image of weakness in the face of a hostile environment pervaded the appreciations and advice of the Chiefs of Staff and Hankey and gave defence policy an almost defeatist and wholly negative attitude. Much of this was undoubtedly based on sound information but it was compounded by the emotional or ideo-logical prejudices of these men: their suspicions and distrust of France and America, their pro-fascist attitude to the Spanish conflict and their admiration of the order, efficiency and might of the revisionist regimes. Eden felt, with some justice, that their image of events was an exaggeration or distortion, rather than a mirror of the real world, and he thought too that strategy was trespassing beyond its proper limits. This latter point was borne out by the Services' role in yet another dispute, this time over the role of France.

The Foreign Office, despite their unwillingness to lead an anti-fascist group in the Mediterranean, nevertheless felt that the events of late

---

[96] C.I.D./303d mtg., 2 December 1937. *Ibid.* The official minutes in Cab.2 do not have this exchange.
[97] Hankey to Chamberlain, 6 December 1937. Cab.21/700.
[98] Cab. Conclusions, 8 December 1937.

1937 underlined England's growing strategic dependence on France, a fact especially prominent in naval planning for the Far East. The same day that Roosevelt first broached his idea of a naval blockade of Japan, the Foreign Office suggested a general expansion of staff talks with the French and mentioned co-operation in the Mediterranean as an important common interest.[99] Next day – 17 December – the French Ambassador, Charles Corbin, proposed wide-ranging naval collaboration with the Admiralty, especially in the Mediterranean.[100] The naval staff suggested that French military policy was being revised towards an offensive strategy in the Mediterranean where Italy, the weak link in the Axis, threatened French communications. The French were trying to induce Britain to adopt a policy of strength in the Mediterranean; strategic co-operation between the British and French navies might persuade Italy to abandon Germany.[101] That interpretation seemed the more credible when General Lelong, the French Military Attaché, sought out Hore-Belisha behind the backs of his professional advisers and pressed him on staff talks; Lelong, too, spoke of offensives against Italy.[102] Admiral Darlan had also written to Chatfield inviting the latter to meet him in Marseille during the First Sea Lord's tour of inspection of the British fleets. Chatfield thought that the French were 'desperately anxious' for naval conversations.[103]

The Services, and particularly the Admiralty, were deeply suspicious of this French campaign. They opposed staff talks of the 1935–6 type and generally regarded conversations with 'grave misgivings', on the grounds that they would impede attempts to settle with Germany. Although Anglo–French naval co-operation in the Mediterranean would be required *if* the fleet moved east, such collaboration before the event might provoke Hitler to denounce the 1935 Anglo–German naval treaty (by which the German fleet was kept to 35 per cent of the British).[104] Although it was supported by an impressive list of technical objections and historical precedents, the argument, as the Foreign

---

99 Foreign Office to C.I.D., 16 December 1937. Annex to C.P. 35 (38). Cab.24/274.
100 Minute by Eden, 17 December 1937. *Ibid.*
101 Vice-admiral Sir W. James to Sir O. Sargent, 23 December 1937. C8804/271/18. (20738).
102 Pownall Diaries, 17 and 24 February 1938.
103 Conf. of ministers, 14 February 1938. Premier 1/308.
104 Chiefs of Staff, 'Staff Conversations with France and Belgium', C.O.S. 680, 4 February 1938. C.P. 35 (38). Cab.24/274. Viscount Norwich, *Old men forget* (London, 1955), p. 220.

Office complained, was wholly political and it naturally found many allies in a Cabinet not noted for pro-French sympathies. Lord Avon recalls that he was 'indignant' about this and had the ruling reversed before his resignation,[105] but in fact it was Chamberlain and Halifax who, capitulating to strong French pressure during ministerial talks in April 1938, went against Cabinet opinion and authorized limited naval and air staff talks. However, these did not embrace the Mediterranean theatre and seem to have made little concrete progress in Europe either. Serious joint staff talks and planning began only in the summer of 1939, and it is fair to say that strategic advice, as well as political prejudice, played a large role in the delay as in the inordinate state of confusion in allied grand strategy in the immediate pre-war period.

Eden's opinion of the Chiefs of Staff and their policies formed the subject of a letter to Chamberlain at the close of January 1938. He thought Britain's allies were neither so weak nor its 'coalition' of enemies so powerful as the Services portrayed them. The links holding the opposing combination together had been exaggerated and were unlikely to bring all three into war together. Strategy also underestimated France and overestimated Italy: 'surely if there was a choice between France and Italy we should not hesitate for a minute'. Eden was disturbed that the Services were so reluctant to discuss the Mediterranean with France and he feared they would take a similar line over air talks:

> I cannot help believing that what the chiefs of staff would really like to do is to reorient our whole foreign policy and to clamber on the band wagon with the dictators, even though that process meant parting company with France and estranging our relations with the United States.[106]

On foreign policy Eden agreed that Britain 'must make every effort to come to terms with Germany' and the obstacles to agreement with Italy could probably be overcome. But in another letter to the Prime Minister he argued that the 'big issues of 1938' were 'Anglo—American cooperation, the chances of effectively asserting white race authority in the Far East and relations with Germany. To all this Mussolini is really secondary.' The Duce was the 'complete gangster' and Britain's moral position would suffer by according recognition to his conquest.[107]

105 Avon, *Facing the dictators, op. cit.* p. 501.
106 Eden to Chamberlain, 31 January 1938. Premier 1/276.
107 Eden to Chamberlain, 9 January 1938. Premier 1/276.

However, Eden was willing to pursue the Italian card, albeit unenthusi-
astically, because Chamberlain was constantly prodding him. Shortly
before Christmas the latter had intervened with Eden to reconcile their
two viewpoints and to get the Foreign Office working on a programme
of Anglo—Italian discussions on all questions, including Abyssinia.
Chamberlain's intention, Wilson assured Hankey, was 'to move as fast
as he possibly can' to get talks opened with Rome.[108] He told Eden
that he shared his dislike for diplomatic bargains, but this was the
wrong way to approach the subject. Britain's object was a general
settlement of the Mediterranean region, part of the overall pacification
of Europe, and as this was in the common interest, every country
should be willing to make a contribution. Britain would offer *de jure*
recognition if general agreement could be brought within reach.[109] It
was an excellent piece of sophistry. To get his 'general settlement' with
Germany Chamberlain was preparing a new partition plan for Central
Africa; to appease Italy he would take the political risk of recognizing
Abyssinia as Mussolini's. Here were England's 'contributions', and it is
hardly worth adding that the wishes of the inhabitants of these regions
figured not at all in this programme of appeasement. Africa was to be
bartered once again in the market-place of European imperialism.

Neville Chamberlain was deeply preoccupied in these weeks with
defence, foreign policy and especially the financial implications of the
rearmament programme. Inskip's Interim Review, the outcome of
months of work with Treasury experts, had come out in mid-December
and, predictably, the document reflected the same conservative
orthodoxy as Chamberlain's June appreciation. It reiterated the
priorities of home defence and the protection of trade and emphasized
the Empire's strength in commerce and raw materials. The maintenance
of credit facilities and a favourable balance of trade gave England
staying power for a long war. Chamberlain had stressed the following
passage at the Cabinet:

> Seen in its true perspective, the maintenance of our economic
> stability would . . . accurately be described as an essential element in
> our defensive strength: one which can properly be regarded as a
> fourth arm of defence, alongside the three Defence Services without

108 Chamberlain to Eden, 7 and 13 January 1938. *Ibid.*; Wilson to Hankey, 7
    January 1938. Cab.21/558.
109 Chamberlain to Eden, 7 January 1938. *Op. cit.*

which purely military effort would be of no avail.[110]

The strains on the rearmament programme coupled with the urgent warnings of London's strategists had convinced the Prime Minister of the need for a dramatic effort to ease the global position with individual approaches to Mussolini and Hitler. Hankey now saw Hitler's coming visit to Italy and French weakness as danger signals that could not be ignored; he warned Inskip to tell the Prime Minister that, 'Unless the number of our potential enemies can be reduced *at once* I submit that our rearmament policy must be changed.'[111] Chatfield too, having just passed through the crisis in the Far East, was using every opportunity to make the same point. Chamberlain cannot have missed the urgency of this advice from his two most senior and influential strategists, but his own choices were even more circumscribed by the pressing need to keep defence spending under control and his wish to avoid tampering with the normal workings of the industrial system.

All of the pressures working on him had led Chamberlain to his decision to appease in Europe and he was not about to be opposed. He and Eden had already quarrelled over Roosevelt's celebrated 'peace plan'; Chamberlain saw the multilateral American approach in conflict with his own plans for bilateral diplomacy and he brusquely dismissed it as misguided idealism. Matters were not helped by Lady Chamberlain's tea-time chats with Count Ciano in Rome, but the dispute which ended in Eden's resignation was not over a personality conflict. At the Cabinet on 16 February, just two days before the two men clashed on the Italian issue, universal gloom prevailed as Inskip's final report was discussed. All bemoaned the fact that the five-year ceiling on defence costs would have to be revised upwards, and Simon claimed that it 'was as serious a matter as any Cabinet had ever had to face in time of peace'. Eden was unresponsive to those who pleaded for an answer from diplomacy, but this time Chamberlain seemed to withdraw his backing. If defence spending were not reduced, the economy would have to be interrupted and taxes increased; otherwise, the nation would face a grim financial future. Chamberlain had agreed to defer these decisions only because he saw hope of an immediate improvement of the international situation.[112] The meaning was clear. On the nineteenth, after the dramatic confrontation in front of Count Grandi, the

110 Inskip, 'Defence Expenditure in Future Years', 15 December 1937. C.P. 316 (37). Cab.24/273; Cab. Conclusions, 22 December 1937. Cab.23/90.
111 Hankey to Inskip, 14 January 1938. Cab.63/53.
112 Cab. Conclusions, 16 February 1938. Cab.23/92.

Prime Minister gave as his reason for seeking urgent talks (*a*) the general state of military unreadiness and (*b*) the growing financial burden of armaments. Britain faced financial dislocation and the loss of its powerful credit position. He wished to make 'one last effort' to alleviate this, and this was why he sought approach to Germany and Italy.[113] The conflict was resolved only with Eden's resignation. The debate was about a matter of timing, not principle, but to the group opposing Eden the Italian issue was all a matter of timing, and had been for months.

The evolution of Britain's Mediterranean policies in the 1936–8 period demonstrated the highly centralized nature of the Government's policy-making process. For two years those responsible for the formation of defence policy had insisted on a settlement with Italy and used their power of denial to obstruct any alternative strategy. On this issue they functioned as a coherent interest group within a divided system and Eden's resignation reflected the weight of their influence; although their conflict with him could hardly have brought about the Cabinet crisis, certainly it did contribute to his isolation. London's strategists saw Mediterranean appeasement as an expedient, as a time-saving device necessary to give the nation extra months in which to rearm without abandoning vital priorities at home or in the Far East, and they advocated it with rare fervour. That the policy of accommodating Italy was unpopular because it condoned that power's programme of counter-revolution and expansion mattered to them little; political risk and moral obloquy must be accepted even though the real reason for the policy – general military weakness – could not be publicly disclosed. And they had their way, a fact that illustrates that the policy process was far more responsive to pressure from within than without.

The usual image of Neville Chamberlain as his own man inflexibly bent on carrying out his personal policies is evidently in need of revision, for the evidence already considered suggests that he was considerably influenced by advice from senior officials. Moreover, it must

---

113 Cab. Conclusions, 19 February 1938. *Ibid.* Hankey made some last-minute efforts to bring Eden around to the majority view but he was secretly relieved at his resignation. He told an unnamed correspondent that the sands had been running out: 'In May Hitler pays his visit to Mussolini, and after that the Rome–Berlin "axis" may become too tight for any agreement . . . I am sorry to say that generally I wake on a thought of how we are to provide for some horror in the next war. Today I felt there was just a possibility of peace.' Letter of 21 February 1938. Cab.63/53. On the immediate cabinet crisis, cf. also the Simon Diaries, entries of 12, 18, 19 February 1938.

be added that his choices were strictly limited by the exigencies of British military and financial weakness. Chamberlain's real failing lay in his willingness to be guided by mediocre advice, not in his alleged aloofness from official advice. Unlike, say, Lloyd George, he was too ready to accept what he wanted to hear and not independent or original enough to challenge the assumptions and prejudices that underlay what was, in the final analysis, the fallible opinion of very fallible men. Under Chamberlain's leadership the serious discussion of policy options tended to be stifled beneath a complacent consensus and the critics who might have made a dent were either sidetracked or wholly excluded from the counsels of the Government. Change typically came in reaction to external events and then it came too late. The system was a little more personalized under Chamberlain but it had not worked much better under Baldwin or his predecessors. The flaw was structural. Meaningful debate — so lacking in the evolution of Mediterranean policy — was not generated because the policy-making machinery was too centralized in its formal workings and too clubby in its informal workings. What was wanting was not better co-ordination but an opposition capable of giving the machinery a dose of healthy self-criticism from time to time.

4. The Most Distant Station: the Dimensions of Mediterranean Strategy, 1936-8

In the evolution of strategy, as Professor Greenfield reminds us,[1] the decisions made and the effect of those decisions are governed largely by feasibility — by conditions determining what, at a given time, it seemed possible to do with the forces at hand; and by the effectiveness of those forces. The conditions influencing strategic choices can vary from the purely physical and geographical constants to the shifting variables of high policy and lowly politics: the priorities of grand strategy, financial restraint, electoral considerations and so on. The study of the process of policy formation is, like the process itself, complex and multi-dimensional, even though this is not always apparent in the efforts of those who would reduce the behaviour of nation-states to one or more deterministic models in the otherwise laudable attempt to make the study more scientific.

These general considerations are particularly apposite for the student of British defence policy in the immediate pre-war period. Strategy was evolved not in the rarefied intellectual atmosphere of mathematical game theory but in the real world of global crisis, post-depression finance, domestic policies and inter-Service rivalry. These, and other such factors, were the components of policy and the historian ignores them at his peril. The very language of British strategy — 'limited liability', 'balancing risks' and so on — suggests that the feasible was very often far from the theoretically ideal. Decisions were seldom born at a given moment as the correct solution to a particular problem; far more likely they were conceived in the womb of conflicting alternatives and compromise and had to pass through a long process of gestation while all kinds of negative restraints came into play before emerging, a hybrid rather than pure offspring of uncertain parentage. Defence policy in the Mediterranean was very much a case in point.

Mediterranean strategy, especially after the close of the Abyssinian

---

1   K. R. Greenfield, *American strategy in World War II: a reconsideration* (Baltimore, 1963), p. 85.

emergency, was a branch of grand strategy and consequently had to
compete against the needs of home and Far Eastern defence. Before
1939 it had last priority in London's allocation of scarce resources;
weakness and heavy risks were deliberately accepted there as the price
of better security elsewhere. In theory, in order to hold the centre of
the Empire and its vital circumference, grand strategy would in, certain
circumstances, abandon control of the Mediterranean and Middle East
to the Axis. This did not mean, however, that the defence of the region
was completely neglected or that the dilemmas of fighting a
Mediterranean war were left unstudied. There was a limit to the margin
of acceptable risk if only because of the political consequences of
military weakness; considerable opposition was mounted to the Chiefs
of Staff's policy of withholding equipment such as air defences from
positions exposed to outside aggression. Italy's rearmament, the Arab
rebellion in Palestine, nationalist opposition to imperial rule throughout
the Middle East and the Axis political and propaganda offensive had
Britain's diplomatic and Service representatives in the area constantly
under pressure, and their demands for London's support inevitably
found some sympathetic ears.

The full extent of England's vulnerability and the risks being taken
were revealed after strategic appreciations of the theatre were drawn up
and the Far Eastern crisis of 1937 had confronted the Services with the
implications of a real evacuation of the Mediterranean. Inroads into the
system of imperial priorities were made in 1938 when the Committee
of Imperial Defence finally acknowledged in principle the need to make
the Eastern Mediterranean and Middle East less dependent on vulnerable
lines of communications and more militarily self-sufficient: Egypt and
the Suez Canal must at least be held. But in other ways the pattern of
deliberate risk was maintained. French offers of strategic co-operation
in the Mediterranean were refused and little attempt was made to
exploit Italy's own colonial weaknesses.

One controversial problem that underlay much of Britain's strategic
thinking about the Mediterranean is worth some preliminary discussion.
How were Italy's strengths and weaknesses perceived by British
planners, and how did their calculations influence their own choices?
Did they overrate Italy, as Eden suggested to Chamberlain shortly
before his resignation? Did they overlook those fundamental weaknesses
that later proved to be its undoing and allow themselves to be bluffed
by a second-rate power? One of the most frequent charges laid at the
door of the military is that, in wishing to err on the side of caution,

they consistently overestimate the strength of their enemies and under-estimate that of their allies. Did the Chiefs of Staff fall into this habit of mind, so easily induced by military unreadiness; was Britain's Mediterranean policy shaped by faulty intelligence?

1. Italy as a Mediterranean power

Italy's strategic capacity was well known to official and unofficial military observers alike in the 1930s. For instance, one of the better contemporary studies of the European military balance[2] demonstrated how Italy's war-making capabilities were subject to very definite and insuperable limitations. Despite its apparent power on paper, its vulnerability in several areas — its lack of raw materials, its dependence upon sea-borne imports, its susceptibility to economic pressure, its weak industrial system and its lack of control over the three 'gates' of the Mediterranean — made Italy almost by definition a second-class power. Italy's strengths lay in its advantageous position in the central Mediterranean and in the fact that its armed forces were generally mobilized. It measured up well in journalistic comparisons of first-line aircraft, manpower under arms, ships building and so on, but these concealed the truth that it had the weakest war potential of any of the big powers.[3] It was, for example, a ranking air power — for a time in the mid-thirties it had been *the* leading air power — but its productive capacity to maintain its forces in wartime was limited by its lack of reserve industry and by its shortages of skilled labour and raw material. Measured in the currency of economic staying-power and industrial capacity, the real bases of strategic power, the Fascist Grand Council's oft-repeated intention to achieve military 'autarchy' looked like the small change of propaganda.

Italian strategic doctrine flowed from the nation's inability to wage a long, exhausting war. General Pariani had admitted that 'Italy is not rich in raw-material resources, and she can therefore not seek a pro-tracted war involving great material expenditure'.[4] Objective conditions imposed the need for a strategy designed for vigorous offensives and swift decisions. Much the same kind of economic reasoning lay behind the German *Blitzkrieg* strategy, but, as Max Werner noted, Italy, unlike

---

2 Max Werner, *The military strength of the powers* (London, 1939), chap. 10.
3 *Ibid.*
4 Werner, *op. cit.* p. 255.

its ally, appeared to lack the offensive capability to implement such a doctrine. So it was left an open question whether its strategy and its economic and industrial potential effectively complemented each other.[5]

The British Chiefs of Staff were at once aware of the same deficiencies in Italy's make-up and determined to exploit them to the full in any Mediterranean war. Italy's essential weakness, they asserted in their comprehensive 'Mediterranean Appreciation' of February 1938, lay in its dependence upon sea-borne imports and in its critical shortages of raw materials.[6] A technical study of the Italian economy carried out at the outbreak of the 1935 crisis had revealed its vulnerability to maritime pressure;[7] the nation lacked liquid and solid fuels and imported other materials — iron ore, copper, timber — by sea or vital land communications of limited capacity. Italy was highly dependent upon seaborne imports of petroleum, much of it from Black Sea sources, and produced only a fraction of its annual requirements, facts that helped explain the fears that an oil sanction might drive Mussolini to attack the leading powers of the League. The same study pointed to Italy's other major strategic flaw: the separation of its African expeditionary force from its source of supply and its absolute dependence upon transit through the Suez Canal. Abyssinia's life-line was in British hands.

Britain's naval planners had these points to the foreground of their appreciations of the Abyssinian crisis. Chatfield noted how, simply by holding the exits to the Mediterranean, Britain could eventually close off the war in East Africa and force Mussolini to the conference table. The mere closure of Suez might be decisive, as it would sever Italy's supply line 'with comparatively little effort to ourselves'.[8] Italy was in a 'fundamentally weak strategic position', he wrote, although it had a

5 Other writers concentrated on Italy's 'imprisonment' within the Mediterranean. Cf. for example, H. Blythe, *Spain over Britain* (London, 1937); a similar approach was taken in an influential German study of the Mediterranean by H. Hummel and W. Siewert, exponents of Carl Haushofer's geo-political studies of strategy: *Der Mittelmeerraum* (Munich, 1936). 'England could easily strangle Italy,' they concluded.

6 Committee of Imperial Defence: Mediterranean, Middle East and North-East Africa: Appreciation by the Chiefs of Staff Sub-Committee', D.P.(P.) 18, 21 February 1938. Cab.16/182. Hereinafter cited as 'Mediterranean Appreciation'.

7 Economic Pressure on Italy', July 1935. C.P. 169 (35). Cab.24/256. Also, Hankey to Chatfield, 24 July 1935. Cab.21/411.

8 Chatfield, 'The Naval Strategical Position in the Mediterranean', D.P.R. 15, 3 September 1935. Cab.116/138.

strong hand in the narrows of the central Mediterranean. Britain's lack of forward naval bases, its deficiencies in anti-aircraft ammunition and its general unreadiness for war might force it to abandon the central seas and the opportunity for an early decision, but in the final reckoning, Chatfield assured his Mediterranean Commander-in-Chief, 'if Italy is mad enough to channelge us, it is at the ends of the Mediterranean she will be defeated'.[9] Sea-borne trade made up 76 per cent of its total imports — 62 per cent through Gibraltar, 3 per cent via Suez and 11 per cent from the Mediterranean and Black Sea — and gave the Royal Navy a potential stranglehold on its economy; and although, to be fully effective, an economic blockade would require belligerent rights and a strict rationing of neutrals, it was clear that the Duce's capability to wage his distant colonial war could be severely checked.[10]

Some of those who saw these advantages and the chance of waging successfully a war of limited violence for the League and collective security regretted a missed opportunity. One British naval officer in a position to know later wrote:

> To us in the Mediterranean Fleet it seemed a very simple task to stop [Mussolini]. The mere closing of the Suez Canal to his transports which were then streaming through with troops and stores would effectively have cut off his armies concentrating in Eritrea and elsewhere. It is true that such a drastic measure might have led to war with Italy; but the Mediterranean Fleet was in a state of high morale and efficiency, and had no fear whatever of the result of an encounter with the Italian Navy ... Had we stopped the passage of fuel into Italy, the whole subsequent history of the world might have been altered.[11]

There was certainly much in this. The next four years would not see another moment when the balance of Mediterranean power would be so favourable for England or another chance to deploy the whole of its power against Italy. But Cunningham's recollections have the advantage of hindsight. The deeply cautious attitude of the Chiefs of Staff was based in a pessimistic appreciation of the present and future global situation, and not simply on the fleet's chances against an obviously weaker power. It is no exaggeration to say that long-term fears of Japan, as much as immediate concern for Italy, operated as an

---

9 Chatfield to Admiral Sir W. W. Fisher, 25 August 1935. Chatfield Papers.
10 Chatfield, 'The Naval Strategical Position in the Mediterranean', *op. cit.*
11 Lord Cunningham of Hyndhope, *A sailor's Odyssey* (London, 1951), p. 173.

important constraint in planning for a Mediterranean war in 1935, and, indeed, right up to 1940. The difference between the conservative sea lords in London and the more aggressive officers in charge of the Mediterranean Fleet was basically one of perspective. That said, however, the Chiefs of Staff's own evidence does tend to verify Liddell Hart's assertion that 'Never again would there be so good a chance to check an aggressor so early.'[12]

The Chiefs of Staff were by and large unimpressed by Italy's victory in Abyssinia, although it came sooner than they had predicted. They were not yet alarmed about the threat to England's naval communications through the Red Sea, and the evidence suggested that Mussolini's war had weakened, rather than strengthened, Italy as a Mediterranean power. Sanctions had had a devastating impact on its shaky economic structure and had aggravated long-standing weaknesses: its foriegn exchange crisis, its lack of gold reserves, and so on. The international boycott had failed in its declared objective of halting the war — indeed, it had forced the Duce to accelerate its prosecution — but one reason why it was lifted in July 1936 was because of growing evidence that sanctions might bring about Italy's financial collapse. As Drummond summed it up, the nation would at best 're-enter an unsympathetic economic world with a broken exchange, a vanishing gold reserve, a heavy unpaid bill for arrears, a disorganized foreign trade and an unbalanced budget'. If sanctions were maintained, the Foreign Office and Treasury calculated, perhaps too optimistically, by September 1936 financial and demobilization problems might bring on a dangerous internal crisis which, Drummond had typically warned, might drive

---

[12] Sir B. Liddell Hart, *Memoirs* (London, 1965), I, p. 290. Most British naval officers, including Chatfield, grew less and less impressed with Italian sea power. After exchanging visits in mid-1938 with the Italian naval command, Admiral Pound wrote Chatfield that his opinion of Italian efficiency was 'exactly as it had been before — just second rate'. Pound to Chatfield 24 August 1938. In April 1939 the British naval attaché in Rome advised the Admiralty that Italian naval officers were not of a high standard and discipline was poor: 'an initial blow at the outbreak of war might have greater effect on the ultimate issue than its strategic value would imply.' R3639/70/22 (23810). Little has been published in English on Italian naval strategy before the war. Useful information is in Kenneth Edwards, *Uneasy oceans* (London, 1939), but the interested reader must consult the Italian official war histories, most of which unhappily deal only marginally with the pre-war period. The compositions of the British and Italian fleets are in the appendices to Roskill, *Naval policy between the wars*, I.

Mussolini to desperate measures.[13] The lifting of sanctions and the government's piecemeal tinkering with the economy (the lira was devalued and measures announced to increase self-sufficiency) did not arrest the process. 'Italy's real strength is wasting in a slow economic decline', Drummond wrote at the end of 1936.[14] For there had been no general demobilization and no economic retrenchment — just more spendthrift imperialism. Italy was forced to retain at immense cost some 70,000 troops in Abyssinia to 'pacify' the post-war resistance and, by mid-1937, had some 40,000 men in Spain and about the same number in Libya. None of this was very profitable. The material rewards reaped from its two large tracts of undeveloped sand and wilderness in Africa were not exactly bountiful and the Spanish commitment, if ideologically satisfying, saw Italy doing much of the donkey-work but Germany carrying home most of the dividends. It looked almost as if Mussolini had deliberately set out to disprove, in his perverse way, the pseudo-Marxist association of profit with imperialism.

As Italian difficulties mounted overseas and the Duce faced his first military defeats in Spain, the reputation of both nation and leader went into decline. The Chiefs of Staff suggested in their 'Review of Imperial Defence' of early 1937 that Italy was more vulnerable than it had been before the 1935–6 crisis. It was over-extended in every direction and had given a hostage to fortune by establishing a colony on the far side of Suez.[15] Military and industrial intelligence showed that Italy's war-making capacity had little of the reserve depth required for protracted modern warfare. Mussolini's air force, so vital to his declared aims in the Mediterranean, had a very respectable first-line strength (approximately 1,800 aircraft in early 1938, of which 1,600 were modern types), but the Italian aircraft industry lacked the capacity, skilled labour and raw materials to maintain this force after immediate reserves

13 Foreign Office memorandum, 3 June 1936; Treasury paper, 28 May 1936. R3284/R3286/2132/22. (20422). This evidence adds a new dimension to Chamberlain's 'midsummer of madness' speech of 10 June.
14 Drummond to Eden, disp. No. 1300, 4 December 1936. R7366/1/22. (20403). The steady deterioration of Italy's economy was studied by the British Foreign Office, whose officials viewed it both as a symptom of weakness — and a source of instability: 'the greater the economic stress the more necessary will Signor Mussolini find it to divert popular attention abroad and to produce foreign scapegoats.' 'Economic Situation in Italy', 3 October 1938. C.P. 251 (38).
15 Chiefs of Staff, 'Review of Imperial Defence', *op. cit.*

had been expended.[16] An industrial intelligence centre report of November 1937 showed that Italy was entirely dependent upon imports of liquid fuels, that stocks were low and that 'all available evidence regarding stocks of this essential war store tends to refute any suggestion of the immediate likelihood of Italy engaging in a war involving large expenditure of liquid fuels'.[17] Italy was 'gravely deficient' in solid fuels as well — more than 12 million tons of coal and coke had to be imported annually — and its reserves of raw materials such as copper, iron and steel, tin, nickel, manganese and timber would last only a few months. Its land transportation system was of strictly limited capacity and its weak industrial base showed up particularly in its engineering and armaments industries; here Italy was increasingly dependent upon Germany. But its essential weakness, the Chiefs of Staff reckoned in their 'Mediterranean Appreciation', was this:

> If the Dardanelles were closed to Italian trade, her economic situation would become critical, and the supply of petroleum products would prove a decisive factor after initial reserves, stocks of which are understood to be extremely low at present, had been expended. If she enjoyed free access to Mediterranean and Black Sea countries, Italy might obtain, so long as she could pay in acceptable value, sufficient raw materials to enable her to pursue a naval and air war for a considerable time, but she would still experience a shortage of rubber, oilseeds, wool, cotton and copper, and could not continue indefinitely.[18]

In the light of this evidence, it is not surprising that Britain's strategists dismissed fascist declarations on military autarchy as prestige-building bravado. Far from being self-sufficient, they noted, Italy would certainly be a heavy liability for its German ally in time of war; whereas if it stayed neutral it might prove a valuable channel for Germany.[19] Nor did the British fear, in the period 1935 to 1940, a Mediterranean trial of strength, a single-handed 'competition in mutual attrition', with Italy, for they knew — and so did Mussolini — that any war between the two powers must inevitably be decided in favour of the British Empire, with its vastly greater resources, maritime

16 C.I.D. Paper No. 1304-B. 'Italian Aircraft Industry', December 1936. Cab.4/25.
17 Inskip, 'The Situation in the Mediterranean and Middle East', 19 November 1937. C.P. 283 (37). Cab.24/273.
18 'Mediterranean Appreciation', App. I.
19 Chiefs of Staff, 'Military Implications of German Aggression Against Czechoslovakia', C.O.S. 698, 28 March 1938. Cab.53/37.

supremacy and control over the exits and entrances to the Mediterranean. 'The position of Italy, *vis à vis* the British Empire', wrote the Chiefs of Staff, 'is thus inherently weak.'[20]

However, this was not the whole story. The threat from Italy had to be seen in the light of Britain's own military weakness in the Mediterranean after the withdrawal of July 1936 and the complications of its global or extra-Mediterranean dilemmas. England's major source of imperial weakness lay in the German programme of military expansion and in the absolute priority fixed to British home defence. In time of peace, nothing could be spared for the Mediterranean without undermining home rearmament; in time of war, Italian belligerency would force diversion of allied forces from the main theatre and add 'immeasurably' to Britain's military anxieties.[21] Seen in this context, Italy's choice of an enemy, neutral or allied role took on a very different meaning for London's military planners. Chatfield, smarting a little from his Mediterranean Commander-in-Chief's criticisms, told Pound in November 1937 why the Cabinet refused to approve his and Sir Miles Lampson's requests for more strength in the region: his letter, incidentally, gives a revealing insight into his true opinion of the Italians:

> ... you say you have got the impression that the Government are averse to consolidating our position for fear of hurting the Italians' feelings, but I do not think that is really the case. There are two points of view about the Italians which have to be considered. The first is that they are thoroughly untrustworthy and probably little better fighters than they used to be, are insolent and bombastic, and the best thing would be to teach them a lesson and answer threat by threat; and the second is that the Mediterranean position is only one of three anxieties (Germany and Japan are the other two), and as we are still hopelessly weak to meet the responsibilities of all three services, and so long as we cannot come to terms with either of our chief opponents, it will be better in the long run to get an agreement with Italy because we have no basic cause of enmity with that country, as we have with the other two. I think this latter factor, together with the unreadiness that I have referred to, has really dominated the thoughts of the C.I.D.[22]

20 'Mediterranean Appreciation'.
21 'Military Implications of German Aggression Against Czechslovakia', *op. cit.*
22 Chatfield to Pound, 23 November 1937. Chatfield Papers.

Time was the crucial dimension. Britain's period of danger, when its global naval strength would be at low ebb, would also see it concentrating all available resources on home defence and the building of a deterrent to Germany. Little could be spared for the Mediterranean before 1939–40, but after that Egypt and Britain's naval bases could be properly equipped: 'until then, and while the German fear exists and we are unready to meet it, the C.I.D. will give the Mediterranean second place'.[23] The Chiefs of Staff sought a pause, a breathing space for at least two vital years in the Mediterranean. The years 1937 and 1938 would be the period of danger, because Italy would enjoy a narrowing margin of superiority *vis-à-vis* England and might feel increasingly tempted to exploit it if its political goals were not satisfied, especially if Britain became preoccupied in Europe or the Far East. But where would it strike?

An offensive strategy aimed at an early decision would best fit Italy's economic incapacity to wage a protracted war; its generally weak strategic posture was thus an added element of instability. Britain's superiority would tell over the long haul, but for a time Italy would enjoy a strong military advantage. In these circumstances its most likely course would lie in obtaining a spectacular local success, and this suggested a lightning *coup* against Egypt, the key to Britain's control of the East Mediterranean and Middle East. By seizing Suez before British reinforcements could arrive, Italy would secure its own communications with Abyssinia and gain a powerful advantage in the war to follow. Italy could be expected to strike at the decisive point and that point was not Gibraltar and not Tunisia, but Egypt; an overland offensive from Libya supported by heavy air strikes seemed to be its most logical strategy.[24]

This inductive reasoning was confirmed by Britain's watch over Italy's military activity in the Mediterranean. The most striking aspect of its military expansion lay in what the Chiefs of Staff called the 'complete re-orientation of Italian air policy'. Mussolini was known to have strong beliefs about the potential of air power for promoting Rome's political influence and in countering Britain's supremacy in sea power; the air arm was the weapon with which Italy would lead its assault against the 'gate-keeper' of the Mediterranean. In 1934 Italy's air force had been a largely obsolescent fleet of 1,000 aircraft — many of which had wooden frames — deployed above the Spezia–Trieste line

23 *Ibid.*
24 'Mediterranean Appreication'.

in northern Italy against France and Germany; no provision for
offensive air operations in the Mediterranean had been made. Under a
remarkable programme of expansion begun that year, annual output
had increased by some 1,200 per cent and the air force had been fully
modernized. The structural weaknesses of the aircraft industry gave its
air power the unsatisfactory reserve figure of under 30 per cent, but by
March 1938 Italy could nonetheless boast a first-line strength of 1,760
aircraft. This alone was reason for concern, but British intelligence also
pointed to a complete re-deployment of air forces into the southern
part of Italy and the Mediterranean after the Abyssinian affair. By May
1937, forty-five bomber squadrons had been established south of the
Spezia–Trieste line and air bases and aerodromes were functioning or
under construction on Sicily, Sardinia, Pantelleria, and the Dodecanese
islands. Italy's regional air superiority over England was in the ratio of
six to one and it was estimated that it could freely deploy 650 aircraft
in an attack on Egypt, which was void of air defences.[25]

The build-up of mechanized land forces in Libya over the same
period constituted the second major threat to the security of British
interests in the Mediterranean and Middle East. The first partially
motorized division had been sent there in the summer of 1935, but in
the course of 1937 three more were sent out, bringing the regular
establishment – excluding the colonial army – up to two mechanized
army corps. This was still a relatively small force, and Britain's planners
understood that the Italians were having problems in Libya with
shortages of fuel and water and would not be able to mount an attack
across the desert for some time. They argued that the build-up was
politically motivated, designed to give Italy bargaining leverage in its
campaign for diplomatic concessions. If this was correct the strategy
was a success, for the effects of the Libyan concentration immediately
complicated Britain's relations with the Egyptian authorities and made

25 Based on: reports by British air attaché to Rome. Cab.21/558; the Embassy's
annual report for 1937. R692/692/22. (22437); air staff note of 21 February
1938. Cab.21/559; 'Mediterranean Appreciation', app. 11, part 11; related
reports by the Chiefs of Staff; Air Ministry and industrial intelligence reports
on Italian aircraft industry. Cab.4/24 and 25. A British appreciation written in
December 1938 concluded that Italy's air force passed its peak of efficiency
and war-readiness at the end of 1936. After that date the war in Spain,
financial stringency and uncertain rearmament planning had taken their toll:
'Today, therefore, the Italian Air Force is in no position to enter a war of the
first magnitude with any hope of pursuing it successfully once the initial blow
has spent itself.' Note by British air attaché (Rome) on Italian air force.
F.O. 371/23796.

its own response as much an issue of imperial prestige as military security. In addition, the Libyan threat seemed more acute when the naval staff pointed out in December 1937 that if Admiral Pound moved his fleet to Singapore, Italy would gain undisputed control of the East Mediterranean and no ships would be available for convoying reinforcements from England and India to the Middle East.[26] Chatfield told Captain Ingersoll during the Anglo–American naval talks of January 1938 that Britain would have to carry out a military occupation of Egypt with Indian troops before the fleet could safely evacuate the Mediterranean.[27] Thus, it was not unnatural that the Foreign Office insisted upon introducing the issue of the Libyan garrison into the Anglo–Italian conversations of 1938 when they finally began.

To summarize, then, Britain's strategic planners saw Italy as a second-class military power advantageously placed to secure local and probably temporary successes in a war in the Mediterranean. Of their capability ultimately to defeat it they had no doubts whatever, but the time that this might take and the losses that they might themselves have to endure would be mainly influenced by the situation outside the Mediterranean. If they overrated Italy it was not because of a lack of knowledge of its vulnerabilities; rather, they, with the Cabinet and Foreign Office, failed to act on the knowledge. The failure was not one of poor intelligence but of a lack of will. The British were bluffed again and again by Italy because they overestimated Mussolini's ability to act in defiance of the sheer realities of power. By acting on the unproved but generally accepted assumption that he would commit a 'mad dog' act rather than lose face they were bound to lose the war of nerves in every Mediterranean crisis. Mussolini was allowed to manipulate risks and to indulge in brinkmanship because the British overrated, not his capacity for violence, but his capacity for irrationality and because they balanced the same risks in a broader global context.

2. Planning for warfare in the Mediterranean and Middle East

The evacuation of the bulk of British naval, military and air forces from the West and East Mediterranean and the Middle East in July 1936 signalled the resolve of the Chiefs of Staff to implement the grand strategy outlined in the pages of the third report of the Defence

[26] Chatfield to Hankey, 7 December 1937. Cab.21/579.
[27] Ingersoll's Report for Leahy, *op. cit.*

Requirements Subcommittee seven months before.[28] The emergency
in the Mediterranean was to be regarded as terminated, British forces
were to resume their pre-crisis dispositions and regional strategy would
again be based on the premise of stable relations with Italy. Balancing
global commitments against available resources, Britain's strategists had
implicitly demarcated the Mediterranean as the theatre in which the
margin of acceptable risk would be pushed to the limit. In order to
concentrate the R.A.F. and the air defence effort in England and to
keep faith with the Government's naval–political commitments in the
Far Eastern Empire, British policies in the Mediterranean were being
constructed upon a weak and fragile foundation of left-over military
resources and dubious political assumptions.

The Baldwin and Chamberlain governments, of course, carefully
disguised that foundation with a smoke-screen of ministerial verbiage
and ostentatious flag-waving: Britain was not about to 'scuttle' from
the Mediterranean. One writer was convinced by this public relations
effort that the Cabinet had endorsed the so-called Mediterranean School
of grand strategy:

> The nation, almost unanimously and without complaint, subscribed
> to a rearmament programme of such magnitude that few states were
> rich enough to compete. Naval and air armaments were added to the
> Mediterranean stock; plans were paid for a base at Cyprus; a promise
> of harbours and landing-grounds was secured from Egypt, and the
> nervous voices of 1935 were drowned in a crescendo of expert talk
> – mysterious but confident – of developments at Malta and
> Gibraltar and their growing power of attack upon an adversary.[29]

As will become clear, the reality of Britain's Mediterranean position
was very far from this contrived image of growing strength and
'mysterious but confident' policy. The truth is that the pre-war defence
of the region was seriously neglected by both the Government's
strategists and ministers. To cite but one example, no strategic planning
of any kind was done for the Mediterranean–Middle East theatre
between July 1936 and August 1937. A general survey of the region –
the so-called 'Mediterranean Appreciation' – was prepared in early
1938, but no Mediterranean war plans were in existence at the time of

---

28 See Chapter 2 on the D.R.C. recommendations for the Mediterranean.
29 Elizabeth Monroe, *The Mediterranean in politics* (London, 1938), p. 10.

the Munich crisis.[30] No co-ordinated tri-Service war plan for the
Mediterranean was worked out before the three regional commands
were finally placed under a Middle East command in August 1939; and
the first Anglo–French strategic planning for the region since the
Abyssinian crisis was still going on when Hitler invaded Poland. The
over-worked and under-staffed plans divisions of the Services were
partly to blame for this situation; but the prerequisites of sound
planning – including available resources and consistent political
guidance – were also missing. Until Chamberlain's Cabinet had decided,
for instance, to revise the strategic formulas to declare Italy an enemy –
or France an ally – the planners were unable to outline anything more
precise than general guidelines for the regional commanders.

Yet, if detailed plans were lacking, the shape of Britain's strategic
dilemmas in the Mediterranean was nonetheless well known. In
November 1938, for example, the naval Commander-in-Chief of the
Mediterranean Fleet, Admiral Pound, outlined the central difficulties
in a series of dispatches to the naval staff in London. Pound argued that
the Mediterranean differed entirely from the navy's other commands
because of technological change and because of its unique geography.
The emergence of long-range bombers and improvements in communications had made the Mediterranean 'a very small place', a fact
especially disagreeable for naval strategists. Under Pound's supervision,
British combined naval and air forces had carried out slow and fast
convoy exercises in the central Mediterranean and in the Atlantic west
of Gibraltar in August 1937 and March 1938. Those exercises had
confirmed Pound's pessimism regarding wartime naval movements
through the Mediterranean: in the face of hostile Italian air power and
submarines, a simple convoy from, say, Malta to Egypt would become
a major fleet operation. Either reinforcements for Egypt should be
completed before hostilities began, he argued, or they should divert
around the much longer Cape route. Paradoxically, then, 'the Central
and Eastern Mediterranean, though seemingly one of the nearest of the
foreign stations, becomes when using the Cape route, the most distant
of all, except China, where it has long been considered necessary to
maintain our personnel at war strength in peace time'.[31]

---

30 Cunningham, *A sailor's Odyssey, op. cit.* p. 195. In September 1938, 'I was
told also to study the war plans, and on sending for them I found they
consisted of no more than plans for the dispatch of the fleet to the Far East.'
31 Pound, 'Situation in the Mediterranean – 1st October 1938', dispatch Med.
01060/0708/8, 14 November 1938. Adm. 116/3900. Of the slow convoy

England's major weakness in the Mediterranean lay in the vulnerability of its line of communications and in the local disparity between Italy's military resources and those maintained by Britain in the Middle East in peacetime. These deficiencies had existed for years, but they had remained latent until Mussolini threatened to test them. The joint planners, in a post-mortem of the Abyssinian fiasco, stated the essential strategic problem:

> While Italy has all her national resources in the Mediterranean, our local forces, in common with our overseas garrisons, have to be restricted to the minimum considered adequate until the arrival of reinforcements. The time and difficulties of reinforcements must therefore largely determine the size of the Army and the Air Forces we should maintain locally.[32]

But 'the time and difficulties of reinforcements' were largely unknown factors. Traditionally, Britain had relied upon naval mobility and small overseas garrisons to defend its interests in the Middle East. The question mark left by the Abyssinian crisis was whether the old policy could now be regarded as sound. Was it simply a matter, as Sir Samuel Hoare asserted publicly — though not privately — of adapting to new conditions; or would a new strategy, involving the consolidation of positions distant from the insecure central basin, have to be evolved for the Mediterranean? The issue was faced — but only in 1938, after two years of coping with the various complications, political as well as strategic, peculiar to the defence of 'the most distant station'.

Of the purely strategic complications, unquestionably the most troublesome was posed by the inadequacies of the Admiralty's naval bases. During the 1935 war scare a grave strategic weakness — long suspected but never tested — had suddenly become critical. Malta, England's sole base between Gibraltar and Singapore capable of holding and repairing heavy capital ships, lay 60 miles from Italian air fields and was judged too tempting to Mussolini and too insecure for the Mediterranean Fleet. Neglect, bred of lean resources and an unresolved dispute between sailors and airmen over whether Malta *could* be

exercise of August 1937, Pound wrote that it 'showed convincingly that the Mediterranean with its narrow waters and short distances from air bases is no place for moving slowly'. Air 2/3302. Of the March 1938 run, Pound recorded in his diary that 'the grave risk to which a convoy passing through the Mediterranean in time of war would be exposed was very clearly demonstrated'. 'A Brief Diary of Important Events (March 1936 to March 1938)'.

[32] J.P. 164, 21 July 1936. C.P. 211 (36). Cab.24/263.

defended, had left the island base with obsolete air and naval defences; and until these were modernized London's planners would be unwilling to risk it as a wartime fleet base. So, on the four occasions in this period when war seemed imminent or possible – August 1935, September 1938, April 1939 and August 1939 – the fleet was ordered from Malta to the only possible alternative in the Mediterranean – Alexandria. With hindsight, it can now be seen that Malta's potential role in Mediterranean warfare was badly underrated[33] – as the naval staff sometimes argued, though with little evidence or conviction. But the debate between the flying and naval experts, part of a larger and older doctrinal conflict about the potential of air versus naval power, was not resolved in the pre-war period; and Malta's defences, though the subject of intermittent discussion at the C.I.D., were never given the financial priority they deserved. The search for an alternative to Malta was therefore a major theme of pre-war Mediterranean strategy.

The Admiralty had dispatched the Mediterranean Fleet to Alexandria in August 1935 with some misgivings. Both Fisher and Chatfield regarded that anchorage, with its shallow harbour and poor repair facilities, as inadequate and the strategy as risky and unsound. The naval staff held to that opinion, but the alternatives were equally un-palatable. Haifa was too small and lay in troubled Palestine. Cyprus looked a better strategic proposition and, until the plan came under Treasury scrutiny, was seriously studied. However, the expenditure and time calculated (£25 million and 10 years building under the most ambitious scheme) were deemed prohibitive; and Chatfield knew too that the construction of a new Mediterranean base would contravene both the D.R.C. formula 'no preparations for war against Italy' and the logic of a settlement with Mussolini. 'Cyprus is out of the question for the immediate needs of the moment', he advised a disappointed Pound. 'It would indeed mainly imply that we had no hope of coming to an agreement with Italy.'[34]

The resolution of the naval base dilemma provided a good illustration

---

33 The air staff, naturally, were the most persuaded of Malta's obsolescence in the face of hostile Italian air power. They calculated in one paper that the Italian air force could obliterate the base's dockyard and repair facilities in one day's bombing! See air staff paper, 'Scale of Attack which the Italian Metropolitan Air Force can Deliver Upon Malta,' n.d. Air 9/35. The War Office generally accepted the R.A.F. view that Malta was indefensible; the army was responsible for air defence and refused to weaken England's defences for Malta's.

34 Chatfield to Pound, 23 November 1937. Chatfield Papers. Also Adm. 1/9559.

of how difficult problems of strategy were apt to be dealt with by the National Government. In a nice stroke of imperial pragmatism, the C.I.D. concluded in 1937 that because England could not afford to spend £25 million on a new base, Egypt would be 'encouraged' to develop, at its expense and potential military risk, improved facilities for the fleet at Alexandria. Foreign Office pleas that such a policy would contravene the Anglo—Egyptian treaty of 1936 and that it would be unwise to leave a major base in the hands of 'a fickle oriental Power' left the C.I.D. unmoved: the decisive criterion was money. Conveniently, the Egyptians themselves presented London with an opportunity to implement the decision. In the summer of 1938 the Egyptian Government requested revision of some of the financial obligations attached to the 1936 treaty; in return for this concession, the Foreign Office sought and won Egypt's acceptance of the Alexandria development scheme.[35]

The effect of this curious compromise of strategic necessity, tight finance and imperial diplomacy was that Egypt's vital role in the defence of the Mediterranean—Middle East theatre was once again underlined. Control of the central Mediterranean, it was assumed, would fall to Italy in the early stages of a war and must be disputed by its opponents. For a time British interests in the Middle East might be severed from their primary supply line and in a state of siege. In such circumstances, England's ability to hold Egypt and Suez could well decide the outcome of the war. 'Egypt', the Chiefs of Staff were clear, 'is first in strategic importance.'

> Whoever controls Egypt can control the Suez Canal; control of Egypt enables us to cut Italy's direct communications with her East African Colonies and is necessary for the security of Alexandria which, in war, would be our main fleet base in the Eastern Mediterranean. The provision of reinforcements for the defence of Egypt, therefore, must have first priority.[36]

Egypt was the hinge to which the security of the entire theatre and, to an important extent, much of the British Empire east of Suez was fastened. For through its territories ran vital sea, land and air communications to India and the Far East as well as to the Sudan and the colonies of East Africa. British planning for the defence of the

---

35 C.I.D./294th mtg., 17 June 1937. Cab.2/6. Minutes by Halifax and Chamberlain, 23 and 31 July 1938. Premier 1/254.
36 'Mediterranean Appreciation', *op. cit.*

Mediterranean and Middle East thus tended in the 1936—40 period to reduce itself to the problem of holding Egypt.

Britain's strategic position in Egypt had undergone some important modifications in August 1936 when the two countries, after years of intermittent talks and dispute, had finally signed a defensive Treaty of Alliance. Although Britain's strategists were wont to grumble about some of the concessions made from London's end, the net effect of this action had indisputably been to strengthen its position in the Middle East. Under the treaty's military clauses, British forces were to be kept at a level of 10,000 troops and 400 pilots; but these figures could be raised at Egypt's request. Britain had been granted virtually unqualified basing privileges in Egypt. London recognized Suez as an integral part of Egypt, but the Cairo Government in turn acknowledged it as 'a universal means of communication as also an essential means of communication between the different parts of the British Empire'. After much haggling, the Services agreed to evacuate their troops from Cairo and Alexandria to the canal zone, but the move was to take place only after Egypt had constructed at its own expense accommodation for the British soldiers. The Egyptian army, for years kept by the English in a state of frustrated impotence, was to be modernized but this process would be supervised by a strong War Office military mission. In brief, these were terms hardly likely to jeopardize British security in the Middle East. On the contrary, through the recognition of Egypt's *de jure* independence the English had drawn much of the sting of Egyptian nationalism and consolidated their political influence in that country and, by extension, in the Eastern Mediterranean. Little had been conceded: the 1936 treaty — much like that signed with Iraq a few years earlier — was a highly unequal instrument in which British imperial interests transcended the concept of Egyptian sovereignty.[37]

37 To a considerable degree, the representations of the Chiefs of Staff and the Australian and South African Governments had guaranteed tough British negotiating terms. The Services — having abandoned Malta and the central Mediterranean during the Abyssinian affair — now viewed Egypt as the vital *point d'appui* and resisted concessions agreed to in earlier negotiations. With the Dominions, they wanted imperial lines of communication, basing rights and freedom of movement guaranteed in perpetuity and resisted any terms that appeared to infringe these principles. Also, they violently and successfully opposed the Foreign Office plan to link the treaty to the League of Nations. See, for examples of military impact on the British terms: C.I.D./227th mtg., 27 April 1936. Cab.2/6A; Dominion Office (D.O.) 114/68. Also, Avon, *Facing the dictators, op. cit.* pp. 390—4; Sir D. Kelly, *The ruling few* (London, 1952); John Marlowe (pseud.), *Anglo—Egyptian relations 1800—1956* (London, 1965).

Given England's weakness in the Mediterranean after the Abyssinian crisis, and in the light of the troubled politics of the Middle East before and during the war, the consolidation of its position in Egypt proved to have been extraordinarily well timed. For to its military vulnerability was added a volatile mixture of nationalist unrest and imperial rivalry: the outbreak of rebellion in Palestine coupled to the Axis politico-propaganda offensive against the *status quo* great powers of the region complicated Britain's already insecure position at the strategic cross-roads of the Empire.

In April 1936, in circumstances indirectly linked to the general atmosphere of crisis in the East Mediterranean, the Arabs of Palestine rebelled against (*a*) Britain's policy – enunciated first in the famous Balfour Declaration of 1917 – of creating the Jewish National Home in that country, and (*b*) the growing number of Jewish immigrants in flight from European fascism.[38] Within weeks an Arab Higher Committee had been formed to direct a general strike, and committees sympathetic to the revolt emerged in all of the neighbouring Arab states, even in the most pro-British kingdoms. In the main, the rebellion was one of indigenous Arab nationalism and did not derive – as both the mandatory power and Zionist movement often suggested – from an Axis conspiracy to create difficulties for Britain in its Empire. Italian and – after Munich – German propaganda, funds and arms shipments fed some moral and material assistance to the rebels; but most objective accounts of the revolt bear out the judgement that it 'was in fact a peasant revolt, drawing its enthusiasm, its heroism, its organization and its persistence from sources within itself . . . it was one of the blind alleys of Arab nationalism.'[39] Nevertheless, in British perceptions Palestine was inextricably linked to the wider international crisis.

The Arab rebellion persisted in varying degrees of intensity and in spite of several shifts in British policy until the Chamberlain Government's capitulation in the White Paper of May 1939. By itself it constituted a troublesome policing operation for the War Office and an unpleasant political dilemma for the Cabinet. Seen against the darkening background of world politics, however, the revolt was a strategic

---

38 The best accounts of the rebellion are J. C. Hurewitz, *The struggle for Palestine* (New York, 1950); John Marlowe (pseud.), *Rebellion in Palestine* (London, 1946); also, Marlowe, *The seat of Pilate* (London, 1959). For a sympathetic study of the Arab nationalist revival, see George Antonius, *The Arab awakening* (London, 1939).
39 Marlowe, *The seat of Pilate*, pp. 137–8.

complication of the first order. For Palestine's role in Middle Eastern and imperial strategy was vital. First, it was supposed to serve as a buffer and reserve for the defence of Egypt and Suez. Second, through it passed England's air communications with India and the Far East and the overland route linking Iraq and Egypt. Third, in contingency planning for the closing of the Mediterranean and Red Sea routes, Palestine lay at the western end of the alternative reinforcement route from India via the Persian Gulf. Fourth, Haifa was the Mediterranean terminus of the pipeline bringing vital oil supplies from the oil-fields in Iraq and Iran. And finally, the same port of Haifa was a potential base for the light naval forces operating in the East Mediterranean.[40] None of these could be deemed secure while the rebellion continued: indeed, far from providing the strategic depth and reserve for the defence of the Middle East nexus anticipated by the architects of the Balfour Declaration, Palestine had by mid-1938 become a crippling liability for an imperial power already badly over-extended and under duress.

As will be seen, at the height of the Munich crisis Britain also faced a concurrent emergency in Palestine that virtually eliminated any possibility of even a small expeditionary force being sent to France at the outbreak of a war in Europe. But well in advance of that climactic date the Services and Foreign Office had recognized the festering rebellion as the focus and emblem of a growing Arab nationalism that could unhinge England's supremacy in the Middle East — particularly if Britain became preoccupied in Europe or the Far East. Traditionally, its supremacy in the region had been maintained by the friendly collaboration of the Arab ruling classes backed by an economy of coercion; but in 1937 and 1938 dispatches from officials in the region poured into the Foreign and Colonial Offices cautioning that the Government's repressive military measures in Palestine and the partition compromise proposed by Lord Peel's Royal Commission in July 1937 were alienating London's best friends and stoking the fires of anti-British nationalism. Sir Miles Lampson, for instance — whom the Zionists considered an arch-foe of the National Home policy — wondered if it was 'wise to maintain a policy which risks alienating all those Arab and Egyptian friends from the Mediterranean to the Persian Gulf whom a century of

---

40 See War Office note, 27 April 1938. Cab.51/11; Chiefs of Staff, 'Strategic Importance of Egypt and the Arab Countries of the Middle East', C.O.S. 824, 14 January 1939; C.P. 7 (39). Cab.24/282; and Chiefs of Staff, 'Strategical Aspect of the Partition of Palestine', C.O.S. 687, 14 February 1938. E879/2/ 31. (21870).

patient effort has won to our side?'[41] As Arab resistance to the partition scheme and Jewish immigration spread and the debate over the efficacy and morality of Palestine policy developed within the British Government, the weight of strategic advice increasingly leaned towards a pro-Arab solution: in the context of the global crisis England could ill afford to alienate the population of so strategic a region.

By 1936, Britain, as the dominant *status quo* power in the Near East, had also to contend with a serious imperial challenge aimed at displacing its influence and overthrowing the arrangements in the region decided in the post-war settlement. Before the Germans entered the arena in November 1938, the campaign from the Axis was largely Italian-inspired and -directed. Its dangers were probably exaggerated: certainly without Palestine to lend some credence to the bombast that poured from Bari radio's daily broadcasts in Arabic and the scattered Axis news agencies in the Middle East, the propaganda offensive could have been countered with ease by the British. But the impression of decline left in Arab minds by English vacillations over Abyssinia, the harshness of the army's tactics in Palestine, and Italy's much-publicized military build-up in Libya created something of a fertile atmosphere for the anti-British campaign. Bari and its German successors dealt at length with English 'atrocities' in Palestine, extolled the Arab resistance, emphasized the weakness of England's global position and left the conclusion to be drawn that the Arab world's salvation lay with the Axis.[42] The War Office and Foreign Office were particularly upset by the use of the radio for anti-imperial propaganda and supported the idea of an all-out counter-offensive;[43] but the Cabinet – while agreeing to the establishment of a B.B.C. Arabic service in January 1938 – preferred to try to silence Bari through appeasement. In this they were temporarily successful, for the Easter Pact of April 1938 purchased a few months of relief (Bari turned its attention to France). It was only in 1939 after the

---

41 Lampson to Eden, tel. No. 645, 16 November 1937. After Munich Lampson warned London that 'we cannot afford to neglect the growing danger to us in this Arab–Muslim movement of cooperation centering on opposition to our Palestinian policy.' Disp. No. 1142, 24 October 1938. E6508/10/31. (21883). On the partition debate, see Norman Rose, 'The debate on partition, 1937–38: the Anglo–Zionist aspect, *Middle Eastern Studies*, 6:3 (October 1970) and 7:1 (January 1971).

42 A good summary is in Lampson's disp. No. 839 of 6 July 1939. P3144/1052/150. F.O. 395/664.

43 Eden, 'Arabic Broadcasts', 13 July 1937. C.P. 185 (37). Cab.24/270; War Office memorandum, March 1937. Cab.51/9. See also, N. Barbour, 'Broadcasting to the Arab world', *Middle East Journal* (Winter 1951).

appearance of the Goebbels propaganda machine in the Near East that
the British began a systematic counter-campaign of their own.[44] And
even this was evidently a rather uninspiring affair: one British observer
complained that even in 1940—1

> our propaganda was still childish and inept . . . The British Empire
> was hawked through the mud villages of the Delta like a dud second-
> hand motor-car. In the face of the witty and virile Axis broadcasts,
> our propaganda was a poor limp thing.[45]

As Professor Hirszowicz and others have ably documented, Axis
attempts to penetrate Britain's mid-Eastern sphere of influence were not
confined solely to propaganda. From 1936 to 1939 the Italians made
several unsuccessful overtures to the Egyptian Government for a non-
aggression pact, renewed their treaty with the Yemen in 1937, carried
on a flirtation with Ibn Saud of Saudi Arabia, and supplied some money
and arms to the Palestine rebels. In the interests of accord with England,
Germany generally refrained from such activities until mid-1938, when
contact was made with the army and nationalist opposition (Wafd) of
Egypt and the first German arms shipments were shipped to Palestine
via Iraq and Saudi Arabia. During the Munich crisis, the British
discovered, both the German and Italian embassies were in touch with
the Egyptian Government and the palace, sowing, as Lampson saw it,
'the dangerous seed of neutrality'.[46] After November 1938 Germany
escalated its anti-British political and propaganda offensive in an
attempt to forge an alliance with nationalist elements in the Arab East,
particularly in the strategic nations of Iraq and Egypt — both of which
the British Chiefs of Staff counted upon as active allies. Britain's later
problems in countering these same elements while waging the war in the
Middle East unquestionably had their roots in the pre-war Axis—

---

44 Cf. F.O. 385/650-651 and W.O. 106/1594C for evidence of Germany's
   propaganda warfare in the Near East. Also Lukasz Hirszowicz, *The Third
   Reich and the Arab East* (London, 1966); and B. Vernier, *La Politique
   islamique de l'Allegmagne* (Paris, 1939). Goebbels visited Egypt in April 1939,
   at which time the lines were set down for the extensive anti-British campaign
   that followed.
45 Alan Moorehead, *African trilogy* (London, 1944), p. 190.
46 Cf. Hirszowicz, *The Third Reich and the Arab East, op. cit.*; E. Dekel, *SHAI,
   the exploits of Hagana intelligence* (New York, 1959), pp. 231–6; Halifax to
   Hore-Belisha, 20 October 1938. J3880/5/16 (21943). Lampson warned the
   Egyptian Prime Minister in October 1938 against 'whoring after strange gods'
   and pointed to the German embassy in Cairo as the fount of conspiracy.
   J3932/3537/16 (22008).

nationalist contacts.[47]

It was to be expected that British officials in the Mid-east who encountered this increasingly hostile political climate would protest their government's deliberate military starvation of the region. Nationalism, Arab or otherwise, feeds on symptoms of imperial weakness,[48] and England had betrayed unmistakable evidence of decline by its policies during the Italo–League dispute. The low priority fixed to Mediterranean defence in the defence requirements debates made strategic sense, but it did nothing to improve the Empire's tarnished image abroad: Egypt, for example, bitterly complained that London was breaking treaty commitments by neglecting its defence and failing to equip its army. Ultimately, awkward problems such as this made the D.R.C. grand strategy untenable; England, as Admiral Pound had warned, could not run its Mediterranean empire 'on the cheap'.

The campaign for the reinforcement and rearmament of British positions in the Mediterranean and Middle East was led from 1937 onwards by Sir Miles Lampson, London's powerful and overbearing Ambassador to Egypt.[49] Obsessed by the dual menace of Arab nationalism and Axis intrigue, Lampson insisted that Britain was risking its supremacy in a strategically vital part of the globe. His constant harping and his biting criticisms of military complacency eventually made his name anathema to the Chiefs of Staff, but his strategy for the defence of the Middle East was probably more consistent than theirs' – and much of it was adopted. With Eden, one of the few Italophobes in the Diplomatic Service, Lampson argued that England must settle with Hitler in Europe, concentrate its military power in the Mediterranean

---

[47] Cf. Anwar El Sadat, *Revolt on the Nile* (London, 1957), for further discussion.

[48] For a good discussion of the impact of Egyptian and Indian nationalism on British imperialism in the inter-war period, cf. A. P. Thornton, *The imperial idea and its enemies* (London, 1959), chap. 5.

[49] The campaign was plotted in advance with Vansittart while Lampson was home on leave in mid-1937. Lampson to Sir L. Oliphant, 15 July 1939. J2850/21/16. (23333). Lampson, a man who was, and considered himself to be, in many ways a reincarnation of Lord Cromer, had great energy, experience and toughness. With the possible exception of Sir Percy Loraine, he was probably the most effective British diplomat stationed in the Mediterranean in the pre-war period. He was not noted for tact, however, and his many interventions in Egyptian affairs – including his notorious ultimatum to Farouk in February 1942 – undoubtedly strengthened anti-British nationalism in Egypt. Lampson deserves a biographer: some material is in, Moorehead, *African trilogy, op. cit.*; Lord Chandos, *Memoirs* (London, 1962); B. S. McBride, *Farouk of Egypt* (London, 1967); and P. Mansfield, *Nasser* (London, 1969).

and force a confrontation with Mussolini. Palestine must also be settled on Arab terms, he insisted – again on strategic grounds.

In the autumn of 1937 Lampson fired the opening broadsides in his battle against London's strategists. Italy had commenced its military build-up in Libya, a fact that made the Egyptians extremely nervous. Egypt's own defences, as Chatfield admitted, were 'most unsatisfactory':

> We had no anti-aircraft defence, no fighter aircraft and the harbour at Alexandria was completely open to attack. The Local Commanders were very naturally apprehensive, knowing full well that no reinforcements in any strength could reach them within a reasonable time.[50]

The Services had revised the defence plan for Egypt and drawn up in some haste a preliminary appreciation of the Mediterranean–Middle East theatre. Reduced to their essentials, these plans called for the use of naval convoys to reinforce Egypt *after* the outbreak of war: one fast convoy carrying fighter aircraft would be sent through the Mediterranean; it would be followed by a series of slow convoys carrying other military equipment and troops – one from India, the remainder from England. The latter might try the Mediterranean route, but if this seemed too dangerous they would have to use the much longer Cape route, taking up to sixty days to reach Egypt. In the meantime, the small, ill-equipped and non-mechanized forces in Egypt – supported by the R.A.F. squadrons maintained in Iraq – would have to hold the Western Desert against Italy's lightly motorized divisions and superior air power.[51]

Lampson and the regional commanders argued that these contingency plans contained several suspect assumptions about the way any future war in the Eastern Mediterranean would be conducted. The plans virtually ignored the possibility of an *attaque brusquée* across the desert as well as the potential dangers of an unresisted bombardment of Egypt's civilian population. The navy would be tied up in convoy operations and Pound had described any idea of slow-moving convoys in the Mediterranean as 'suicidal'. The War Office was warned by the General Officer Commanding in Egypt that his garrison might be able to hold out for only two weeks. The plans had been complacently and uncritically conceived and, it was being implied by the critics, reflected

50 C.O.S./220th mtg., 22 October 1937. Cab.53/8.
51 'Interim Appreciation of the Mediterranean, Middle East and North East Africa Theatre', J.P. 233, Cab.16/182. The 1937 draft scheme for the defence of Egypt is in J4613/244/16. (29011).

an antiquated and rigid approach to modern imperial defence. The reliance upon naval mobility to reinforce infantry garrisons had served an earlier era of military technology; but the strategy had been dated by developments in air communications and by new principles of land warfare. Arguing that Egypt was as crucial to British security as the defence of French frontiers, Lampson contended that the convoy system should be discarded as the basis of Mid-eastern defence and that the alternative — 'local self-sufficiency' — should be adopted: reinforcements should be sent to the East Mediterranean *before* the outbreak of hostilities so that the region could be defended for two months without external assistance.[52]

Lampson's initial pleas for immediate reinforcements and for higher priority for Mediterranean defence met a wall of bureaucratic indifference in London. Eden, it will be recalled, had made an earlier unsuccessful bid for a programme of Mediterranean rearmament, and the Chiefs of Staff and C.I.D. were still opposed to any action 'which would result in a diversion of our limited resources from our main objective which is the security of this country against German aggression'.[53] It was this that necessitated the taking of 'horrible risks' in Egypt.[54] The Government's top financial advisers were also attempting to reconcile, as Inskip put it, safety and solvency,[55] and there was therefore little support for the Lampson–Vansittart strategy for Egypt. Two unrelated developments, however, subsequently forced the Chiefs of Staff to reverse their stand on this issue. First — and this needs no further documentation — the Far Eastern crisis in the winter of 1937–8 confronted the Services with the implications of an actual naval evacuation of the Mediterranean, and convinced them that 'The greater the tension in the Far East, the more important becomes the necessity for security in the Mediterranean.'[56]

In the second place, the Government's review of defence policy had

---

52 See the collection of telegrams and dispatches in Cab.21/578; and Lampson's tel. No. 682, 30 November 1937. Cab.21/579; Hankey to Chatfield and Chatfield to Hankey, of 6 and 7 December respectively. *Ibid.* Pound's and Chatfield's views on convoys in the Mediterranean can be found in Adm. 1/9533.
53 Chiefs of Staff, 'Situation in the Mediterranean and Middle East', 19 October 1937. C.P. 259(37) Cab.24/272.
54 Hankey to Vansittart, 2 November 1937, Cab.21/578.
55 Inskip, 'Cost of Defence Requirements', T(reasury) 161/855/5.48431/01/1.
56 Chiefs of Staff, 'Defence of Egypt', C.O.S. 686, 14 February 1938. Enclosure in C.P. 41(38). Cab.24/275.

finally evolved — after months of debate and several postponements — a policy on the contentious question of a role for the British army. In essence, the review virtually eliminated any Continental commitment (by ranking it at the bottom of its list of priorities), and the army's share of the defence budget had been drastically pared. Almost by default, the army's role in imperial defence was now defined as its essential role.[57] The War Office was also re-examining the army's role, and the minister supervising this departmental review, Leslie Hore-Belisha, was at the time much influenced by the ideas of the controversial military writer Captain B. H. Liddell Hart. Liddell Hart's conception of the army's proper role in modern imperial defence had led him to propose the establishment of strategic imperial reserves — at various key locations in the Empire, including Palestine and Egypt. His theory of the autonomous strategic reserve was given prominent attention in Hore-Belisha's Cabinet proposals of 10 February 1938:

> Because of the special difficulties of the Mediterranean passage it is desirable to locate part of the Imperial strategic reserve, as well as its sources of supply, east of the Mediterranean passage.[58]

The idea of a Middle East reserve, formed in part with armoured units, was given C.I.D. assent in February 1938 and reinforcements were quickly dispatched to Egypt. Admitting that it was largely 'a question of balancing risks' between the three global theatres, Chatfield explained that the Chiefs of Staff had concluded after their 'Mediterranean Appreciation' review that the unstable situation in the Middle East demanded military measures. Building Egypt's land and air defences up to self-sufficiency for a sixty-day period would involve some denuding of home defence, but the Services were now willing to take that risk.[59]

---

[57] W. K. Hancock and M. M. Gowing, *Britain's war economy* (London, 1949), pp. 22–5; P. K. Kemp, *Key to victory* (Boston, 1957), pp. 23–4; Inskip, 'Defence Expenditure in Future Years', December 1937. C.P. 316 (37). Cab.24/273; Cab. Conclusions, 22 December 1937. Cab.23/90.

[58] Hore-Belisha, 'The Organization of the Army for its Role in War', 10 February 1938. C.P. 26(38). Cab.24/274. On the evolution of this policy paper and the influence of Liddell Hart, see Liddell Hart's *Memoirs*, II, pp. 89–103. For a different assessment, cf. D. C. Watt, 'Sir Warren Fisher and British rearmament against Germany', *Personalities and policies*, pp. 113–4. An important overview of the implications of the budgetary and army decisions of 1937–8 is, N. H. Gibbs, 'British strategic doctrine, 1918–1939', in M. Howard (ed.), *The theory and practice of war* (London, 1965).

[59] C.I.D./310th mtg., 17 February 1938. Cab.2/7. Also, C.O.S. 686, *op. cit.* On India's enhanced role in Mid-east defence, see the report on 'India: Defence Questions' (Annex 2). C.P. 187(38). Cab.24/278.

This decision represented the first real modification of the D.R.C. strategy for the Mediterranean described earlier in this study. To some extent, it thereby anticipated the Government's reversal of imperial priorities in the spring of 1939 when England reverted to a concentrated naval strategy. In Liddell Hart's idea of a Middle Eastern *place d'armes* can also be seen the germ of the 'Mediterranean first' concept that dominated the 1939 debates on grand strategy and that was later implemented — though more because of circumstance than design — in the war. The decision frankly acknowledged the changed and weakened nature of Britain's status in the Mediterranean and reflected a shift in official thinking away from the rather complacent defence requirements strategy towards the new approaches to imperial defence advocated by critics such as Sir Miles Lampson and Captain Liddell Hart.

At the same time, however, one can exaggerate the significance of what the actual decision-makers must have seen as slight deviations from established policy. In other ways the British continued to neglect the various dimensions of Mediterranean defence. To recall remarks made earlier, strategic choices are often governed by feasibility, and in 1938 — and much later — there were strict limitations on what could be done for 'the most distant station' without jeopardizing the security of that most vital station — the British Isles. And, as will be seen, after Eden's departure there was little enthusiasm within the Chamberlain administration for political or military acts that might offend Mussolini and destroy the Government's new 'Stresa' policy. The British, for instance, made no attempt to exploit Italy's colonial difficulties by aiding, with the French, the resistance in Abyssinia;[60] indeed, the granting of *de jure* recognition could only ease those problems. At the military level, there was very little co-ordination of intelligence, communication or command in the Middle East, and the implementation of the decision to raise a mobile reserve in Egypt was delayed until September 1938.[61]

The best evidence that no general change in Mediterranean strategy was contemplated by the Services or Cabinet in this period is provided by their attitude to staff co-operation with the French. It was shown

---

60 The French intrigued in the resistance from 1937 onward but the British became involved only after May 1939 (it was first discussed during the Munich crisis). See del Boca, *The Ethiopian War 1935–1941, op. cit.*; and Lt. Col. Yves Jouin, 'La participation française a la résistance éthiopienne', *Révue Historique de l'Armée*, 4 (1963).

61 Liddell Hart, *Memoirs*, II, pp. 193–4; and F.M. Lord Wilson, *Eight years overseas, 1939–1947* (London, 1950).

earlier how the Chiefs of Staff resisted French calls for staff conversations on the Mediterranean — Chatfield had even wondered whether it was to England's advantage to be allied to France in the event of an Anglo–Italian war.[62] In April the C.I.D. agreed that, in view of Chatfield's fears about the Anglo–German Naval Agreement and the conversations then under way with Mussolini, it was undesirable to extend the scope of the Anglo–French staff talks to the Mediterranean; in fact, no naval talks were deemed necessary, a remarkable conclusion in view of Chatfield's constant warnings about the naval period of danger and England's global predicament. Only when the French bitterly protested against the navy's exclusion from the staff talks did Chamberlain and Halifax overrule the Services and order naval conversations to commence. But much to the frustration of the French navy — Admiral Darlan alluded to 'the would-be assassin who tries to stab you in the back with his stiletto' — the English declined to discuss even the possibility of war in the Mediterranean; and those few naval exchanges that took place in Paris over the summer of 1938 appear to have been quite useless.[63]

This example alone reminds the student of the period that Britain's military weaknesses — usually mentioned as one of the decisive arguments for appeasement — were in part a matter of political choice. In the Mediterranean, as already seen, geography, scarce military resources and vulnerable communications all conditioned England's strategic posture; and to that extent, strategy was indeed determined by 'feasibility'. But it was also determined by politics: by, for instance, the decision to give the Far East higher priority than the Mediterranean; by the commitments given to Australia and New Zealand in 1937; by the decision to starve the Middle East of military resources in order not to weaken home defence or financial solvency; and by the decision to shun strategic collaboration with the French. Italy, as previously demonstrated, was also vulnerable in many ways, yet it is a fact that the British consciously eschewed any attempt to exploit that vulnerability. Planning, intelligence, co-ordination were all badly neglected — as the coming crisis in Central Europe was to prove.

---

[62] C.O.S./228th mtg., 28 January 1938. Cab.53/8.

[63] See F.O. 371/21653 for further material. Chatfield dominated the Chiefs of Staff on this issue, and it is interesting to note that his successors at the Admiralty, Admirals Backhouse and Pound, were both far more anxious for staff co-operation with the French in the Mediterranean. How much had these rebuffs to do with Darlan's later Anglophobia?

The dimensions of Mediterranean strategy from 1936 to 1938 might therefore by described as inevitable military weakness compounded by confusion and neglect. If appeasement succeeded, the dangers that inhered in this policy would remain latent. But what if Mussolini's future attitude to England remained malevolent; or what if he turned his hostility to France; and what if Germany threatened vital British interests in the Balkans and East Mediterranean? How wide was the margin of acceptable risk in the Mediterranean? Given Britain's imperial weakness and the growing menace to its interests in the Far East and Europe, how long could its strategy of defence in two hemispheres be maintained if the security of its traditional line of communications could still not be ensured? These were the kinds of questions soon to reopen the unresolved debate over British grand strategy.

5. From Acquiescence to Containment: the Search for Policies in the Balkans and Mediterranean, April 1938 to April 1939

Britain's appeasement of Italy — a policy the implementation of which had caused or contributed directly to the resignation of two Foreign Secretaries in as many years — entered a new phase with the conclusion of the Perth–Ciano negotiations in Rome on 16 April 1938. Those discussions cannot be analysed in detail here, but it may be noted that their outcome, the Anglo–Italian Agreement (or Easter Pact), was, as Neville Chamberlain had insisted it must be, a comprehensive one covering most of the areas of imperial rivalry.[1] Both sides agreed again to respect the *status quo* in the Mediterranean and Red Sea; an annual exchange of strategic information dealing with movements of forces and so on was arranged; agreement was reached on disputes over territorial spheres of influence in Arabia, Abyssinia and Lake Tsana; Britain agreed to grant *de jure* diplomatic recognition of Italy's conquest of Abyssinia; and Italy indicated that it intended eventually to withdraw its 'volunteers' from Spain. However, Chamberlain and Viscount Halifax, the new Foreign Secretary, apparently in deference to domestic political sentiment concerning the war in Spain, agreed to an uncharacteristic tactic (originally proposed as a face-saving device by Halifax to Eden) that had effect of withholding *de jure* recognition until the Spanish question was 'settled' — that is, ceased to be a cause of international friction. Franco's spring offensive once more failed to bring him victory, and consequently the London–Rome accord remained in abeyance for several months while a petulant Mussolini stormed threats and satisfied his anger by wrecking similar negotiations with France.

Whatever their other benefits, the Rome talks cannot be said to have

---

[1] For an assessment, cf. D. C. Watt, 'Gli accordi mediterranei anglo–italiani del aprile 1938', *Rivista di Studi Politici Internazionale*, 26 (1959). Perth's account of the negotiations in his disp. No. 392, 22 April 1938. R4251/23/22. (22411).

resolved for England the nagging problem of its Mediterranean security; and it had been primarily on this issue that the advocates had put their case. The troop reductions in Libya amounted to fewer than 10,000 in five months and those were returned in September; the exchange of military information had no strategic value to either side; and although the temporary easing of Italy's propaganda was a relief, the crisis in Palestine remained acute and Dr Goebbels' organization soon filled the vacuum in the Middle East. But most important, Italy's status in any future war was no more certain than it had been; as Halifax admitted to Chamberlain in June:

> Italy is not likely to make an unprovoked attack upon the British Empire, and in the event of the Empire being involved in war with Germany she would probably struggle hard to maintain her neutrality.
>
> But I suppose it is also probably true that Italian policy is likely to remain opportunist, and that in any such war she might be expected eventually to throw in her lot with what she considered likely to become the winning side. Nor can we exclude as a further element of doubt the influence that we must expect to derive from the pattern exercised by the existence of the Rome—Berlin axis, and by the presence of Germany on the Brenner.

And, far from describing the region as secure and the need for further rearmament there as ended, Halifax concluded, as Eden typically had, that 'the stronger we can show ourselves in the Mediterranean the more likely this is to swing the opportunist policy of Italy in our direction'.[2]

Chamberlain had confided to Halifax the previous August that the main objective in having talks with Italy was to get back to the pre-1935 position, when that power had been safely excluded from the Government's list of enemies.[3] That end had not been attained, any more than the earlier 'gentleman's agreement' had 'solved at a stroke', as Inskip had fondly predicted, Britain's global crisis. The Easter Pact did not even bring temporary security: for as the conflict in Central Europe loomed in the summer of 1938, the Chiefs of Staff were forced to keep a reluctant eye on the Mediterranean, a fact that may account in part for their very negative attitude to Continental commitments. As early as March, the Government's military planners had cautioned the Cabinet that just two divisions 'seriously deficient in modern

---

2 Halifax to Chamberlain, 2 June 1938. Cab.21/562.
3 Chamberlain to Halifax, 7 August 1937. Premier 1/276.

equipment' could be dispatched to the Continent, and then only at the expense of Britain's own interests in the Mediterranean. Should Italy and Japan attack as well, then the Empire would be in the 'gravest danger' and the Mediterranean would have to be relinquished to Italy.[4] And it was precisely this type of danger that the conciliation of Italy was to have eliminated.

On the diplomatic side of the account sheet, on the other hand, the British were satisfied with the outcome of the Rome talks and committed to following them up. Chamberlain noted that it was 'very clear' that 'the Anschluss and the Anglo—Italian agreement together have given the Rome—Berlin axis a nasty jar';[5] and for once Vansittart spoke for the Government when he told Hugh Dalton that Mussolini's anger over events in Austria should be exploited in order to detach him from Hitler.[6] There was more behind this than a 'divide-and-rule' strategy, for Italy represented the last desperate hope of those determined to restore a European balance without dividing the Continent into blocs. The Government had decided in mid-March to guarantee neither France nor Czechoslovakia, and the consensus of opinion was that England must hold itself aloof and attempt to fashion a new balance of power. Italy, rather than the despised Soviet Union, must be enticed to take up a balancing role: Gladwyn Jebb, Halifax's private secretary, and Cadogan both held out the prospect of a new 'Stresa front' blossoming from the talks in Rome.[7]

That Cadogan could refer after the *Anschluss* to the 'Stresa' policy as 'the best hope that I can see' is itself a revealing commentary on British foreign policy in the summer of 1938. Clearly it could only be an interim policy at best, one that might postpone graver decisions — such as Winston Churchill's 'Grand Alliance' or a definite commitment in Central Europe. Italy was, in truth, quite unfit for the exalted station of Europe's balancer, especially in the aftermath of *Anschluss*, an event that had manifestly reduced its power to influence Germany. The shift in balance of power within the Axis in the spring of 1938 meant that Italy's only guarantee against Hitler's encroachments would

---

4 Chiefs of Staff, 'Military Implications of German Aggression Against Czechoslovakia,' C.O.S. 698, 28 March 1938. Cab.53/37.
5 Keith Feiling, *The life of Neville Chamberlain* (London, 1946), p. 354.
6 Dalton Diaries, 12 April 1938.
7 Cadogan and Halifax memoranda, 17 and 18 March 1938. In F.O. 371/21674. Also D. N. Dilks (ed.), *The diaries of Sir Alexander Cadogan 1938—1945* (London, 1971), pp. 62—6.

be the maintenance of the Italo–German arrangement – but on Germany's terms. Mussolini, Dalton correctly retorted to Vansittart, 'would calculate that he would gain more by hanging on to Hitler than by leaving him'.[8]

The new 'Stresa' policy – which was little more than the familiar 'Vansittart line' of isolating Hitler by appeasing Mussolini – was a chimera because Italy was fast becoming irrelevant in Europe's diplomacy. Its weakness *vis-à-vis* Germany, for instance, was particularly evident in the Balkans after Hitler's take-over in Austria. Nazi economic penetration of the region had been under way since 1934 when the German regime, excluded from world markets by the protectionist policies of the powers (the Ottawa agreements and so on) and suffering from chronic shortages of foreign exchange, instituted a complex system of exchange controls, fixed pricing and barter arrangements designed to create a Danubian zone of self-sufficiency and dependency within which Germany could obtain foodstuffs, oil and other raw materials and sell its manufactured goods. This policy, implemented by Dr Hjalmar Schacht, Germany's Finance Minister, was facilitated by French disengagement from the Little Entente after 1936 and by Italy's loss of its Balkan markets during the sanctions episode. It proved such a brilliant success that by 1938 the economies of Roumania, Bulgaria, Hungary, Yugoslavia, Greece and Turkey were all to some degree tied through bilateral agreements to the *Reich* economy.[9]

The British regarded this phenomenon with some ambivalence, for, on the one hand, German economic expansion was seen in official London as natural and inevitable and the region itself was tacitly regarded by Britain's trading spokesmen as Berlin's sphere of influence. The Balkans accounted for 16 per cent of Germany's foreign trade by 1937; for Britain, however, it made up just 2 per cent of its trade.[10] Moreover, the time for action had passed and Germany's regional preponderance was already a *fait accompli* that Chamberlain at least was not willing to challenge. Indeed, the Prime Minister wondered if it might not be a healthy development: 'Might not a great improvement

8 Dalton Diaries, 12 April 1938.
9 Details and statistics in H. S. Ellis, *Exchange control in Central Europe* (Cambridge, Mass., 1941); and Antonin Basch, *The Danube Basin and the German economic sphere* (London, 1944); German foreign economic policy is examined in Arthur Schweitzer, 'The foreign exchange crisis of 1936', *Zeitschrift fur Staatswissenschaft*, 118 (April, 1962).
10 See Table 1 for statistics showing the shift in the relative positions of Britain and Germany in the trade of Greece and Turkey, 1929–37.

Table 1: Germany and Britain in the Trade of Greece and Turkey:
Percentages of Imports (*I*) and Exports (*E*), 1929–37

	Greece				
	Germany			*Britain*	
	I	*E*		*I*	*E*
1929	9·4	23·2		12·7	11·7
1930	10·4	23·2		13·0	12·5
1931	12·2	14·0		13·3	15·0
1932	9·6	14·5		13·7	23·4
1933	10·2	17·9		14·4	18·9
1934	14·7	22·5		16·7	17·4
1935	18·7	29·7		15·5	12·6
1936	22·4	35·4		16·1	12·2
1937	27·2	31·0		11·0	9·6
	Turkey				
	Germany			*Britain*	
	I	*E*		*I*	*E*
1929	15·3	13·3		12·2	9·6
1930	18·6	13·1		11·2	8·9
1931	21·3	10·7		11·4	8·6
1932	23·3	13·5		12·3	9·9
1933	25·5	18·9		13·5	8·9
1934	33·8	37·4		9·9	5·8
1935	40·0	40·9		9·8	5·4
1936	45·1	51·0		6·6	5·4
1937	42·1	36·5		6·2	7·1

Source: League of Nations, International Trade Statistics, Geneva, 1938

in Germany's economic situation result in her becoming quieter and less interested in political adventure?' he mused.[11]

On the other hand, if that optimistic future failed to materialize and Hitler used his advantage for political dominance, where would England try to contain him? If Chamberlain was not worried about German economic penetration of South-East Europe, the governments of that region decidedly were, and it was to London that they turned after the *Anschluss* as an alternative. Cadogan could casually dismiss French fears over German 'hegemony' as 'awful rubbish',[12] but there were nagging anxieties all the same that Germany's policies would soon carry it to the shores of the Mediterranean and into the Near East where England had vital imperial interests. At some undefined point on the map of Southern Europe the strategy of acquiescence would have to be replaced by one of containment or even 'encirclement'. Was the zone of disinterestedness to include, for instance, Roumania's oil reserves and Black Sea ports, or the borders of Greece and Turkey, powers of vital interest to the British navy? If not, how could the integrity of these nations be defended: through foreign aid, diplomatic pressure or military guarantees? In other words, where was the line of British commitment to be drawn, and by what methods would it be defended?

There was no precise answer to these questions, nor were the questions posed in this manner: London typically reacted to events in South-Eastern Europe and coped piecemeal with developing individual situations. Before April 1939 Britain resisted the idea of a Mediterranean guarantee system on the grounds that this must conflict with its Far Eastern commitments. The Foreign Office wished to compete economically with the Germans, but there was little support for this in the rest of the Government. With one important exception, the British stubbornly declined to play their containment cards and literally had to be forced by Hitler and Mussolini finally to take the initiative.

The exception to the strategy of acquiescence was Turkey. Situated at the strategic cross-roads between the Black Sea and Mediterranean and the Balkans and Middle East, Kemal Atatürk's young republic occupied a pivotal position in British appreciations of that part of the world. As mistress (after July 1936) of the Dardanelles, buffer between fascism and the troubled British Moslem empire, and an acknowledged

11 Foreign Policy Committee (F.P.)/30th mtg., 1 June 1938. R5362/94/67. (22432).
12 Dilks, *The diaries of Sir Alexander Cadogan 1938–1945, op. cit.* p. 73.

independent power among weak dependencies, Turkey's importance in Continental and Mediterranean diplomacy was daily growing. England had learned a hard lesson well during its bitter struggles with the Turks in the 1914—18 war and its lengthy aftermath, and its leaders were determined, as Neville Chamberlain put, to avoid repeating that 'disastrous mistake'.[13] Even had the grim historical precedent been missing, however, strategic logic would have dictated the priority given to the search for a neutral or friendly Turkey. Strategy, in fact, dominated Britain's pre-war Turkish policy.

The method used by London to fashion, first, a *rapprochement*, and, second, an alliance with the Turks might be described as a series of well-timed concessions to Turkey's strategic, diplomatic and economic demands. In plainer language, the British attempted — with considerable success as it turned out — to outbid Germany for Turkey's rather expensive friendship. It was neither original nor idealistic; yet, judged against Turkey's subsequent wartime and post-war role, it could probably be described as one of the few bright spots in an altogether bleak era of English diplomatic history.

Britain's attempts to appease Atatürk's regime can be traced to the 1933 sessions of the disarmament conference, where diplomats of the two powers began discussion of Turkey's grievances.[14] But progress was slight, and the British understood that it must remain so while support was withheld from the Turkish demand to re-fortify the Straits (which had been demilitarized, opened to international navigation and placed under international supervision under the Lausanne Convention of 1923). When later consulted on this issue, the British Service chiefs were clear that the strategic advantages obtained from the demilitrization of the Straits were not important enough, nor secure enough in the face of Turkey's rising power, to warrant diplomatic resistance to this specific demand (namely, remilitarization, not revision of the entire Lausanne treaty).[15]

Significantly, that conclusion coincided with the Services' belated awareness of the Italo—League crisis and the weakness of their own Mediterranean position. In their appreciations of a possible war with Italy the Chiefs of Staff stressed Turkey's vital role and urged that it be lured into the British orbit, if necessary through unsolicited concessions

---

[13] Cab. Conclusions, 11 May 1938. Cab.23/93.
[14] Sir G. W. Rendel, *The sword and the olive* (London, 1957), p. 100.
[15] Cf. War Office note and comment by the Chiefs of Staff (C.O.S. 387 and 389) of 19 July and 6 August 1935 respectively. Cab.53/25.

on the Straits.[16] The Foreign Office managed, however, to bring the Turks, Greeks and Yugoslavs into temporary mutual-support arrangements, a method that seemed safer than lifting the lid from Europe's pandora's box, treaty revision.[17] Thus, the issue was suspended until late March 1936 when, the Germans having sprung the lid, Turkey's Foreign Minister, Rüştü Aras, advised Eden of his determination to have Lausanne partially revised.[18] Days later Britain's influential ambassador in Ankara, Sir Percy Loraine, dissuaded Atatürk from reoccupying the demilitarized zone *à la mode hitlérienne*, but the Turks shortly moved on the diplomatic front to have the inevitable acknowledged in law. Britain, following agreed tactics, indicated its sympathy.

In pre-conference bargaining, however, the Turks surprised and annoyed the British by raising the stakes to demand revision of the Lausanne clauses under which non-Black Sea powers enjoyed the freedom in time of peace and war to move naval forces into the Black Sea — a privilege naturally much in favour in London. This went well beyond Turkey's original demands and challenged the whole concept of the internationalized Straits. The Turkish draft treaty, presented as basis for discussion at the Montreux conference in June 1936, imposed rigid limitations on non-Black Sea tonnage entering that sea and omitted reciprocal restrictions on Black Sea (for example, Russian) warships passing into the Mediterranean. England's incensed negotiators made the not unreasonable deduction that Soviet pressure and Russia's traditional interest in the Straits lay behind this new Turkish move, and they suspected too that Aras was under the personal domination of Maxim Litvinov, the Soviet Foreign Minister. The conference thereafter resolved itself into a conflict between two antagonistic viewpoints: on the one hand, the Russian interest in closing the Straits in wartime and keeping open its only access to warm water; on the other, Britain's objectives of retaining freedom of the Straits while excluding Russian

16 C.I.D./271st mtg., 14 October 1935. Cab.2/6.
17 Admiralty–Foreign Office correspondence of January 1936, in E269/26/44. (20072).
18 My analysis of the 1936 negotiations on the Straits is based on the Foreign Office records (F.O. 371/20072-20081). Useful summaries are in E4633 and E5074/26/44 (20080). The Admiralty apparently pulped their archives of the Montreux conference. Secondary accounts are in: J. Shotwell and F. Déak, *Turkey at the Straits* (New York, 1940); G. Warsamy, *La Convention des Détroits* (Paris, 1937); M. Toscano, *La Conferenza di Montreux e la Nuova Convenzione degli Stretti* (Milan, 1938). Text of the Montreux convention of 20 July 1936 in, Command 5249: Turkey No. I (1936).

naval power from the Mediterranean. A new instalment in the historic rivalry between the dominant Black Sea power and the dominant Mediterranean power over mastery of the Straits — now with an added ideological difference to fuel the conflict — was being played out, and Britain's hand was not a strong one. As the English perceived their dilemma, should Russia be resisted to the point where the conference would fail, an outcome sure to antagonize the Turks?

The British naval staff, originally the keenest advocates of friendship on Turkey's terms, hated the prospect of losing the strategic advantages obtained from Lausanne, but they professed to be even more anxious about the effect that a closure of the Straits might have on the naval balance in Europe. When the Cabinet heard on 15 July that the Montreux conference would soon collapse unless Britain made substantial concessions, the First Lord was prepared to accept that as the lesser risk:

> There was a grave danger that the result [of British concessions] might be that Germany would seek to escape from the Anglo—German Naval Agreement. As soon as the Black Sea was closed to warships and thereby made safe for Russia it would be possible for Russia to concentrate all her naval effort in the Baltic. Germany, on the other hand, would not be able to send her ships into the Black Sea. This was a different situation from the one in which the Anglo—German Naval Agreement had been concluded. The question at issue, therefore . . . was as to whether it was worthwhile to run the risk of losing the Anglo—German Naval Agreement . . . for a very dubious Treaty.

This was a rather extravagant scenario, even for the Admiralty, and fortunately for future Anglo—Turkish relations the Cabinet decided to appease Atatürk instead.[19] The British delegation at Montreux were instructed to accept the Soviet proposal for the closure of the Straits in wartime, Turkey being neutral. In return, Litvinov was persuaded to make reciprocal concessions — most of which also worked to Turkey's advantage — and a new convention was initialled that granted the Turks full and sovereign control of the Straits. Interestingly, in their strongly anti-Soviet mood the British as yet had no hint that the Russians were quite as dissatisfied as themselves with the outcome. The word at the Foreign Office was that Montreux had demonstrated Turkey to be a Soviet satellite, but the reality was that the Turks had exploited a great

[19] Cab. Conclusions, 15 July 1936. Cab.23/84.

Power deadlock to win a brilliant diplomatic success: out of their mutual suspicion and hostility, London and Moscow had each concluded that the least dangerous solution to the conflict would be to restore Turkey's role as gate-keeper of the Dardanelles.[20]

The substantial concessions extended to the Turks quickly yielded the fruit of Anglo–Turkish *rapprochement*. Relations improved so rapidly, in fact, that in early 1937 Dr Aras advised Sir Percy Loraine that in his opinion Turkey's best interests henceforth lay with British friendship. Turkey, he told the delighted ambassador, would surely ally itself with England in another war: not immediately, perhaps, but certainly if Italy became involved. Loraine's assessment of these remarks underlined the growing mutual interests of the two powers, the common denominators of a future alliance.[21] First, the Turks openly despised Mussolini and feared his revisionist aims. Determined to see the Dodecanese islands freed from Italian control, they supported Britain in its conflict with Rome and welcomed its rearmament. Second, the Turks were clearly hoping for British diplomatic support in their dispute with France over the contentious Hatay (Sanjak of Alexandretta) question.[22] Third, Loraine thought that they might also be seeking relief from an oppressively close relationship with Russia. (In the summer of 1937 Aras confided to the Ambassador that his visit to Moscow had left a 'slight but "insidious" rift' in Turco–Soviet relations and went on to complain that the Soviets had tried to stretch Turkish obligations, 'to have the Turks in tow'.[23] This would account for

20 The rivalry did not end there of course. See F. Marzari, 'Western–Soviet rivalry in Turkey, 1939', *Middle Eastern Studies* (January 1971 and June 1971).
21 Loraine to Eden, 24 and 28 February 1937. E1414/315/44. (20861).
22 Early in 1937 Eden took on the delicate task of mediating between Turkey and France in an attempt to head off a clash in the already troubled Near East between two potential allies. He was able to persuade the Turks not to take unilateral action outside the League and in May 1937, thanks to British mediation, a compromise solution for the Hatay's administration was worked out. But the Turks soon began their campaign again for the transfer of the territory to the Turkish nation and the French, fearful of the dangerous situation in the Mediterranean, capitulated. The British disapproved of Turkey's revisionism but were unable and unwilling to risk a confrontation with it. Although the Hatay dispute lingered until the eve of the war – thus complicating Franco–Turkish relations – its resolution on Turkish terms was regarded as inevitable in London; mediation having failed, the British played a minor role in smoothing the way for France's capitulation and the reconciliation of the two powers. See F.O. 371/20845-46 and 21909-11 for Britain's attitude to this question.
23 E4434/386/44. (20861).

Turkey's fearful and suspicious reaction to Litvinov's policy during the Nyon conference.) And finally, Loraine argued, the Turks were anticipating direct economic assistance from London in their struggle to avoid becoming another dependent of the expanding German *Reich*.

As events developed, it became clear to the British that neither Mussolini nor Stalin threatened Turkish independence in the same way as Germany's dynamic economic expansion throughout South-Eastern Europe. Loraine and other diplomats in the Balkans had grown steadily uneasy about Dr Schacht's tactics and Germany's penetration of the weak agrarian economies of the region. The *Anschluss* did not revolutionize this process, but it did give Hitler control of the financial—communications centre of the Danube — Vienna — as well as Austria's economic stake in the Balkans.[24] Britain now faced the probability, Halifax warned the Foreign Policy Committee, of Germany's economic, cultural and political domination of Central and South-Eastern Europe. The Turks, Greeks, Roumanians and Yugoslavs — who constituted the Balkan Entente — were seeking to avoid that future and the first three of these were expecting direct British assistance to counter-balance the *Zollverein*. Halifax opposed anti-German policies of 'encirclement', but he did favour taking up the challenge in a limited way, giving priority to countries bordering on the Mediterranean. England, he urged in — for him — rather unfamiliar language, should throw its resources into the scale to redress the balance of power: 'the success of such a policy would count two in a Division'.[25] But what type of diplomacy could fashion such a balance?

Broadly speaking, Halifax later explained,[26] there were two strategies open to London. The first, 'policies of power politics', would mean political guarantees, binding military conventions, staff talks and so on. These were regarded by the Chamberlain Cabinet as dangerous measures of last resort. Such a policy would encumber Britain with extra commitments, 'almost certainly leads to war, will be unpopular in this country and is uncertain in its operation'. Here the 1914 precedent was clearly influencing Britain's decision-makers: if the Balkans became directly linked to the Great Powers, might not Germany and England find themselves once again dragged into catastrophe? With this antecedent shaping his vision, Halifax offered a more cautious alternative.

[24] See Industrial Intelligence Centre (I.I.C.) report, 25 March 1938. C3594/541/ 18/ (21702).
[25] F.P. (36)/30th mtg., 1 June 1938. *Op. cit.*; also, C.P. 127(38). Cab.24/271.
[26] C.P. 257(38). Cab.24/280.

Britain should put its economic and financial resources and its consuming capacity to work for political ends. By extending loans and credits and purchasing products such as Greek tobacco and Roumanian wheat and oil, Britain could sustain the economic integrity of a few of the Balkan countries while offering them an alternative to Berlin's style of 'friendship'. This strategy's political purpose was covert and would not impair the chances of an Anglo—German settlement — in mid-1938, still a major objective of British foreign policy.

In articulating his strategy for a foreign aid programme for the Balkans, Halifax was able to point to an impressive precedent established by the Cabinet: namely, the Anglo—Turkish Guarantee Agreement and the Armaments Credit Agreement, both of 27 May 1938, by which London had extended industrial and arms credits valuing £16 million to Turkey. At Nyon in September 1937 the Turks had delighted Chatfield with the news that Turkish orders for warships would be offered to British shipbuilders. The following February the order list of twenty-six warships (including four destroyers and eight submarines) plus heavy gun-batteries for the Dardanelles was presented in London with a request for credit terms. The naval staff, who favoured a British-sponsored expansion of the Turkish fleet and were eager to have British guns installed at the Straits, informed Halifax of their strong backing of the order: 'We regard this matter of such vital importance that we should be prepared to accept reasonable delay in our own programme of naval rearmament if this were necessary to meet Turkish requirements.'[27] Additionally, the Turks had also presented in London a request for industrial credits worth £10 million. Britain was being invited to finance most of Turkey's second five-year industrialization, and, Loraine correctly admonished his superiors, if it declined the Germans were more than ready to fill the vacuum.[28]

The ever-cautious Board of Trade and Treasury were cool to these projects, feeling that they involved dubious breaks with financial orthodoxy and substantial credit risks. But Halifax was able to deploy the strategic argument, as well as an interesting variant of 'the row of falling dominoes' image, to establish that the diplomatic game was worth the economic candle. For Halifax, German expansion in South-Eastern Europe was directly linked to the question of imperial security

---

27 Duff Cooper to Halifax, 14 April 1938. E2274/67/44. (21918); Admiralty memorandum of 4 May 1938. Adm. 116/4195.
28 Loraine to Halifax, 7 April 1938. E2125/797/44. (21932).

in the Mediterranean and Middle East — particularly after the *Anschluss*:
Germany is now a direct neighbour of one of Turkey's associates in
the Balkan Entente, Yugoslavia, while nothing but a friendly or at
any rate a docile Hungary separates Germany from another of
Turkey's associates Roumania. As things stand at the present, it is
difficult to see what is going to stop the expansion of German
influence over and through these two countries to the boundaries of
an equally docile Bulgaria, and over and through Bulgaria to the
boundaries of Turkey.

Beyond Turkey . . . lie the lands of the Middle East (Syria, Iraq,
Palestine, Saudi Arabia, Egypt) through which run our sea or air
communications with India. The maintenance of our influence in
those regions is not a simple matter at the best of times. Palestine is
of course making it much more difficult and I can say without
hesitation that without a friendly Turkey it would become quite
impossible. If Turkey fell, however reluctantly, within the German
orbit — and the fact that Germany has been taking about 40% of
Turkey's exports is a formidable factor in the situation — German
influence would spread freely through the Middle East, encouraging
our enemies in these regions and above all making good the lack of
cohesion and organization which is their principal weakness.

It is therefore scarcely too much to say that Turkey has become
not the main, but the only obstacle to the *Drang nach Osten.*[29]

It was a powerful brief and one that left Chamberlain 'greatly
impressed'. The Prime Minister backed the credit scheme in the Cabinet,
arguing that England must avoid the disastrous mistake through which
it had ended up fighting Turkey in the war. But he also admonished
that the Turks were in a 'very special and exceptional position' and that
the terms being offered 'involved a grave departure from precedent'.
The Cabinet approved the £16-millions credit to Turkey but gave
Halifax no mandate for the further use of financial resources for
political ends.[30]

The Turkish decision appeared to represent a shift in official
thinking from the strategy of appeasement and acquiescence to one of
containment and resistance, and the Foreign Office were ready to use it
as the model for a general offensive in the Balkans. Halifax wired his

[29] Halifax, 'Credits for Turkey', 7 May 1938. C.P. 112(38). Cab.24/276.
[30] Cab. Conclusions, 11 May 1938. Cab.23/93. Texts of the agreements in
Command 5754 and 5755 of 1938.

advisers from the League meetings in Geneva that he was 'quite prepared to initiate a drive for the extension of British influence in the Balkans'.[31] But there was scant sympathy for this view in the other concerned departments of the Government — for instance, in the orthodox corridors of the Treasury where the call for the political use of financial reserves was regarded as irresponsible. Chamberlain shared this latter opinion and he also suspected certain of Halifax's advisers of ambitions to encircle Germany, a policy he was sure would precipitate war. Britain must not block Germany's economic expansion in Central and South-Eastern Europe, for that natural and inevitable process might make Hitler more quiescent and ready to come to a general political settlement. Chamberlain even took to Munich — but did not use — a document prepared by Sir Horace Wilson that amounted to an explicit waiving of all British economic interest in that region.[32] For special reasons Turkey necessarily lay outside the boundaries of disinterestedness, but beyond this exception Chamberlain and his colleagues were unwilling to practise containment or 'encirclement' while preaching economic and political appeasement.

Inter-departmental machinery was created in mid-1938 to study the region of Central and South-Eastern Europe and to make recommendations, but the new committee was dominated by the voices of imperial protectionism and pre-Keynesian finance and its reports were written within the sceptical assumptions of those schools of thought.[33] Not surprisingly, it seems to have functioned as a bureaucratic restraint on the Foreign Office rather than as an initiator of new policy. To cite the most important instance, the Foreign Office consistently argued that Greece, along with Turkey, should be given first priority in the committee's deliberations:

> . . . a friendly Greece is essential, while a Greece subservient to Berlin would constitute a menace to be avoided at all costs. If the defence of Egypt be a criterion, then first in importance comes the consolidation of British influence in Turkey and Greece. On the same criterion, Bulgaria and Yugoslavia take second place, and Roumania

---

31 R4755/94/67. (22342).
32 Wilson's document and Vansittart's criticisms of it, in R8044/94/67. (22344).
33 Known as the Interdepartmental Committee on Economic Assistance to Central and South-East Europe, it was chaired by Sir Frederick Leith-Ross, the Government's Chief Economic Adviser, and attended by representatives of the Foreign Office, Treasury, Board of Trade, Department of Overseas Trade, Bank of England and so on.

and Hungary come last.[34]

Like Turkey, Greece was regarded by British naval planners as 'an essential part of the defensive complex of the Eastern Mediterranean, a Levantine rather than a Balkan state'.[35] In the early stages of the Abyssinian crisis, British plans were drawn up on the assumption that, in place of Malta, the Mediterranean Fleet would use the anchorage at Navarino (known as 'Port X') as its forward base for operations against Italy.[36] The control of the Aegean, it was acknowledged, would be vital for the interruption of Italy's eastern trade and communications, and some British naval people presciently pointed to the island of Crete as the vital centre of the eastern basin where a future Mediterranean war might be decided.[37] Greece also was a power of considerable importance in the Balkan *Entente*, and Britain's investment in its economy and its share of Greek trade, although not decisive factors, could not be written off. With these interests at stake, Halifax argued, it was 'of the highest importance at the present moment that Greece should not be allowed to pass under German influence, in view of the political, economic and strategic consequences which would ensue'.[38]

But there was little agreement in London as to how this might be prevented. On several occasions in 1938 the government of General Ionnis Metaxas hinted at or formally proposed an Anglo–Greek alliance. This immediately raised all the problems that Halifax had outlined in his argument against strategies of powei politics in the Balkans. The Services were not consulted, but in 1936, it will be recalled, they had advised against a guarantee of Greece on several grounds: it would conflict with England's other imperial commitments; it would alienate Italy; Greece would prove more of a strategic liability than an asset.[39] In 1938, it was true, the real menace to Greek independence now emanated from Germany rather than Italy, but Lord Perth was

---

[34] C.P. 127(38). *Op. cit.*

[35] M. Howard, *The Mediterranean strategy in the Second World War* (London, 1968), pp. 10–11.

[36] See Marder, 'The Royal Navy and the Ethiopian Crisis, 1935–36', p. 1331. In the first weeks of the emergency Chatfield was prepared to seize Navarino if necessary; by December, however, Admiral Fisher and the air staff had persuaded the Chiefs of Staff that the anchorage was too exposed to air attack, and 'Port X' was left a question mark.

[37] For example, Captain H. Packer (naval attaché, Athens), 'A Review of the Strategical Situation in the Eastern Basin of the Mediterranean', March 1939. Adm. 1/9941.

[38] Foreign Office to Air Ministry, 15 September 1938. Air 2/3412.

[39] C.P. 211 (36). Cab.24/263.

nonetheless sure that Mussolini would regard an Anglo–Greek alliance with the 'gravest suspicion' and interpret it as a device of anti-Italian politics.[40] Perth's warnings were especially significant in view of the British Government's plans to use the Duce as an ally in the search at and after Munich for a general European settlement. Halifax therefore rejected the guarantee solution and posed the alternatives of economic aid, increased trade, and the assisted re-equipment of the Greek armed forces:

> it may well be essential to our ultimate security to promote our political influence by economic measures in South-Eastern Europe today: or perhaps it would be fairer to say that to permit our political influence in these countries now to go by the board may well have, in the long run, a most serious effect upon that security. That is why I am so anxious that we should do what we can now to promote that influence, particularly and above all in Greece.[41]

But within the limits and assumptions of orthodox finance and economics these political interests could not be guaranteed. The Leith-Ross committee, while favouring increased economic activity in Roumania, was unable to persuade Britain's tobacco interests to increase their imports of Greek tobacco, and the Board of Trade and Treasury were reluctant to extend credits to a shaky and unpopular regime already heavily indebted to foreign financiers.[42] Moreover, London's strategists had evidently retained their suspicions of Greece's real strategic value, for they declined to revise their own rearmament plans in order to step up arms sales to that nation.[43] There were risks in this negative strategy, as Leith-Ross himself admitted: for if England had to look forward to fresh emergencies and crises in the post-Munich period, then might there not be a greater danger in refusing financial assistance than in granting it? And the answer to that question was in turn rooted in a much larger unknown – 'whether we can look forward

40 Perth to Ingram, 6 July 1938. R6161/5888/67. (22351); and Perth to Halifax, tel. No. 671, 13 October 1938. R8238/361/19. (22362).
41 Halifax, 'Central and South-Eastern Europe', 10 November 1938. C.P. 257 (38). Cab.24/280.
42 See the committee's second interim report of December 1938, 'Assistance to Roumania and Greece', R10352/94/67. (22345). We are not directly concerned here with Anglo–Roumanian relations, but it may be worth noting that Chamberlain was persuaded by King Carol in November 1938 that Britain should counter Germany's influence by increasing its economic activity in Roumania. During the winter of 1938–9, increased imports of Roumanian wheat were authorized.
43 Admiralty and War Office notes of October 1938. R8555/361/19. (22363).

to a general appeasement in Europe'.[44]

Neville Chamberlain did not share history's subsequent verdict that Munich had been at worst a criminal or immoral act, at best a disastrous setback for the policy of appeasement. On the contrary, another of Hitler's major 'grievances' had been appeased — tragic though that fact might be for the people of Czechoslovakia — and the Prime Minister and his closest colleagues and advisers were determined to continue their quest for the elusive general European settlement. At Munich, Britain had negotiated from a position of unacceptable weakness, so it must push on with rearmament; but this would be wed to an activist, conciliatory foreign policy. Wrote Sir Alexander Cadogan, 'Munich, like many other promising initiatives, is likely to remain without effect if we let the opportunity pass and do not follow it up.'[45]

The boundaries of Germany's sphere of influence in Central Europe and England's in the Mediterranean and Empire, tacitly discernible in the wake of Hitler's new bloodless conquest, would form the geopolitical foundation of the political settlement. Any thought of 'encirclement' or of containment was now ruled out of the question. Munich signalled an end to any significant British role in the affairs of Central and Eastern Europe. 'Henceforward', Halifax argued in a long, revealing letter to Sir Eric Phipps, 'we must count with German predominance in Central Europe. Incidentally I have always felt myself that once Germany recovered her normal strength, this predominance was inevitable for obvious geographical and economic reasons.' German expansion in that region was 'a normal and natural thing', he went on, but it would have to be resisted in Western Europe.[46] The Foreign Secretary mused in similar but even franker language to U.S. Ambassador Joseph Kennedy: Hitler would be permitted to 'go ahead and do what he liked in Central Europe' while England sought its future in the Mediterranean and Empire and with America.[47] To the Foreign Policy Committee Halifax spoke in near-identical terms and emphasized the new importance of the Mediterranean in the post-Munich world. England, he repeated, could not prevent Hitler from doing as he wished in Central Europe.

We must, however, become as strong as possible and aim at securing

---

[44] Leith-Ross, 15 November 1938. R9139/94/67. (22345).
[45] Memorandum of 8 November 1939. C14471/42/18. (21659).
[46] Halifax to Phipps, 1 November 1938. F.O. 800/311.
[47] *F.R.U.S.*, 1938, I, pp. 85–6. See also the memoranda by Cadogan in Dilks, *The diaries of Sir Alexander Cadogan 1938–1945*, pp. 116–20.

the vital cord of the British Empire, namely, our communications through the Mediterranean by ensuring the friendship and goodwill of Portugal, Spain, Italy, Greece, Turkey and Egypt, to which we could certainly add the Dominions and probably the United States.[48]

In this further retreat from the European heartland into Mediterranean and imperial isolation, stable relations with fascist Italy would have renewed significance. That was why the Chamberlain Cabinet agreed in October to accede to Mussolini's demands that the Anglo–Italian agreement – held in abeyance since April because of British preconditions regarding the Spanish conflict – should immediately be put into force. Halifax explained that he wanted to 'do all we could to liberate Signor Mussolini by degrees from the pressure to which he was subjected from Berlin'.[49] 'Although we do not expect to detach Italy from the axis', he advised Phipps, 'we believe the agreement will increase Mussolini's freedom of manoeuvre and so make him less dependent on Hitler, and therefore freer to resume the classic Italian role of balancing between Germany and the Western Powers.'[50] Vansittart may have been sidetracked, but his spirit certainly lived on in Britain's Mediterranean policy. In November the agreement duly came into force.

Hopes for an early settlement with Hitler were disappointed by the savage anti-Jewish German pogroms of November and by secret reports received in London about this time that indicated the Führer's displeasure with Munich and his intention to turn against England. Chamberlain was not about to abandon his programme of appeasement, however, and told Vincent Massey, the Canadian High Commissioner, 'that his determination to arrive at a stabilization of Europe was too deep-rooted to be affected by the disappointments of the last few weeks.'[51] Still, public reaction to Hitler's latest anti-Semitic barbarism made any approach to Berlin 'very difficult'. The Prime Minister had therefore decided to attack the Rome end of the Axis: he was to visit

---

48 F.P. (36)/33d mtg., 21 November 1938. Cab.27/624.
49 Cab. Conclusions, 26 October 1938. Cab.23/96; and Halifax, 'The Anglo–Italian Agreement,' 21 October 1938. C.P. 231(38). In F.O. 371/22414.
50 Halifax to Phipps, 1 November 1938. *Op. cit.*
51 'He said – and I think quite rightly – that it is necessary to take a very long-range view of conditions in Europe and to keep the ultimate goal in mind despite the setbacks which may occur from time to time.' Massey to Mackenzie King, 15 November 1938. W. L. M. King Papers, M.G. 26 Jl. Vol. 255. Public Archives of Canada, Ottawa.

Mussolini in January.[52] Spain would be the first item on the agenda, he wrote privately:

> But of course I want a lot more than that. An hour or two *tête à tête* with Musso might be extraordinarily valuable in making plans for talks with Germany, and if I had explored the subject first with France, we might see some way of getting a move on. In the past, I have often felt a sense of helpless exasperation at the way things have been allowed to drift in foreign affairs, but now I am in a position to keep them on the move, and while I am P.M. I don't mean to go to sleep.[53]

The Rome summit was an integral part of Britain's long-range planning for appeasement. The underlying vision was of a conservative Europe dominated by the four Great Powers (excluding, of course, Russia) and disarmed of major diplomatic and ideological friction. Chamberlain's ambitious programme of appeasement envisaged a role for Italy grandiose enough to tickle even Mussolini's ego: first as direct participant in the ending of the Spanish war and in reconciliation with France; next as balancer or 'armed arbiter', with England, in negotiations on disarmament and Germany's outstanding grievances. But before he could play his designated part in the fashioning of this new concert the Duce must regain his independence and resume that 'classic Italian role' of Europe's balancer. If nothing else, this was a rather optimistic reading of Italian diplomatic history. Another – albeit less flattering – classic Italian role was that of Europe's most expensive whore. Mussolini was sensitive about this unsavoury chapter of the nation's past and claimed that it belonged to the pre-fascist era. But his own price was certainly inflating. In December the Fascists raised the public bid to 'Tunis, Corsica, Nice' in an ill-mannered outburst that incensed the French but brought only mild reproaches from the British Foreign Office.[54]

The historian who has read the various official and private accounts of the Mussolini–Chamberlain discussions of 11–13 January 1939 may find it difficult to credit Chamberlain's subsequent opinion 'that the journey has definitely strengthened the chances of peace'.[55] Whereas

---

[52] F.P. (36)/32d mtg., 14 November 1938. Cab.27/624.
[53] Keith Feiling, *The life of Neville Chamberlain* (London, 1946), p. 389.
[54] Cadogan warned Lord Perth that these kinds of demonstrations might force Chamberlain to cancel his visit; Perth replied that Mussolini would regard cancellation as a personal insult, 'a thing that he never forgets or forgives'. *Documents on British Foreign Policy, 1919–1939*, ser. 3, III, pp. 473–4, 478.
[55] Feiling, *op. cit.* p. 393.

the Prime Minister and Halifax found the Duce quiet and reasonable and took comfort in his silence on his dispute with France,[56] the Italians appear to have perceived only weakness and desperation on the part of the British. These, said Mussolini, 'are the tired sons of a long line of rich men, and they will lose their empire'. Ciano concluded, 'The British do not want to fight.'[57] The long-range effect of the conversations was still more serious, for Stalin apparently was informed (evidently erroneously) that Chamberlain had encouraged the idea of Germany's expansion into the Ukraine; and that suspicion was to have profound repercussions for England later in the year.[58] Within days of the British delegation's return to London the Italians had renewed their claims against French territory and initiated mobilization measures that continued to disturb London and Paris up to the occupation of Albania. In the light of these negative results, and considering that the British delegation had expressly set out for Rome to show Mussolini that the democracies were not 'on the run' and would not make unjustifiable concessions,[59] one must agree with Count Ciano's conclusion that the visit was a 'fiasco'. Nonetheless, Neville Chamberlain persisted in his esoteric view that it 'was highly successful and achieved all and more than I had hoped from it. I did not expect immediate results, but it has produced a relation from which we may draw valuable consequences before long.'[60]

Against this wider backdrop of relentless acquiescence in both Europe and the Mediterranean, the less dramatic issue of Britain's attitude to the Balkans remained unresolved. At the end of 1938 the Foreign Office received information that the military staffs of the four

---

56 *D.B.F.P.*, ser. 3, III, pp. 517—29; these include the official accounts of the Rome discussions.

57 Malcolm Muggeridge (ed.), *Ciano's diary, 1939—43* (London, 1947), pp. 9—10.

58 See M. Toscano, 'Italy and the Nazi—Soviet Accords of August, 1939', in his *Designs in diplomacy* (Baltimore, 1970), pp. 48—123. The official British account records Chamberlain as having mentioned the Ukraine and Western Europe as regions where rumours had Hitler marching next. But neither this nor the various private accounts — Cadogan's, Harvey's, Ciano's, etc. — convey any impression that Chamberlain actually encouraged the idea of a move against the Ukraine.

59 Dilks, *The diaries of Sir Alexander Cadogan 1938—1945*, pp. 134—5.

60 Chamberlain to Lord Tweedsmuir (Governor General of Canada), 7 February 1939. John Buchan Papers. Queen's University Archives, Kingston, Canada. This letter indicates that Chamberlain's oft-noted optimism in February and March may have derived largely from Franco's victory in Spain. With that war over the powers could move on to other settlements.

Balkan *Entente* nations had secretly convened after Munich and re-inforced their mutual obligations. They wanted England to keep strong forces in the Eastern Mediterranean and hoped that it and France would attempt to defeat Italy at the outset of any Mediterranean war. The total military man-power of the Balkan *Entente* was about five million, but poor communications would hamper their early deployment against Germany. 'Not one of the four countries has munitions enough to conduct a big war for more than 10 to 15 days and they will all be entirely dependent upon Great Britain and France for replenishments. Therefore they consider the maintenance of our sea communications in the Mediterranean to be vital for them and for us.'[61]

This intelligence only confirmed the many reports received in London after Munich from Balkan countries demanding material assistance in their struggle to avoid being swallowed by the encroaching Nazi empire. Munich had obliterated the final barrier to German penetration of the Danube and now virtually nothing stood between Hitler's swelling ambition and Berlin's actual presence on the shores of the Black Sea and East Mediterranean. Central Europe might be casually dismissed, but was Hitler also to be permitted 'to go ahead and do what he likes' until he controlled Roumania's oil or Greece's naval bases? Halifax and his advisers had extended the line of commitment to Greece for strategic reasons, and argued that the policy of the 'free hand' must cease at its borders.[62] But the Government's purse-holders and the Leith-Ross committee remained sceptical and vetoed Foreign Office efforts to utilize financial and economic resources in competition with Germany over Greece. Some £2 million in non-commercial credits were found for Greek naval purchases,[63] but no progress was made on the more fundamental question of large-scale economic assistance to the Metaxas regime.[64]

Failing such assistance, Halifax had warned, nothing short of a political—military alliance would arrest Germany's steady penetration of Greece. Metaxas was eager for this, but the Foreign Office had declined on the grounds that it would be interpreted as encirclement by Berlin and Rome, both of which figured in the Government's plans

---

[61] Sir R. Campbell (Belgrade) to Ingram, 19 December 1938. R8262/233/67. (22347).
[62] Cab. Conclusions, 19 October 1938. Cab.23/96; and Halifax, 'Central and South-Eastern Europe', 10 November 1938. C.P. 257(38). Cab.24/280.
[63] Adm. 116/3949.
[64] Cf. F.P. (36)/37th mtg., 8 February 1939. Cab.27/624.

for a general European settlement, and that it would conflict with Service commitments in the Far East. On similar grounds the British had refused in the autumn of 1938 to enter a pact with France and Turkey.[65] On the very eve of the Prague crisis, amidst reports and rumours of Italian plans to seize Albania, Foreign Office officials were reconsidering the idea of an Anglo–Greek alliance. They concluded that the disadvantages outweighed the merits of such a measure of 'last resort' and decided not to enter into negotiations for the moment; but if Italy seized Albania, then London should immediately offer Greece an alliance.[66]

However, it was Turkey rather than Greece which again became the Balkan focus of London's attention in the Prague and Albanian crises. At the beginning of March the Chief of the Naval Staff, Admiral Sir Roger Backhouse, had informed a special C.I.D. strategical appreciation subcommittee of the necessity of having Turkey for an ally in any general war. For reasons analysed later in this study the naval staff had tentatively decided to try to defeat Italy in the very early stages of a war, and Turkey, as mistress of the Straits, held a key to the success of this policy. The closure of the Straits would deny Italy its vital sea-borne oil supplies and seal the only Mediterranean 'gate' not controlled by the British.[67] Another appreciation written about this time – by the British naval attaché in Athens – emphasized that as the Eastern Mediterranean would possibly be sealed from the west in wartime, the active support of Greece and Turkey would be essential to allied forces operating there. In its struggle to gain control of the eastern basin the British fleet would need naval anchorages, mastery of the Dardanelles and the support of the Graeco–Turkish navies. No effort, he urged, should be spared to ensure their active friendship in a war in the Mediterranean.[68]

The advice was good, but as events unfolded in Central Europe and then the Mediterranean, it was the Turks who first had to play the role

---

65 E5185/67/44. (21923).
66 'The Possibility of an Anglo–Greek Alliance', 13 March 1939. Annex V in
   J.P. 394. Cab. 55/15. The Services were even more reluctant to guarantee
   Greece, and argued now – as they had in 1936 – that its frontiers were
   difficult to defend and that it would prove more of a liability than an asset.
   Right up to the April guarantee, indeed, they argued that England should seek
   Greece's neutrality.
67 S.A.C./1st mtg., 1 March 1939. Cab.16/209.
68 Captain H. Packer, 'A Review of the Strategical Situation in the Eastern Basin
   of the Mediterranean,' *op. cit.*

of anxious suitor to England's reluctant virgin. Some weeks before the Prague occupation of 15 March, it appears, the Turks had 'weighed the advantages of an already tentatively formulated agreement with the Soviets in the Black Sea against an, as yet, unformulated agreement with Britain in the Mediterranean, and had decided that the second alternative took precedence'.[69] They quickly seized the opening provided by a British inquiry regarding Turkey's attitude to the Prague *coup* to launch their own project for an Anglo–Turkish alliance in the Mediterranean. Halifax was assured on 21 March by Aras, the Turkish Ambassador, that as a matter of 'fixed policy' his nation was ready to go to all lengths with England in the Mediterranean. Turkey would depart from neutrality only if it became allied to Britain. But the Turks first wanted reassurance on two points: first, would they have Britain with them; second, could they count on direct British assistance?[70] Then at the end of March, having received no encouraging sign from the British side, Aras appeared again at the Foreign Office to make an 'unofficial' and far-reaching proposal for a containment front including Britain, Turkey, the Soviet Union, Poland and Roumania (and perhaps France, if Franco–Turkish relations improved). In Aras's concept the latter four powers would make a non-aggression pact and agree to combine against any party threatening it; Britain would guarantee the whole arrangement. This time Halifax was almost rudely sceptical, questioning the logic of the whole idea, and Aras was unable to persuade him that it had any merit.[71] In effect, this amounted to a cold douche that accurately reflected official policy.

Against the aforementioned strategic advantages of an alliance with Turkey, the British had to weigh its likely political and diplomatic effects, particularly in the Mediterranean region. On 17 March the Foreign Office was warned by the Roumanian minister in London, M. V. Tilea, of an impending German economic ultimatum to his country. Next day the Cabinet learned that the Chiefs of Staff felt that German access to Roumania's oilfields would enable it to neutralize a British blockade; Hitler's political domination of Roumania would be still more serious, as the Nazis could then march straight to the Mediterranean. Chamberlain, in a seminal statement, announced an end

---

[69] F. Marzari, 'Western–Soviet rivalry in Turkey – 1939', I, in *Middle Eastern Studies* (January 1971), 66. Also, Sir H. Knatchbull-Hugessen, *Diplomat in peace and war* (London, 1949), p. 145.

[70] *D.B.F.P.*, ser. 3, IV, No. 472.

[71] *Ibid.*, No. 590.

to his policy of conciliating Germany and spoke of the need for a peace front in resisting further aggression.[72] Turkey was among the states contacted initially, but at the next Cabinet — on 20 March, a day before Aras's first call on Halifax — Chamberlain worried that its inclusion in the peace front might offend Mussolini. 'Italy would not regard the approaches to Paris, Moscow or Warsaw as being directed against her, but she might do so if Turkey were also to be approached.'[73] Three days later the Prime Minister explained — correctly — to T.U.C. and Labour Party leaders that the events in Central Europe had been 'excessively disagreeable' to Mussolini. London and Paris had spotted a chance to loosen the bonds of the Axis and they had consequently decided to exclude the Turks from consultations on the peace front.[74] Chamberlain then sent off another letter to Mussolini expressing concern over the international situation and requesting Italy's help in restoring Europe to peace. The only effect of this latest supplication was to encourage a new aggression: 'Mussolini will answer after striking at Albania,' Count Ciano confided to his diary. 'This letter strengthens his decision to act because in it he finds another proof of the inertia of the democracies.'[75]

Chamberlain's policy was more or less consistent with the highly ambivalent advice he was getting from the Chiefs of Staff on the merits of allying with the Turks and Greeks. The Services found it hard to overestimate the positive effects that Turkish intervention could have on the military balance in the East Mediterranean, but if a pact with Turkey finally decided Mussolini on a war alliance with Hitler, 'then we might stand to lose more than we should gain by the treaty'. Further, they still counted Greece a military liability. The Chiefs of Staff concluded by dumping the entire problem into the lap of the Foreign Office.[76] It was an indecisive, almost contradictory report, which probably made scant impression on a political leadership still

[72] Cab. Conclusions, 18 March 1939. Cab.23/98.
[73] Cab. Conclusions, 20 March 1939. Cab.23/98. The Cabinet agreed that this had 'great force'.
[74] C4317/15/18 (22967).
[75] *Ciano's diary 1939–43, op. cit.* p. 54. Mussolini had indeed found the Prague *coup* disagreeable ('every time Hitler occupies a country he sends me a message') and for a few days he contemplated shifts in policy. But his prestige recovered, and he concluded, 'We cannot change our policy now. After all we are not prostitutes.' *Ibid.* pp. 46–54.
[76] Chiefs of Staff 'Alliance with Turkey and Greece', C.O.S. 383, 31 March 1939. Cab.55/15.

faithful to the religion of detaching Italy.

That religion was put through yet another severe test on Good Friday, 7 April, when Mussolini's forces overwhelmed and occupied tiny Albania — an utterly gratuitous act whose only motivation seems to have been the Duce's sense of eclipsed prestige. Albania was no vital interest of England's and even though the aggression was an obvious violation of the Anglo–Italian agreement, Halifax and Chamberlain were still reluctant to provoke Mussolini. What finally precipitated British action was the rumour of a pending Italian move against Corfu.[77] The Strategical Appreciation Committee advised the Foreign Policy Committee through their spokesman, Lord Chatfield, that plans were under consideration for an offensive against Italy in the event of war. Turkey's role in these plans for pivotal and every effort should be made to bring it into an alliance, even if it meant giving Greece a parallel guarantee. Britain should also strive to construct a Balkan bloc and to mediate Bulgaria's differences with the four members of the *entente*. On 10 and 11 April the Foreign Policy Committee acted on this strategic opinion and decided (*a*) to give a definite guarantee to Greece while (*b*) attempting to bring the Turks into a comprehensive mutual support agreement.[78] Under French pressure Halifax reluctantly included Roumania in his public announcement of the Greek guarantee, but the crucial events from London's perspective were the dispatches that passed between the Foreign Office and Ankara on the twelfth and thirteenth. Halifax in effect offered the Turks everything Aras had suggested in March, including guarantees against both Italy and Germany.[79] The immediate outcome of this *démarche* was the Anglo–Turkish declaration of 12 May 1939 in which the two powers announced their intention to conclude a long-term agreement and meanwhile to support each other 'in the Mediterranean area'. Subsequent negotiations for an Anglo–French–Turkish treaty were prolonged by difficulties over the Hatay question, over Turkey's large demands for economic assistance and by Soviet interference, and the treaty was not signed until 19 October — at a moment when the British

---

[77] Cf. Harvey, *The diplomatic diaries of Oliver Harvey*, pp. 274–6; and Dilks, *The diaries of Sir Alexander Cadogan 1938–1945*, pp. 170–2. Halifax and Cadogan took the line that Britain should 'steer between provocation and impression of impotence. If you are too bellicose, you provoke Dictators into doing something irrevocable. If you are too passive, you encourage them to think they can do anything.' *Ibid.* p. 171.

[78] *Ibid.*; Notes of a conference, 10 April 1939. W5991/105/80. (23982).

[79] Marzari, *op. cit.*; *D.B.F.P.*, V, nos. 128, 138, 155, 157.

were actively seeking to keep Italy and the Balkans out of war.[80] From the perspective of this study, however, the crux of the matter is that from mid-April 1939 the British Government was committed to the defence of the East Mediterranean.

The acceptance of the obligations and guarantees of April 1939 marked a partial shift in British diplomacy from appeasement and acquiescence to one of containment: partial, because the Government refused to denounce the Anglo–Italian agreement and still hoped to bring France and Italy together. From the perspective of global strategy, however, these events marked a profound departure from the goal of a 'tranquil Mediterranean without commitments' enunciated by the Chiefs of Staff in 1936; indeed, the guarantees to Greece and Turkey seemed in direct conflict with the Admiralty's long-standing obligations in the Far East. In fact, however, the essential principles of grand strategy were undergoing a major reassessment in the spring of 1939 and the future role of the Mediterranean in imperial defence was central to that review. The grand strategy debates of 1938–9 are a key source for understanding Britain's actions in April 1939 and subsequently, during the last summer of peace in Europe.

---

80 The negotiations are reviewed in Sir L. Woodward, *British foreign policy in the Second World War*, vol. 1 (London, 1970), pp. 24–7.

6. 'England's First Battlefield': a Mediterranean Offensive ?

The various efforts to achieve a diplomatic settlement with Italy after 1935 were undertaken by Britain to buy time for rearmament, to alleviate pressures on financial and military resources and to purchase security for imperial communications. There were, to be sure, also diplomatic reasons for these efforts, but the real thrust and sense of purpose came from strategy. It has been shown that the policy of Mediterranean appeasement flowed logically from British strategic doctrine: indeed, the policy was an integrated part of grand strategy, a necessary complement to the rigid priorities of defence established by the Defence Requirements Subcommittee. From the same perspective of strategy, however, the policy was less than a raging success, and by early 1938 the Chiefs of Staff had been forced to divert forces from home defence to Egypt — a decision that clearly violated both the letter and the spirit of the D.R.C. line. The war scare of September 1938 acted as a forcing-house for dissent by raising many further doubts about the merits of established strategy for the Mediterranean. Within a few months a wide-ranging debate on British grand strategy had been joined within the Government and was still unresolved when Hitler attacked Poland.

Almost in defiance of Halifax's admission shortly after the conclusion of the Anglo—Italian talks in Rome that Italy would remain opportunistic, vulnerable to German pressure and an unknown factor if war broke out, British military planning continued to be based on the dubious assumption of Italian neutrality.[1] In July 1938 the C.I.D. approved a scale of air defence for Malta and Aden that did not take into account the contingency of a hostile Italy,[2] a typical decision hardly reflecting Mussolini's relentless animosity. Naval opinion was to the effect that the *Anschluss* had weakened Italy fundamentally,[3] but it was not at all certain that this was to England's advantage. On the

---

[1] Halifax to Chamberlain, 2 June 1938. Cab.21/562; C.I.D./326th mtg., 2 June 1938. Cab.2/7.
[2] C.I.D./331st mtg., 27 July 1938. Cab.2/7.
[3] Admiralty note, 21 May 1938. W8006/11/41. (22618).

contrary, Britain's interest in excluding Germany from the
Mediterranean depended on a strong and independent Italy, and
Mussolini's Italy was by 1938 in decline, dependent and therefore also
dangerous. The postponement of the implementation of the Easter
Pact, the breakdown of Franco—Italian negotiations and the continuing war in Spain kept Anglo—Italian relations in an 'intermediate
and dangerous phase' and lent credibility to the opinion of some
officials that a European war would quickly spread into the
Mediterranean.[4]

On the eve of the Czech crisis the Rome Embassy argued that Italy
might keep faith with its sullied diplomatic tradition and sit on the
fence for a price;[5] but no assurance of its neutrality — such as that
given by Sir Percy Loraine a year later — could be made. Some hope
was taken from evidence of Italy's weakness and from its reluctance to
mobilize, but the sudden appearance of an extra 10,000 troops in Libya
in mid-September created a 'great sensation' in Whitehall and precipitated the dispatch of the Mediterranean Fleet from Malta to Alexandria.
War Office estimates put the Libyan garrison at 67,000 troops, with
stores sufficient for an immediate attack on Egypt by at least one army
corps.[6] But Egypt was only a fraction of the strategic dilemma.

As tension and rumours spread through Europe's diplomatic system
in September 1938 over Hitler's intransigence on the Czech—Sudeten
conflict, Britain faced a concurrent crisis in the East Mediterranean that
placed an almost intolerable strain on its military capabilities. Full-scale
rebellion had broken out in Palestine during the summer and was
expected to reach a climax in the autumn. British forces from Egypt
had already reinforced the over-extended garrison in Palestine, but at
the end of August a request was forwarded to London for another full
division of troops to crush the revolt. The request was initially refused
because of the European situation, but the Colonial Office pressed for
urgent reinforcements on 7 September. The War Office again refused to
dispatch an English division but promised to gather units from India,
Egypt and Britain so that its equivalent could be sent. This should not
involve 'serious interference' with the intermediate contingent ear-
marked for possible duty in France. These proposals were approved,
but only after strenuous protests by several ministers, particularly

4   Minute by Nichols, 26 July 1938. R6557/23/22. (22413).
5   Sir N. Charles to Halifax, disp. No. 785, 24 August 1938. R7253/899/22.
    (22438).
6   See Foreign Office minutes in J3594 and J4013/3/66. (22032).

Inskip and Halifax, who regarded the European situation with the 'utmost anxiety' and cautioned against tying up large numbers of troops in the Middle East from where it could take months to retrieve them.[7]

The same strains of conflicting commitments were painfully in evidence on 14 September when the Chiefs of Staff submitted their deeply pessimistic analysis of the military balance. Although Italy's attitude remained obscure, British dispositions would have to be framed for the worst contingency. Although its intervention might be more of a liability than an asset for Hitler, nevertheless, it would also seriously embarrass Britain and France. And if Japan took advantage of the situation, Britain might have to evacuate the Mediterranean to send a fleet to Singapore:

> We consider that, as we must take account of Italian and Japanese intervention in formulating our initial plan, the first commitment of our land forces, after the security of the United Kingdom should be the security of Egypt and of our interests in the Middle East. At the same time, it may be most desirable, and even absolutely essential, ultimately to despatch a Field Force to France. Consequently our aim should be to preserve the Intermediate Contingent for this purpose, and to provide the necessary reinforcements for the Middle East from other sources.
>
> The despatch of reinforcements to the Middle East will be all the more necessary owing to the deterioration of the position in Palestine. We regard with grave concern the possibility of the spread of disaffection to other Moslem Countries, involving us in a steadily increasing military commitment in the Middle East, and one which would be a most serious embarassment to us in the event of war with Germany.

No air reinforcements would be available for overseas interests, even though Egypt's air defences were still 'very weak'. In summary, wrote the Chiefs of Staff, the defeat of Germany would require prolonged, unlimited war — war that might well involve the entire British Empire.[8]

The political and military dimensions of the crisis in the Middle East continued to distract the Cabinet and C.I.D. right up to the climactic final week in September and the conference at Munich. Malcolm

---

7 Note of a conference held at the Colonial Office, 7 September 1938. Cab. 21/595.
8 Chiefs of Staff, 'Appreciation of the Situation in the Event of War Against Germany', 14 September 1938. C.P. 199(38).

MacDonald, the Colonial Secretary, had raised the spectre of 'full scale Arab rebellion' and devised a plan for a conciliatory statement on Palestine — immigration would be suspended and partition abandoned — in the event of war.[9] Italy's wavering attitude complicated planning and finally forced the Chiefs of Staff to order reinforcements from Palestine to Egypt: the defence of Egypt and Suez must be the first priority. The long neglect of defensive planning for the Mediterranean, and the lack of co-ordination of intelligence, organization and command within the theatre, necessitated hasty and *ad hoc* decision-making in an atmosphere of crisis. Was it the fleet's first responsibility to keep open the Red Sea for reinforcements from India; or should it concentrate in the Eastern Mediterranean to interrupt Italy's communications with Libya and its Black Sea trade? Should Malta be defended; what would be the role of naval forces in the Western Mediterranean? And how might the allies exploit Italy's strategic weaknesses: the vulnerability of its industrial north to air attack; its dependence on sea-borne trade; its exposed colonial communications and the isolation of its East African army?

These questions remained undecided because they turned on the co-operation of France, and the staff talks that had taken place over the summer of 1938 had excluded, at British insistence, any discussion of the Mediterranean or of a hostile Italy. Consequently, neither side had a clue as to the other's intentions. The British, for instance, had no knowledge of French plans in Tunisia where fourteen divisions stood behind the Mareth line. Nor had they any indication of the planned dispositions of the French fleet. An emergency exchange of vice-admirals was ordered to facilitate naval talks, but the only important decision taken committed the French to retain two capital ships in Atlantic ports. The best information received, and this very general, came late in September, during General Gamelin's visit to London. The English learned that the French expected a hostile Italy and that this would tie down forces that should be used against Germany: up to fifteen divisions would have to be kept in Tunisia and the French Alps. Gamelin anticipated Italian air attacks against the French sea-coast and Tunisia and he was anxious about the vulnerability of Suez. Any French offensive across the Alps could not be ordered before spring, but an action against Libya was a possibility (although he also hinted at plans

9   E5603/1/31. (21864).

164

for seizing Spanish Morocco).[10]

One other important strategic question that was left unresolved until late in the day was the effect of Italian neutrality on Britain's plans for economic warfare against Germany. As the Foreign Office informed President Roosevelt, Britain's initial role in a war with Hitler would be the enforcement of a general blockade.[11] The economic warfare plans had recognized that Italy could not be handled vigorously as other neutrals, but they had not suggested any relaxation of contraband control in the Mediterranean. Despite its restricted economic capacity, Italy could act as a channel for German trade and reduce the effectiveness of the British blockade; in fact, a neutral Italy might be more valuable to Germany than an Italy allied in arms. A strict rationing of Italy would probably decide Mussolini on war, so in stark terms the choice came down to a neutral Italy with an ineffective blockade or a hostile Italy with an effective blockade. The Chiefs of Staff provided guidance on this point only a week before Munich, and their position illustrates their anxiety over the Mediterranean:

> In the initial stages of war with Germany, it is of the highest importance that Italy should be kept out, so that we have time to develop our defensive position in the Middle East, having in mind possible future eventualities both in the Mediterranean and Far East. Another very important consideration is that we need time to clear our merchant ships from the Mediterranean.[12]

In other words, so critical was Britain's military situation in the Middle East that the Services were willing to risk the effectiveness of their one trump — their ability to exercise superior naval and economic power against Germany — in order to keep Mussolini on the fence.

Here, in the menace to empire, was a major incentive to resolve the Czechoslovak crisis on Hitler's terms. A study of the documents confirms that weaknesses in home air defences, exaggerated estimates of Nazi air power, and the old fear of the 'knock-out blow' certainly influenced the British political and military leadership in September 1938. But so too did the concurrent crisis in the East Mediterranean and the fear of a Japanese move against Western interests in the Far East.

---

10 Notes of a meeting with Gamelin on military aspects of the Czechoslovakian crisis, 26 September 1938. Includes notes by General Lelong, French military attaché to London.
11 Cf. *D.B.F.P.*, ser. 3, VII, Appendix IV.
12 Sir C. Newall (Chief of Air Staff) to Halifax, 23 September 1938. R7762/899/22. (22438).

The fact uppermost in the minds of British strategists was that they faced the possibility of simultaneous war in three corners of the Empire at a moment when resources were divided among theatres and strained to the very limit. Britain's army was ear-marked for Palestine as much as for France, a fact that militated against any concentration of military force in either theatre; its naval power at its pre-war ebb, the period of danger that had so troubled Chatfield having arrived.[13] London's planners were convinced that they faced not only war on unfavourable terms with Hitler, but also a series of chain-like catastrophes in the Empire overseas. Whether this apocalyptic vision was realistic is not to the point: what matters is that it appears to have been the genuine appreciation of the global situation in London. For a government such as Chamberlain's the threat to the Empire — and here one must also recall the wholly negative attitude of the Dominions[14] — must have loomed at least as large as that across the Channel. It could be argued, indeed, that for such men that threat would be sufficient reason to sacrifice Czech independence and to seek a 'peace at any price'.

In view of the above evidence, it would seem reasonable to assume that Britain's leaders would have set about immediately after their narrow and humiliating brush with disaster to put their imperial defences in some order. There was pressure from the Foreign Office and Services in this direction, but the political leaders blocked any measures that could conceivably have antagonized Mussolini. When, for instance, the Chiefs of Staff urged Halifax to agree to staff talks with the French on joint Mediterranean defence, the Foreign Secretary replied that 'he was inclined to discourage any extension of the scope of staff conversations in regard to help by this country to France, although he might be willing that Staff conversations should be extended to cover French assistance to this country'.[15] That at least had the virtue of frankness, if not selflessness. Halifax and Chamberlain felt that Mussolini's willingness to assist their capitulation at Munich fully

13 See Duff Cooper, 'The Naval Situation', 2 September 1938. Cab.21/591: 'The critical period of international relations through which Europe is now passing could not have arisen at a time less desirable from a naval point of view.' Just 10 capital ships were fully operational at this time.

14 For a pessimistic military appreciation of likely Dominion assistance, see the memorandum by Pownall in the 1938 volume of his diaries. Also, D. C. Watt, 'The influence of the Commonwealth on British foreign policy: the case of the Munich crisis', in *Personalities and policies* (London, 1965), essay eight.

15 Cab. Conclusions, 22 November 1938. Cab.23/96; C.O.S./261st mtg., 10 November 1938. Cab.53/10.

vindicated their past appeasement of Italy, and they were determined — as their decisions to implement the Easter Pact and to chase the 'general settlement' will-'o-the-wisp to Rome demonstrated — to exhaust the possibilities of a conciliatory policy before entering into strategic co-operation with the French. Even the Foreign Office's modest attempt to replace the standing assumption of Italy's neutrality in the event of war with a more realistic assessment was not integrated into official doctrine until early 1939.[16]

The most telling critique of strategy came from the Mediterranean station itself. In a series of dispatches written in November 1938, Admiral Pound argued that had war broken out in the Mediterranean, British forces in the Mediterranean would have been subjected to severe attrition by Italian aircraft, submarines and light surface vessels. The vulnerability of Malta and the absence of repair facilities in the East Mediterranean would add to the naval difficulties and impede efforts to interrupt Italy's sea communications. He was convinced that British and French grand strategy should be revised to include a two-front invasion of Libya by Anglo–Dominion and French forces on the out-break of war. This action would have far-reaching political effects among the minor powers of the Mediterranean and would also ameliorate the problem of naval communications. It might even bring about the early elimination of Italy from the war. Pound requested large increases in the light naval vessels, including submarines, attached to his command and concluded that, next to these, the most 'vital and urgent need on the Mediterranean Station' was the formulation of a general war plan.[17]

This was the first official reference in British strategy to a Mediterranean offensive, later to become a central theme of the 1939 debates on grand strategy. The role of the fleet was not outlined in detail, but Pound seems to have envisaged a conservative policy of supply, control of vital zones and some harassment of Italian trade and communications. His accompanying analysis of Mediterranean strategy

16 The Foreign Office argued that Germany was in such a strong position to influence Italian policy that planning should be based on the new assumption that, 'although Italy is anxious to keep out of a general European conflagration, her entry into the war on the side of Germany must be regarded as the most likely hypothesis'. C.I.D. Paper No. J.I.C. 78, 16 November 1938.
17 Pound to Admiralty, disp. Med. 01061/0708/9, 14 November 1938. Adm. 116/3900.

— discussed earlier[18] — emphasized the disadvantages of convoy and naval warfare 'on the most distant station'. Pound's dispatches and another proposal to concentrate the Mediterranean Fleet in the Western Mediterranean in time of war were discussed at a special conference on naval strategy held at the Admiralty in November 1938. The naval staff demonstrated that the limited land and air forces available for Egypt could only hope to fulfil their defensive tasks; the fleet would be needed in the eastern basin to harass Italian communications and to control the Suez approaches.[19] However, this was not the last word on the subject.

The sea lords, now under the direction of Admiral Sir Roger Backhouse, Chatfield's successor as Chief of Naval Staff, knew well enough that the adoption of an offensive strategy for the Mediterranean would carry important implications for naval policy in general, particularly in the Far East. It will be recalled that when the Chiefs of Staff were asked by the Australians in 1937 to examine the possibility of an Italian intervention during a Pacific crisis, they replied that, even though security in the Mediterranean would be jeopardized, no anxieties or risks in that region would be permitted to interfere with the dispatch of the main fleet to Singapore.[20] This statement, it has been argued, amounted to a wider formulation of a long-standing political and strategic commitment to the Far Eastern Dominions. And as the decision to give the Far East strategic priority had actually been a political decision, so any reversal of priorities or change of strategy in one theatre would inevitably create friction within the Commonwealth.

In Australia, as it happened, the contradiction between Britain's capabilities and its far-flung commitments had become the subject of some anxious debate during the Far Eastern crisis of late 1937. Chamberlain's speech of 8 March 1938 on the priorities of defence had brought troubled queries from that Dominion,[21] and during the

18 Cf., Chapter 4.
19 E. Bridges to Cadogan, 25 November 1938. C14653/13/17. (21592). This letter shows that the entire range of Mediterranean strategy was under review. No minutes of the conference are to be found, but the outcome of the meeting — which Pound attended — is recorded in a plans division note of December, P.D. 07306/38. Adm. 116/3900. Also see, Maj. Gen. I. S. O. Playfair, *The war in the Mediterranean and Middle East* (London, 1954), pp. 17–18.
20 C.O.S. 590, 31 May 1937. Cab.53/31.
21 J. A. Lyons to N. Chamberlain, tel. received 10 March 1938. Reply of 11 March. Premier 1/309.

summer the Australians — evidently uncertain about the British guarantee — remained undecided about their own strategic policy. Backhouse later recalled that at the time of the September war scare the Australians had been in a 'state of agitation' over their defences. Stanley Bruce, the High Commissioner, had been in daily contact with his government and had had several meetings with the British naval staff. Australia had requested, and had been refused, the immediate dispatch of a battleship to Eastern waters.[22] Whether this was the source of Bruce's frenetic diplomatic activity during the Czech crisis is unclear,[23] but he confessed to Backhouse in November that he personally doubted the credibility of the naval guarantee. In his own recollection of these conversations, Bruce recalled that the naval staff had assured him that a fleet of at least seven capital ships would immediately move to Singapore in the event of trouble with Japan, regardless of the Mediterranean situation.[24]

Seen against the background of the growing crises in Central Europe and the Mediterranean, and in view of England's diminished strength in capital ships, these reassurances were probably ill-considered. A reversal of a key principle of imperial defence could not, of course, come from the naval staff, but it would surely have been more astute to admit the grave problems that Bruce himself had detected in British strategic doctrine. At the very least, they should have been placed before the C.I.D. and Cabinet. Once again, however, the bulky and uncritical defence committee system failed to generate a timely debate on a vital aspect of strategy.[25] What was wanting in the post-Munich period was a general reappraisal of grand strategy, much like those undertaken in 1934 and 1935 by the old Defence Requirements Sub-committee; but by the time this was finally begun, in March 1939, the opportunity for reflective analysis had passed and the debate was caught up in an atmosphere of crisis and near-panic.

In part because of this delay, by February 1939 British naval doctrine was still mired in the orthodox response to the 'worst possible

---

[22] C.O.S./267th mtg., 13 January 1939. Cab.53/10.

[23] Cf. Watt, 'The influence of the Commonwealth on British foreign policy: the case of the Munich crisis', *op. cit.*

[24] Record of a meeting held at the Dominions Office, 11 July 1939. Annex to C.I.D./362d mtg., 26 June 1939. Cab.2/9.

[25] Oliver Harvey blamed Inskip for these failings: 'the C.I.D. machine with Inskip in command goes slower and slower, the Committee for Impeding Defence as Strang calls it. Inskip must certainly go.' Harvey, *The diplomatic diaries of Oliver Harvey*, p. 229.

case', war on three fronts:

> A British Fleet would have to be sent to the Far East to give cover to
> New Zealand, Australia, our Eastern possessions and to our com-
> munications in the Indian Ocean, including those to Egypt and the
> Middle East, while sufficient naval strength would be retained in
> home waters to contain the German Fleet. We should have to
> depend on the French Fleet to restrict Italian naval action in the
> Mediterranean.[26]

This was standard and familiar stuff, taken almost verbatim from the
D.R.C. text. Yet just two weeks later, while discussing the same 'worst
possible case', Backhouse mentioned that it might be some time before
a fleet could move to Singapore: hence, that base's seventy-day 'period
before relief' would have to be increased.[27] What had brought about
this sudden and radical departure from a basic principle of grand
strategy?

The answer was to be found in the convergence of a new set of
diplomatic circumstances with a developing debate among naval
planners over the fleet's correct dispositions. Late in January, following
the visit of Chamberlain and Halifax to Rome and amidst rumours of
an impending German menace to Holland, the Foreign Policy Committee finally authorized staff conversations to proceed with France on
the hypothesis of war against Germany and Italy in combination.
Chamberlain ordered joint plans to be formulated for the Mediterranean
and Middle East in particular, even though it was recognized that this
would mean 'a far more binding commitment than has hitherto been
contemplated'.[28] Then, on 6 February, during the tense conclusion of
the Spanish war, Chamberlain − at Halifax's urging − declared publicly
'that the solidarity of interest by which France and this country are
united, is such that any threat to the vital interests of France from
whatever quarter it came must evoke the immediate cooperation of this
country'.[29]

At the same time, misgivings were being expressed within the
Admiralty about the navy's capacity to handle concurrent crises in two
hemispheres. As Chatfield had warned, the capital-ship situation had
steadily worsened because of the naval modernization scheme, and 1939
was to be the worst year. A dramatic improvement would occur in 1941,

[26] C.O.S. Paper No. 832, 1 February 1939. Cab.4/29.
[27] C.O.S./276th mtg., 15 February 1939. Cab.53/10.
[28] F.P.(36)/36th mtg., 26 January 1939. Cab.27/24.
[29] Dilks, *The diaries of Sir Alexander Cadogan*, p. 147.

but for the present the fleet's strength would not exceed twelve capital ships before September 1939, when *Renown* would finish construction. Of the twelve, *Revenge* and *Hood* were refitting and would rejoin the fleet in late summer. For the first half of 1939, then, the Royal Navy would be led by just ten capital ships. But by April the German fleet would be able to dispose two battle-cruisers and three pocket-battleships of the *Deutschland* class. To contain these and to prevent an escape by the fast German raiders onto the Atlantic trade routes, the naval staff estimated that they would require at least six capital ships in home waters. This would leave just four (later five, perhaps six) ships to lead a Far Eastern fleet, and such a force would not be large enough to engage the Japanese fleet. Also, if England was already at war with Italy the formation of a Far Eastern fleet and its evacuation from the Mediterranean would be a difficult and dangerous operation involving delays.[30]

These calculations explained the presence of the most controversial paragraph in the 'European Appreciation, 1939–40', a major strategic review that the Chiefs of Staff presented to the C.I.D. on 24 February 1939. The otherwise orthodox discussion of the Far East concluded on a jarring and apparently contradictory note:

an assurance was given at the Imperial Conference in 1937 that in the event of war with Japan we should send an adequate fleet to Eastern waters irrespective of the situation elsewhere, and the Dominions of Australia and New Zealand rely primarily upon that promise for their security. The strength of that fleet must depend upon our resources and the state of the war in the European theatre.[31]

Chamberlain promptly noted that this seemed to conflict with the 'categorical and unqualified' 1937 guarantee: should the Dominions be warned of the new situation? Admiralty spokesmen dwelt at length on the capital-ship position and on the dangers of abandoning the French

---

[30] Backhouse, 'The Dispatch of a Fleet to the Far East', Paper No. S.A.C. 4, 28 February 1939. Cab.16/209. An earlier indication of this thinking may be found in a naval briefing of October 1938. F10819/10819/61. (22176). See Adm. 1/9897 for the fleet's planned dispositions in event of war on three fronts before the 1939 decisions. When the two German battle-cruisers came into commission in 1938 the Admiralty had returned its own battle-cruisers – stationed in the West Mediterranean since 1936 – to home waters. Adm. 1/9919.

[31] Chiefs of Staff, 'European Appreciation, 1939–40', Paper No. D.P.(P)44, 20 February 1939. Cab.16/183A.

in the Mediterranean, and for the first time raised the possibility of a movement of the American Pacific fleet to Honolulu. Lord Chatfield, Inskip's newly appointed successor as Minister for Co-ordination of Defence, attacked the new policy as unduly pessimistic: on the basis of an appreciation, Chatfield remarked somewhat irrelevantly, Nelson's inferior fleet would have lost the battle of Trafalgar. It would be far better to suffer losses in the Mediterranean than to permit Japan to seize control of the western Pacific and Indian Ocean. Moreover, he added, any weakening of the Far Eastern guarantee would raise political problems within the Commonwealth.

A second theme of this key debate concerned Mediterranean strategy. The appreciation, accepting most of the arguments of Pound, Lampson and others, recommended a policy of self-sufficiency in the Middle East. In order to ease the difficulties of reinforcement, and to meet the possibility of a naval evacuation of the Mediterranean, the Services proposed to raise British army establishments in the Mid-east to a level where they could deal for up to three months with 'a considerable degree of disaffection among the Arabs while at the same time meeting the maximum possible scale of land attack from Libya'.[32] The central recommendation was for the creation of a reserve 'Colonial Division' in Palestine from the Middle East infantry brigade already there and from a second brigade. Co-ordination of intelligence, communications and command would be improved within the theatre. Only small increases in air strength were possible; nevertheless, the Chiefs of staff argued, British naval and land forces might, in concert with the French, be able to bring immediate pressure to bear against Italy.[33]

At Chatfield's suggestion a special Strategical Appreciation Sub-committee (S.A.C.) of the C.I.D. was created to study the 'European Appreciation', to organize a new set of strategic priorities and to recommend policy for the British delegation to the Anglo—French staff talks, scheduled to open at the end of March. The new committee was to meet weekly over the critical six-week period from 1 March to 17 April 1939, and, as such, it came to play an important role in British policy-making during the Prague and Albanian crises. Its advice to the Foreign Policy Committee on the question of guarantees in South-East Europe and the Mediterranean has already been noted. But it was also the source of new initiatives in Anglo—American relations. Politics and

32 *Ibid.* para 176.
33 C.I.D./348th mtg., 24 February 1939. Cab.2/8.

diplomacy, in fact, so dominated the S.A.C. debates that strategy was given a hasty and superficial review. Unrealistic policies were recommended because they seemed politically attractive and there was a good deal of amateurish dabbling in grand strategy. It developed that the Mediterranean was the source of most of the confusion and ignorance, and so much of this persisted over the summer that it is no exaggeration to say that England and France went to war without a Mediterranean strategy.

The earliest S.A.C. meetings, held before the Prague crisis, saw the Admiralty, supported by the Chiefs of Staff and Foreign Office, press for a revisionist naval strategy. Arguing that correct strategy demanded the concentration of decisive strength at the decisive point at the decisive moment, the naval staff wanted to 'hold two of our enemies with a minimum of strength while delivering a crushing blow against the third'.[34] If England and France could strike Italy hard at the outbreak of hostilities, Italy might be quickly eliminated and the course of the war greatly changed. Backhouse and Lord Stanhope, the First Lord, sketched a Mediterranean naval offensive: Turkey must be brought in and the Dardanelles closed to Italian trade; and in the western basin, Italo—German sea-borne trade could easily be strangled at Gibraltar, unless hostile submarines were based in Spain; the fleet would not idle at Alexandria but would move quickly to harass Italy's communications and to bombard the Libyan seaboard. Italy could be 'pinched out' by such a strategy — supported by France and by land and air offensives — and the Mediterranean cleared at the outset of war. Ships could then be released for duty in the Far East. The Foreign Office supported this policy, as such a display of force must have a positive political effect, especially on Greece, Turkey, Egypt and the other Arab states; whereas an evacuation of the Mediterranean would have serious repercussions, especially on Anglo—French relations. The revisionists further argued that the 1937 commitments on the Far East were 'optimistic' now because Italian neutrality could no longer be assumed and imperial security was menaced by Arab nationalism. However, the C.I.D. should inform the American Government of the changed strategic situation in the hope that Roosevelt would order the fleet to Honolulu.

Chatfield, architect and now lone advocate of orthodox strategy,

---

[34] Cf. memos by Drax and Stanhope, Adm. 1/9897. Stanhope hinted at another motive of the Admiralty when he noted it was important to impress the public: if not, 'we shall not get many more capital ships'.

attacked these theses, but his argument, though fervent, was grounded more in emotional imperialism than in reality. He made the interesting revelation that the naval staff had supported the categorical guarantee of the Dominions in 1937, not only to encourage them to support imperial defence, but also to prevent them re-insuring with the United States. England must not retreat from this guarantee: far better to risk the Mediterranean than the Empire itself. France, he went on, should be forced to assume greater naval commitments in the Mediterranean and Atlantic.[35] But Chatfield lacked the authority of his old position as well as the support of his old ally on strategic issues, Sir Maurice Hankey (who had retired in 1938); and there was in any case no effective way to rebut the Admiralty's point that Britain's naval capabilities had not kept pace with its commitments.

Influential unofficial strategists participated as well in the grand strategy debates and seem to have contributed to the shaping of official thinking, particularly on the 'Mediterranean first' issue. Admiral Sir Herbert Richmond privately advised the naval staff to attack sea communications and he had also advocated naval bombardments of the Italian coast.[36] Captain Liddell Hart's articles in *The Times* returned to a favourite theme: an attack on the 'soft spots' of an enemy coalition would bring victory indirectly and with an economy of force. His historical 'lessons' directly influenced offensive-minded planners at the Admiralty.[37] Another active proselytizer was Winston Churchill, who advocated a Mediterranean offensive in his 'Memorandum on Sea-Power, 1939', sent to Halifax and Chamberlain near the end of March. 'England's first battlefield', Churchill pronounced, 'is the Mediterranean.'

> All plans for sealing up the ends must be discarded in favour of decisive victory there. Our forces alone should be sufficient to drive the Italian ships from the sea, and secure complete command of the

---

[35] S.A.C./1st and 2d mtgs., 1 March and 13 March 1939. Cab.16/209. Also, Foreign Office notes in W3784/108/50. (23981), and Foreign Office to Admiralty, 22 March 1939. W4831, *ibid.*

[36] Richmond to Drax, 4 January 1939. Archives of Admiral Sir R. A. R. Plunkett-Ernle-Erle-Drax. Churchill College, Cambridge. Box 2/File 8.

[37] See, for example, Liddell Hart's article in *The Times*, 8 February 1939. Drax, referring to this analysis, remarked that, applying the same rule to the next war, it would be easier and quicker to smash Italy. The plans division, of which he was a member, worked out detailed plans for naval attacks of strategic centres on the Italian coast. See memoranda of February and March in Drax Archives, Box 2/File 11.

Mediterranean, certainly within two months, possibly sooner . . .
Not to hold the Mediterranean would be to expose Egypt and the
Canal, as well as the French possessions, to invasion by Italian troops
with German leadership. We cannot tolerate this on any account.
Moreover a series of swift and striking victories in this theatre,
which might be obtainable in the early weeks of the war, would
have a most healthy and helpful bearing upon the main struggle with
Germany.[38]

It was a timely intervention, which may well have influenced the outcome of the S.A.C. debates. 'I find my thoughts going very much with
yours,' Halifax replied. Chamberlain discussed the idea with Churchill
and was assured by Chatfield — now converted — that the strategy was
sound, although it might take up to six months to finish Italy.[39]

Within a month of its appearance as a serious proposal, and with
remarkable ease, the nebulous concept of a Mediterranean offensive had
been circulated among, and accepted by, the British political and
military leadership.[40] It is within this context, this radically changed
climate of strategic opinion, that the Government's response to the
events of mid-March and early April must be analysed. In the new
strategy of an attack on the 'soft spot' of the Axis, commitments could
be an asset rather than a liability, and in some cases — Turkey, for
instance — mutual guarantees were an absolute necessity. The construction of a guarantee system in South-East Europe and the East
Mediterranean was a logical counterpart to an offensive war strategy.
If Chamberlain continued to hope that Mussolini would stay out of war,
he nevertheless was beginning to take out insurance against the failure
of appeasement. This emerges most clearly from a brief analysis of his

---

38 W. Churchill, 'Memorandum on Sea-Power, 1939', 25 March 1939. Premier
1/345. Copies were sent to Chamberlain and Halifax on 27 March and the
paper was forwarded to the embassy in Washington as representative of
official thinking. Publicly, Churchill asserted that it might be a definite
advantage to have Italy as an enemy: Germany would find it a liability and
it would make an easy and vulnerable target. *New York Herald Tribune*,
14 April 1939.
39 Premier 1/345; and W5721/108/50 (23982).
40 For instance, Oliver Harvey wrote in his diary on 20 March: 'One thing
certain, that Italy ought to be dealt with drastically if she shows signs of
moving against us. If we knock out Italy, the Mediterranean and the Balkans
are relieved and we shall be free to deal with Japan and Germany . . . So long
as Italy is actively hostile or doubtful, we cannot send ships off to Far East
or be sure of Canal or Egypt, valuable forces being pinned down for defence
in the Mediterranean.' *The diplomatic diaries of Oliver Harvey*, p. 265.

attempt to draw the United States into the Far Eastern vacuum.

During the crisis of September 1938 Franklin Roosevelt and Ambassador Joseph Kennedy had arranged to keep two American cruisers stationed conspicuously in British waters. A month later Roosevelt used his closest English friend, Colonel Arthur Murray, the Liberal M.P., to pass a message of support to Neville Chamberlain. If Britain became involved in war with the dictatorships, it would have — in so far as the President could achieve it — the industrial resources of the United States behind it. America would be forced to resist any attack on Canada and events might also force it to protect Australia.[41] This background is essential to an understanding of Chamberlain's next moves. In the aftermath of the Prague occupation, the Australians were again highly nervous about their own defence: Prime Minister Lyons had telephoned Chamberlain personally to inquire into English intentions. On the same day — 19 March — Chamberlain told a group of ministers that, on recalling Roosevelt's 'very friendly attitude in Naval affairs', he wondered whether Dominion fears might be eased through another approach in Washington. If war broke out in Europe, the United States might be asked to dispatch a fleet to Honolulu to deter Japan.[42] Next day Chamberlain began to extricate himself from the binding 1937 guarantee: in the event of war against Germany, Italy and Japan, 'a combination never envisaged in our earlier plans', he wired the Australians, the size of the British Far Eastern fleet would depend on the timing of Japan's entry into the war and the losses suffered by England and its opponents in the Mediterranean and Europe.[43] At the same moment, however, two approaches were being made to America.

During the previous winter, most of the American Pacific fleet had been temporarily transferred to the Atlantic for exercises in the Caribbean, and also to honour the World Fair in New York. The British naval staff, facing the possibility of war in Europe, were anxious that the U.S. fleet be returned to its Pacific stations and, if possible, move to Honolulu: this, they felt, might well deter Japan from advancing against British interests. Halifax and Chatfield accordingly informed Kennedy of the dilemmas of naval strategy and of the new plan to start

---

[41] On 14 December 1938 Murray passed on these messages to Chamberlain — who was 'delighted' by the reference to American industrial resources and 'highly interested' in those to the Dominions. Murray's memorandum and other material on this informal exchange are in Premier 1/367. I am grateful to D. C. Watt for information from the papers of Lord Murray.

[42] Note of a conference, 19 March 1939. C3859/15/18. (22967).

[43] Chamberlain to Lyons, tel. of 20 March 1939. Premier 1/309.

war operations against Italy: to facilitate this, would the United States consider returning their fleet to the Pacific 'at the psychological moment' to keep Japan quiet?[44] Roosevelt replied that he would announce in mid-April that the fleet was being moved back to the Pacific.[45] The British had made a separate *démarche* through Lindsay in Washington to the effect that the Anglo–American naval conversations broken off in January 1938 should be resumed. A warning was added that the European situation might restrict the navy's ability to reinforce Singapore. Again Roosevelt agreed, this time with the condition that absolute secrecy be ensured.[46]

These were encouraging developments. Roosevelt's attitude promised relief from Dominion pressures and from the oppressive burden of defending the Far East. This must have been of great psychological importance at a moment when the British were contemplating far-reaching political commitments nearer home and a concentrated strategy in the event of war. For the weakest link in the 'Mediterranean first' policy was the threat of a Japanese intervention, and Roosevelt now seemed willing to strengthen this link. The way was open for the construction of a peace front in Europe that could be turned into a war alliance, especially in the Mediterranean.

The fact that the British leaders, including Chamberlain and Halifax, had been contemplating a much more positive strategy in the event of war explains something of their actions in the aftermath of Hitler's Prague *coup* in mid-March. It makes some sense of their eagerness to accept a whole new set of commitments in Europe and the Mediterranean, commitments that a month earlier would have been direct conflict with strategy. To put it another way, it was the revolution in British strategy that cleared the way for the diplomatic revolution of late March–early April 1939. On the other hand, it is also true that the Chamberlain Cabinet were 'pushed along by events',[47]

44 Kennedy to Cordell Hull, 22 March 1939. F.R.U.S., 1939, II, p. 88. The Commonwealth High Commissioners were told of this action, but Halifax warned them it was very private and they should 'forget it'. C4415/15/18. (22968).

45 Lindsay to Halifax, tel. No. 130, 24 March 1939. F2942/456/23. (23560).

46 Halifax to Lindsay, tel. No. 131, 19 March 1939; and Lindsay to Halifax, tel. No. 124, 21 March 1939. F2879/F2880/456/23. (23560). The British Cabinet were apparently not told about the staff talks and Kennedy was not consulted; at the Washington end, Sumner Welles and Roosevelt dealt with Lindsay: Cordell Hull was evidently kept in the dark, probably because of his adverse reaction to the exposure of the earlier Ingersoll conversations.

47 Taylor, *The origins of the Second World War*, p. 254.

rumours and public opinion in a psychological atmosphere of great uncertainty. A system of guarantees designed to bolster a Mediterranean offensive would clearly not have included Poland, or even Roumania. The Polish guarantee, as the war amply demonstrated, was undertaken by Chamberlain without reference to British strategic capabilities: it could not be directly implemented and was actually a rather contrived bluff. In fact, as will be seen, the British and French military staffs intended to fulfil their commitments to Poland *indirectly* via the Mediterranean offensive!

The Albanian *coup*, of course, only reinforced the trend in British policy that argued for decisive action in the Mediterranean. The vital *point d'appui* was Turkey, whose assistance must be won, even at the cost of a parallel guarantee to Greece. The Admiralty again urged the importance of the return of the American fleet to the Pacific,[48] especially in the light of French panic over the Mediterranean. Both Daladier and Bonnet warned the British Ambassador that Albania was the prelude to a big Axis offensive from the North Sea to Egypt. The French were particularly anxious that Britain should not abandon the Mediterranean in case of war: this would be 'catastrophic'. The allied forces should concentrate on winning the war in the Mediterranean through the quick defeat of Italy.[49] A message was passed from Paris to London via the U.S. Navy Department to the effect that France would immediately make terms with Germany if the Mediterranean Fleet withdrew to Singapore; and the French underlined their point with a major reinforcement of their forces in the Mediterranean, Tunisia and French Somaliland.[50]

In fact, French fears over British naval intentions were groundless. At no time in March or April was the idea of a Far Eastern reinforcement seriously contemplated. On the contrary, the Admiralty had concluded on 5 April that, because of the capital-ship position and the political war of nerves in the Mediterranean,

> ... there are so many variable factors which cannot at present be assessed, that it is not possible to state definitely how soon after Japanese intervention a Fleet could be despatched to the Far East. Neither is it possible to enumerate precisely the size of the fleet that

[48] Notes of a conference, 10 April 1939. W5991/105/80. (23982).
[49] See Phipps' telegrams of 8, 9 and 10 April in *D.B.F.P.*, ser. 3, V., Nos. 96, 103, 106 and 115.
[50] Lindsay to Halifax, tel. No. 163, 11 April 1939. W5922/108/50. (23982); and Gén. Maurice Gamelin, *Servir*, I (Paris, 1946–7), pp. 403–7.

we could afford to send.[51]

The Strategical Appreciation Subcommittee concluded its review of grand strategy in mid-April and Chatfield placed its recommendations before the C.I.D. in early May. His sparse outline articulated the main interlocking themes of the new approach:

> It was not open to question that a capital ship force would have to be sent to the Far East, but whether this could be done to the exclusion of our interests in the Mediterranean was a matter which would have to be decided at the time. If we took on more enemies than we had the strength to combat, we must try to knock out one of them before the others could cause us serious injury. As regards the question of whether we could knock out Italy before the Japanese caused us irreparable damage, the stationing of the United States Navy in the Pacific was an important factor.

The political situation had undergone a drastic change and England was now committed to Greece, Turkey and Roumania. Chamberlain supported the new approach, arguing that the defeat of Britain would seal the fate of the Dominions, and Halifax contributed an optimistic assessment of the Far East. With a million men in China and their resources impaired after two years of war, the Japanese 'would think very carefully before embarking on any further major aggressive enterprise'. On this sanguine note, soon to be rudely dispelled, the C.I.D. approved the new strategic doctrine and ordered two further initiatives to strengthen the Far East: America was to be informed of the new strategy, and Singapore's reserves and defences would be reviewed.[52]

Thus, in a matter of some nine weeks, British grand strategy, whose principles had gone virtually unchallenged for years, had been revised fundamentally. The key was to be found in the global naval situation, particularly in the dynamics of the German and British naval rearmament programmes. The German navy was now regarded by the Admiralty with real alarm, and not simply because of Hitler's denunciation of the Anglo–German Naval Agreement on 28 April. In the event of war with Germany and Italy, the naval staff planned to leave *seven* of their ten capital ships in home waters, and this would be increased to nine as the two ships on extended notice rejoined the fleet.

---

[51] 'Despatch of a Fleet to the Far East', S.A.C. Paper No. 16, 5 April 1939. Cab. 16/209.
[52] C.I.D./355th mtg., 2 May 1939. Cab.2/8.

The threat of an escape by the new German raiders into the Atlantic was the new element in the Admiralty's equations.[53] It left very few ships for duty elsewhere and it would be futile and dangerous to evacuate the Mediterranean in order to send a small fleet against Japan. Better to knock out Italy, clear the Mediterranean and then attend to the Far East where, hopefully, America would keep Japan quiet.

It was via this circuitous route that the naval staff arrived at the idea of the Mediterranean offensive. As an exercise in logic it was almost French in conception, but as practical strategy it was open to question on several counts. First, could France and Britain co-ordinate a strategy and allocate the forces needed to eliminate Italy in the early stages of a war? Second, what would happen in the event of a fresh crisis in the Far East, particularly if America failed to play its assigned role? Third, how would the contingency of Italy's neutrality be handled? And finally, what contribution would the strategy make to the main European struggle? Was it a strategy for victory or a strategy for avoiding Continental commitments?

[53] Revised section of Admiralty war memorandum (eastern); about May 1939. Adm. 116/3863. The 10 ships would be disposed as follows: North Sea—5; Channel—2; East Mediterranean—3. In other documents the naval staff argued the need to keep 'at least six' heavy ships in home waters.

7. A Summer of Illusions

The grand strategy approved by the British Committee of Imperial Defence in May of 1939 was the offspring of global weakness and the ancient psychological tendency of men under duress not to question that which they wish to hear.

There thus coexisted within the strategy factual and dispassionate analyses of the increasingly grave military equation, on one hand, and, on the other, a hastily conceived 'solution' to the equation whose assumptions and implications had scarcely been probed. Illusions and superficial thinking had a good deal to do with the adoption of the 'Mediterranean first' policy and with the resultant confusion and inactivity that typified allied strategy in the early months of World War II.

London's joint military planners had warned in late March that this could well be the case when they were instructed to formulate plans 'to knock Italy out of the war at the outset'. They responded by refuting the entire strategy. In the first place, strategic initiative rested with the strongest powers, and in the early stages of a war this meant the Axis. Before England and France could develop an offensive they must first secure their home territories and colonies. Germany was estimated — and here a severe intelligence error compounded caution — to have twice the striking power of the combined Anglo—French air forces, so that few bombers could be spared for operations against Italy. Land operations across the Alps would pose great difficulties and an offensive against Libya would not necessarily force Mussolini to the peace table. Italy's manifest weaknesses could certainly be exploited through the allies' superior naval and economic power, but probably not soon enough to defeat it 'at the outset'. More fundamentally, the joint planners pointed out, the S.A.C. strategy ignored the principles of grand strategy worked out in three years of continued study. They and the Chiefs of Staff had always argued that Britain's initial strategy must be mainly *defensive*, and this applied to the Mediterranean. Italy would be defeated, but not immediately. There was grave danger in reversing this strategy as the result of 'a hasty review in time of crisis.[1]

---

1 Joint Planning Subcommittee, 'Allied Plans Against Italy', J.P. 382, 27 March 1939. Cab.55/15. In their warning on the 'Military Implications of an Anglo—

This reproachful assessment of the new policy appears to have gone completely unheeded. Probably it went unread too — along with a similar warning to the planners on guarantees to Roumania and Poland. That was unfortunate, for not only was the appreciation an accurate portrayal of British capabilities, but it also correctly anticipated that France would give priority to its own defence. At the first sessions of the Anglo—French staff talks in London the French sketched out a strategy in three phases. The first objective of French policy would be to resist an Axis offensive, to stand on the defensive behind the Maginot Line and develop its reserve strength. The next objective would be to 'encircle' the enemy and to exert economic pressure. And finally, when resources were ready and a favourable moment presented itself, France would move to the counter-offensive. But it would not be against Germany: 'The most profitable objective for a counter-offensive would be found in Italy.'[2]

The French and British staffs had both argued that a second front must be opened up to relieve pressure on Poland. This was a question of self-interest, for if the Poles were easily defeated Germany would then attack in the West. But where, if Germany was not to be attacked directly, would this front be created? The answer was: in the Mediterranean! To the French an offensive against Italy might open up a flank from which to attack Germany. They had detected a 'weak point in Germany's defensive armour':

> The result of successful operations against Italy would be to open up Germany's weak flank, namely, Austria and Czechoslovakia, a part of the country which, though difficult for military operations had not been fully assimilated into the German Reich.[3]

The British learned that the French had even maintained, in staff talks with the Poles, that a Mediterranean offensive would directly assist Polish defence — or so the British military attaché in Paris was told by Colonel Petibon, Gamelin's aide:

> The thesis which is being maintained by the French is that their main offensive must be initially in the Mediterranean area and not against Germany, and the advantage to Poland from such a course is that

French Guarantee to Poland and Roumania', J.P. 387, 28 March 1939. *Ibid.*, the planners noted that Italian hostility might be a net liability for Hitler but it would also compound England's military dilemma.

2 Anglo—French staff conversations (A.F.C.) 1939, 2d mtg., 29 March 1939. Cab.29/160.

3 A.F.C. 1939/13th mtg., 3 May 1939. *Ibid.*

success will enable her to be supplied via the Mediterranean and Black Sea.

The road from Paris to Warsaw was clearly going to be circuitous. The French added that they would also create 'diversions' on the western front to draw German divisions away from Poland. The Poles were reportedly 'a little disappointed that the French were not prepared to go bald-headed for the Germans, but the French had maintained their point of view that the first offensive must be in the Mediterranean area'.[4]

What the Poles were not told — but the English knew — was that France had no intention of attacking Italy proper in the early stages of a war. A French staff paper acknowledged that Mussolini's swift defeat would require a major land and air offensive against Italy, particularly its industrial north. An attack could be mounted by twenty-five to thirty French divisions across the Alps, but only from June to September and not before France had received 'considerable' reinforcements from England.[5] Most of the French air force would be needed on the western front and there would be no chance for a systematic air campaign against Italy. Conditions were far more favourable for an offensive from Tunisia — where France had fourteen divisions that would be used in North Africa — against Libya, but this would depend upon the attitude to Spanich Morocco. The French, it emerged, were deeply concerned about British weakness in the Middle East, and argued that it menaced French interests in the area. France needed a secure Suez Canal to transport 4 million tons of oil a year from the Mosul oil-fields and to supply its forces in Syria.[6]

Like their British counterparts, French military planners had no

4 The attaché's letter to the War Office of 18 May is quoted in paper D.P.(P.) 59. Petibon added that 'should the German offensive be made in the West, the Poles are to take the offensive. In this case the French make no suggestions as to objectives, but suggest only that they should not be too ambitious and that there should be no question of trying to reach Berlin in a day'. The last piece of advice was probably unnecessary in view of the fact that any Polish offensive would have to come from the horse cavalry!
5 French delegation, 'General Appreciation of the Problem of an Offensive Against Italy', 31 March 1939. Cab.29/160.
6 A.F.C. 1939/5th mtg., 31 March 1939. *Ibid.*; also, Anglo–French naval staff conversations, 2d mtg., 31 March 1939. *Ibid.* From the latter the British learned that the main French fleet would be based at Mers-el-Kebir, but they failed to get a firm commitment on the dispositions of the two French battle-cruisers, *Strasbourg* and *Dunquerque*, which the Admiralty wanted stationed at Brest for Atlantic duty. There is some information on the staff exchange in Sir J. Slessor, *The central blue* (London, 1956), p. 230–1.

intention of attacking Germany directly, and neither delegation had anything but the vaguest idea of how the directive to 'knock out Italy' was to be implemented. The British were especially vague because there were no Mediterranean war plans in existence when the staff talks began, and regional commanders had passed through the Albanian crisis without even general instructions from London. Only in mid-April were they informed of the proposed objectives of allied operations: to render Italy's position in Libya and Abyssinia untenable; and the methods: at sea, attacks on its colonial communications and control of its maritime trade; on land, Egypt's defence, a French offensive against Libya; and the organization of insurrection among the Tribes of Abyssinia and Libya; in the air, defence, and, where possible, attacks on Italian depots and communications.[7] This was a modest set of plans, invoking the traditional methods of maritime pressure, and it was certainly a more accurate reflection of British capabilities than the nebulous concept of a Mediterranean offensive.

After the Albanian crisis – when English ships were caught loitering in Italian ports – the Mediterranean Fleet was again moved to the eastern basin, primarily because of Pound's fears of a fresh Italo–German 'stunt' but also because of an impending visit by the German navy to Spain.[8] This meant that control of the central sea would not be disputed at the outset of war and Malta would be in jeopardy. Although the military estimate of the Libyan menace had been revised because of British reinforcements and potential French assistance, the Middle East was still far from being the *place d'armes* it became during the war. In the air there was a severe shortage of long-range bombers, as well as fighters, general reconnaissance aircraft and air defences; and any offensive on land was ruled out because of the lack of mechanized forces and artillery.[9] Egypt, however, had been given first priority in the 'European Appreciation' and the services now took a lively interest in the Middle East: co-ordinated command and intelligence were to be established by the summer, and the Chiefs of Staff had agreed to view

7 C.O.S./290th mtg., 19 April 1939. Cab.53/11. These objectives closely resemble those set out in the 'Mediterranean Appreciation' of February 1938, a document reflecting a wholly defensive approach to Mediterranean warfare in the initial stages of a conflict with Italy.

8 Pound to Admiralty, 18 April 1939. Adm. 116/3844.

9 The joint planners admitted in August that regional air forces were 'unduly weak, even if all the expected reinforcements arrive, in comparison with the air forces which Italy can dispose against them'. C.O.S. 932(J.P.), Cab.53/51. Also F.M. Lord Wilson, *Eight years overseas, 1939–1947* (London, 1950).

the region as a single integrated whole, a considerable advance on their earlier complacency. Still, Miles Lampson's pessimistic cables worried that nationalist and neutralist opinion, stirred by unemployment, student dissent and Axis propaganda, would make Egypt an unreliable ally. An Italian invasion supported by heavy air attacks might bring on an internal collapse behind British lines, and the young Egyptian army — in whose ranks the spread of nationalist grievances had been detected — would be a very uncertain element.

After the Italians had sent another 30,000 troops to Libya and had seized Albania, the Egyptian Government panicked, ordered its army mobilized and asked that the British garrison be raised above treaty limits. Lampson, now worrying about the Red Sea route and the role of the Palestine reserve in war, requested the dispatch of a 'Middle East expeditionary force', and, when this was refused, asked for the immediate dispatch of the Indian brigade group ear-marked for war duty in Egypt.[10] That was opposed by the India Office, and the Colonial Office refused to send troops from Palestine.[11] Lampson's constant refrains and his assessments of the military situation (which were not shown to the British military command in Egypt) annoyed the Chiefs of Staff; they pointed out that the Ambassador's all-too-frequent dispatches ignored the Services' other commitments and over-estimated Italy's capacity to attack across the desert. In brief, the strategists made a sharp distinction between the apparent and the actual military threat.[12] There is evidence that Lampson and the Foreign Office could make the same distinction and that they were really trying to use the panic in Egypt to increase the British military garrison beyond the limits of the 1936 treaty. Halifax was told by his advisers 'that the opportunity to increase our garrison in Egypt at the request of the Egyptian Government is one which may never recur, and that if, in quieter times, we were faced with an ill-disposed King and Government we might bitterly regret having thrown away the opportunity'. This forward imperial policy, however, was frustrated until late July when the Chiefs of Staff relented and agreed to the prompt dispatch of force 'Heron'

---

10 See his dispatches and the comments of the Chiefs of Staff, in Cab.21/581.
11 Marquess of Zetland to Halifax, 16 May 1939. J2016/21/16 (23330).
12 Lampson, wrote an official who served with him in Cairo, 'believes from past experience that the War Office are entirely unimaginative and never act except when under political pressure'. J1859/21/16 (23330). At one point Lord Gort, C.I.G.S., used 'picturesque language' to describe Lampson's campaign and asked the Foreign Office to 'tick him off' — a request refused.

from India.[13]

As Pound noted in a fresh appreciation of Mediterranean strategy shortly before leaving that station to succeed Backhouse as Chief of Naval Staff, Britain must stand on the defensive in the Mid-east if war came with Italy. The navy could take the offensive, but it would make its contribution over a period of time and that might be cancelled by attrition from enemy submarine and air attack. From his observation of the wars in China and Spain Pound drew the lesson that warships were far from immune to attack from the air − one of the first assessments by a British naval officer of this 'unknown' factor of warfare on the basis of actual events rather than unverified speculation. Pound's pessimistic conclusions − which essentially confirmed those he had drawn from the convoy exercises of 1937−8 − were a far cry from that complacent attitude of many naval officers to air power which Professor Marder calls the 'valor of ignorance'. Pound went on to argue that Italy was in a strong position to attack Malta, Alexandria and the Mediterranean Fleet, but Anglo−French forces could not retaliate; therefore he called for an allied bombing force to be established in Tunisia where attacks could be made against Sicily and southern Italy. In this way Malta might still be defended and control of the central sea made possible.[14]

In May Anglo−French staff talks were held at the regional level in North Africa, the Middle East and the Red Sea to work out detailed joint plans. The talks on North Africa were held at Rabat between generals Ironside and Nogués, and the outcome proved to be a sharp setback for the prospects for any Mediterranean offensive. The French warned Ironside that Spanich Morocco had been reinforced since Franco's victory in Spain, and this would influence their dispositions. If Spain entered the war with the Axis − Spain had signed the anti-Comitern pact in April − France would seize Spanish Morocco before attacking Libya. Even if it did not, it might be two months before any major offensive could be staged against Tripoli. No amount of persuasion had been able to move the French on this point − which conflicted with their assurances during the London staff talks. Nor were the British able to get a clear picture of French priorities from the other regional meetings. At the conference on the Middle East, for instance,

13 J2093/21/16 (23330); the 'Heron' decision was taken because of the fresh
   crisis with Japan in June and July. C.I.D./367th mtg., 21 July 1939. Cab.2/9.
14 Pound to Admiralty, 'Strategy in the Mediterranean', disp. Med. 0447/031/
   8, 10 May 1939. Adm. 116/3900.

the English learned that they might receive reinforcements from Syria for Egypt's defence, but at the same time the French unveiled a plan for a second Salonica expedition. Pound's proposal for an allied air strike force in Tunisia was considered by the staffs, but because of the overriding menace of German air power neither was willing to release units for duty in southern France or North Africa.[15]

All of this tended to confirm the warnings of the joint planners that the *early* elimination of Italy from an enemy coalition could not be guaranteed. Italy was certainly vulnerable; but, given the situation in Europe, it would be spared the type of direct and overwhelming violence that would force it to surrender or that might bring about internal revolt against the Fascist regime. As the planners summed up in July, 'There are no decisive Military measures that we can take against Italy at the outset ... Italy may well be in a position to hit us more effectively at the outset than we can hit her, by such measures as air attack on Malta and Egypt.' The only kind of operations open to the allies in the early stages of a Mediterranean conflict would be against Italy's colonies, its sea communications and its trade;[16] but even here, where results would tell over the long haul, there were significant obstacles in the way of an effective joint strategy. The lack of agreement between England and France was partly political, involving a dispute over the national and imperial interests that should take priority in planning. But it was also the inevitable reckoning of an attempt to compress into two or three months discussions of planning, coordination, organization and intelligence that should have been covered long before. Here was the fruit of London's earlier indifference to strategic co-operation with the French.

Aside from being a rather dubious proposition of allied strategy, the

---

15 Admiralty to Admiral Cunningham, disp. M04978/39. 6 July 1939. Adm. 116/3900. Accounts of the Anglo–French staff discussions in C.O.S. 209th mtg., 19 July 1939. Cab.53/11; C.I.D. Paper D.P.(P.) 65; and Air 9/116. Naval talks between Admirals Andrew Cunningham and Vice-Admiral Ollive, commanders of the British and French Mediterranean fleets respectively, were held on Malta from 27 to 29 July. Record in Med. disp. 0721/0700/11. 2 August 1939. Adm. 1/9905.

16 Joint Planning subcommittee, 'Plans for Action Against Italy' C.O.S. 942 (J.P.). 12 July 1939. Cab.53/51. Also, Cunningham, *A sailor's Odyssey* (New York, 1951), pp. 210–11. Cunningham, Pound's successor as Mediterranean C.-in-C., recalled that the theory of the 'knock-out blow' against Italy was held in 'political circles' in London. It was, he wrote a 'fallacious belief'. This was overly modest: the theory originated, as we have seen, within the navy and later was propounded by ministers and other political figures.

Mediterranean offensive concept also rested upon two shaky assumptions about the Far East. First, it calculated that Japan would stay quiescent and provoke no further trouble with England. Second, it suggested that Japan would be influenced by American actions and that the United States could be induced to play an activist role in the Far East. This badly misread the intentions of both Washington and Tokyo. In June 1939 – virtually in defiance of Halifax's optimistic appreciation of the Far East in early May – Japanese harassment of the British imperial concession at Tientsin, China, escalated into a serious crisis and exposed England's vulnerability on the circumference of its empire. As in 1937, naval action was debated and, as before, ruled out because of the Mediterranean situation and the size of the available fleet. The crisis also defined the narrow limits of American intervention.

Earlier in the year the Admiralty had dismissed an idea of Sir Robert Craigie, British Ambassador to Japan, to the effect that a squadron of capital ships should be stationed permanently in Singapore. The naval staff had pointed out that the restricted numbers of heavy ships and new commitments in the Mediterranean made Craigie's proposal impossible. Yet they appreciated the political arguments behind the thought:[17] Britain's Far Eastern diplomacy operated in a vacuum of power as the *potential* dispatch of the fleet could not be judged a deterrent or instrument of persuasion. Singapore was a giant, unloaded revolver.

Craigie and the Far Eastern division of the Foreign Office returned to these themes during the Tientsin incident, and the question of a major reinforcement of British naval forces in the Far East came seriously under review in June. In their first appreciations the Chiefs of Staff were totally pessimistic and negative: just two capital ships could be spared and a force of this size would be useless. They were inclined to deprecate naval movements and to seek instead America's active intervention.[18] Chatfield, however, thought this report 'unduly black' and suggested that, if the Government were willing to take the risk involved in evacuating the Mediterranean, a fleet led by seven capital ships might be sent east in mid-September. This would leave five, possibly six, in home waters, but none in the Mediterranean; if Britain withdrew from the latter area the French would probably shift their

---

17 *D.B.F.P.*, ser. 3, VIII, app. I, pp. 542–50: Additional Correspondence on the Naval Situation in the Far East.
18 Chiefs of Staff, 'The Situation in the Far East', C.O.S. 928, 18 June 1939. Annex to D.P.(P.) 61. Cab.16/183A.

two battle-cruisers from Brest to the Mediterranean. This last consideration worried the naval staff who wanted the French ships in the Atlantic where they could help contain Germany's fast raiders. To keep the French at Brest the Admiralty would have to show the flag in the Mediterranean.[19]

The decisive argument against a Far Eastern reinforcement was that the action might trigger diplomatic and political disaster nearer home. If the Mediterranean Fleet moved east, how could the Government's commitments to France, Greece and Turkey be met, and what would be the reaction of Arab nationalists? Above all, would it not create a situation, Chamberlain asked Labour Party leaders, 'in which Hitler would say to Mussolini, "Come on now and drop all these hesitations" '?[20] Once it was evident that the United States would not intervene directly, the choice was stark and painful. For Chamberlain it was

> clear that we could only send an effective Fleet to the Far East at the cost of abandoning our naval position in the Mediterranean. This was conclusive in favour of making every endeavour to reach an early settlement of the dispute at Tientsin. It was clear that we should only be prepared to run the risks involved in sending a Fleet to the Far East if Japan made our position there quite intolerable.[21]

As in late 1937, the Mediterranean sharply restricted Britain's freedom in the Far East and forced it to invite America's support. This came to nothing, however, and the C.I.D. decided to 'shorten British lines' in China; or, as Ambassador Kennedy put it, 'they must back out the best way they can.'[22]

Chamberlain's description of American policy during this difficult period as 'wary but helpful'[23] was accurate enough. Roosevelt was attempting to guide his amendments to the Neutrality Act through Congress and the British understood by now how their own actions and speeches could undermine his hand. Presumably this is what Chamberlain meant when he remarked that the surest way to lose the Americans was

---

[19] C.O.S./304th mtg., 20 June 1939. Cab.53/11; F.P.(36)/52d mtg., 19 June 1939. Cab.27/625; Chiefs of Staff, 'Situation in the Far East', C.O.S. 931, 24 June 1939. Cab.16/183A; Dilks, *The diaries of Sir Alexander Cadogan, 1938–1945, op. cit.* pp. 186–95; and Harvey, *The diplomatic diaries of Oliver Harvey, op. cit.* p. 298.
[20] Dalton Diaries, 28 June 1939.
[21] F.P.(36)/53d mtg., 20 June 1939. Cab.27/625.
[22] F.R.U.S., 1939, V, pp. 205–6; C.I.D./362d mtg., 26 June 1939. Cab.2/9.
[23] Annex to C.I.D. minutes of 362d mtg. *Ibid.*

by running after them.[24] Kennedy noted that Roosevelt would be unable to make any gesture of support in the Far East unless (*a*) American interests were attacked, or (*b*) Germany attacked in the West.[25] Roosevelt's fear of adverse publicity — especially on matters of strategic co-operation — was vividly illustrated by the elaborate precautions taken to secure the June naval staff talks in Washington from the press. Commander T. C. Hampton, the Admiralty's deputed officer, was sent incognito to Washington for talks with the chief of U.S. naval operations, Admiral W. D. Leahy; but it was only with great difficulty that Hampton managed to extract even a personal opinion — let alone any commitment — from the American officer. The Admiralty considered the talks useful[26] — Hampton gave the Americans another frank account of Britain's naval predicament — but it was obvious that planning could not be based on the expectation of U.S. intervention in the Far East. Roosevelt's surprising congressional defeat on the neutrality issue at the end of June was further proof that the United States would remain an indeterminable factor.[27]

This was decisive for British strategy. Every major aspect of grand strategy was complicated by this fresh crisis in the Far East and by Japanese unpredictability. The naval staff were reluctant to give up their Mediterranean offensive, and argued that, even though it might not be possible to 'knock out Italy' in a very short time, allied naval and air forces could greatly weaken its war-making capacity by concentrating attacks on its oil stocks. 'With Turkey on our side it should be possible to prevent any seaborne supplies reaching Italy and it is

---

24 Dalton Diaries, *op. cit.* Dalton reported Chamberlain as saying that the U.S. attitude was 'decisive' because of British naval weakness. America was encouraging Britain to stand firm and helping where it could, but it was not ready for joint action. Chamberlain favoured further aid to China even though it would be lost money.

25 Halifax to Lindsay, tel. No. 647, 27 June 1939. F6469/1/10. Cab.21/569.

26 Hampton's report of 27 June 1939 and Admiralty comments, in Adm. 116/3922. This document is interesting for the light it casts on naval–congressional relations in pre-war Washington. Leahy was extremely nervous — even though the talks were held at his home — and Hampton discovered that the report of the Ingersoll conversations of January 1938 had hardly been read inside the Naval Plans Division: in order that officers called to testify before congressional committees would not have to lie, virtually no one had been willing to read it!

27 The Congress, Chamberlain wrote Tweedsmuir on 7 July in a rare outburst, 'are incorrigible. Their behaviour over the Neutrality Legislation is enough to make one weep, but I have not been disappointed for I never expected any better behaviour from these pig-headed and self-righteous nobodies.' John Buchan Papers.

believed that the stocks in the country 'would only allow of a major war being conducted for a period of 4 to 5 months.' But an aggressive naval bombardment strategy would enhance the risk of high attrition and it was here that the Far East cast a long shadow into the planners' appreciations. If Japan seemed unlikely to move with the Axis against British interests or if Britain had an American guarantee, then the navy could risk the loss of two or three capital ships in a decisive effort against Mussolini. However,

> if there is any doubt as to the attitude of Japan and the United
> States of America, we cannot, with our present strength, afford to
> risk the loss of these ships, as not only would this serious
> reduction in our Capital Ship strength afford every inducement to
> Japan to come in against us, but if she did so we should have in-
> sufficient ships to send to the Far East even if we abandoned the
> Eastern Mediterranean.[28]

Inevitably, London also came under strong Commonwealth pressure, especially from Australia, to honour its Pacific commitments. Bruce told Chamberlain and a group of other ministers that the British tele-gram of 20 March had come as a 'bombshell' to the Australian Govern-ment. He reminded the Admiralty heads of their repeated assurances on the naval guarantee after Munich and demanded to know the exact nature of British war plans. It was an apt commentary on the state of strategic thought in mid-1939 that the only response —'undecided' — was quite honest.[29] The Australians continued to press for diplomatic appeasement in the Mediterranean, urging Chamberlain and Halifax to persuade the French to make concessions to Mussolini.[30] With full Commonwealth support required if war came, these views could not be dismissed: in fact, Bruce's arguments prompted the British to use leverage with the French in July in yet another futile attempt to bring about a Franco—Italian reconciliation — on Mussolini's terms.[31] There

---

28 First Sea Lord, 'Plans Against Italy', C.O.S. 946, 18 July 1939. Cab.53/52.
29 Two meetings were held with representatives of New Zealand and Australia
   to explain the changes in strategy. The first, with Chamberlain presiding, was
   on 28 June; the second, with Chatfield in the chair, on 11 July. Bruce told of
   a conversation he had had with Roosevelt in early May on his return from
   leave in Australia. Roosevelt had said, 'You need not worry.' Cf., Annex to
   C.I.D./362d mtg., 26 June 1939. Cab.2/9.
30 Menzies to Chamberlain, 15 June 1939; and Chamberlain to Menzies, 23
   June 1939. Premier 1/324. Also, record of meeting between Halifax and the
   High Commissioners on 11 July. C10103/15/18. (22975).
31 Halifax to Phipps, 7 July 1939. F.O. 371/23795.

was some anxiety in London that the changes in strategic policy might produce a reaction in Australian politics in favour of 'neutrality' or pan-Pacific self-help under the aegis of America.[32] Here was additional argument in favour of a return to the old policy of detaching Italy, if necessary with the traditional methods of diplomatic seduction.

Britain's growing predicament was the more acute because the Mediterranean was the only theatre in which any kind of early offensive action had been contemplated. Both the British and French staffs – and certainly their political chiefs as well – had convinced themselves that action against the weaker Axis partner would open up a 'second front', from which the Poles would gain assistance. The 1939 grand strategy debates reflect the deep-seated reluctance of British policy-makers to become committed to a direct military confrontation with Germany. No doubt this was in part inspired by an exaggerated picture of the German war machine, but it must also have derived – as did appeasement – from the memories of a generation 'bled white' on the Western Front from 1914 to 1918.

When the Chiefs of Staff outlined in late June the various courses of air action that might aid Poland directly, ministers hastily returned to the call for an offensive against Italy. Vigorous activity in the Mediterranean might have far-reaching effects, for the Italian population was strongly averse to war.[33] Chatfield told the Service chiefs of his hope that an Anglo–French success – if only in Africa – would damage Mussolini's regime; and other ministers spoke of the need for a 'spectacular success in Africa' that would have repercussions in the Balkans, America and Japan[34] (not to mention on domestic public opinion). To Lord Lothian, Ambassador-designate to the United States, the prospects seemed even better: a European war might be totally averted. He wrote to General Smuts in June that if Hitler attacked Poland and Roumania,

> our first task should be to smash Italy, and if we succeed in doing this and Russia comes in Fascist Imperialism will wither away, and we may be able to make a settlement with Germany which will last.[35]

The historian must wonder if it was only coincidental that the strategy of 'smashing' Italy involved little risk of a direct provocation of Hitler –

---

[32] Cf. Foreign Office minutes, 24 May 1939. C10764/15/18 (22975)

[33] C.I.D./360th mtg., 22 June 1939. Cab.2/8.

[34] C.O.S./309th mtg., 19 July 1939. Cab.53/11; C.I.D./368th mtg., 24 July 1939. Cab.2/9.

[35] J. R. M. Butler, *Lord Lothian* (London, 1960), pp. 233–4.

particularly if it was not complemented by some kind of air attack on Germany. An indirect or parallel response 'on the littoral' — as Hankey described the 1915 Dardanelles campaign — to German aggression against Poland would not necessarily precipitate the type of un-restrained, irrational violence that would make inevitable another exhausting total war. To this extent, the concept of 'Mediterranean first' was consistent with the course of British foreign policy throughout the 1930s and it also anticipated the diversionary projects that characterized allied strategy in the 'twilight' winter of 1939—40.

What would the allies do if Italy simply stayed out of the war? The French had posed that question and admitted that it must create a 'very thorny problem', for it would eliminate the chance of exploiting the weak end of the Axis.[36] It would also, of course, bring up the nasty choice of moving against Germany or doing nothing at all. In spite of their constant use of the Italian card in the summer of 1939, Britain's policy-makers apparently thought that Mussolini's chances of standing aside were virtually nil. The Italo—German 'Pact of Steel' of 22 May was perceived as the logical development in a now highly unequal partnership, and Sir Percy Loraine had warned his superiors after his first encounter with Mussolini: 'I fear the die is cast and that the only argument is the visibility of overwhelming strength.'[37] Vansittart told the C.I.D. in late July that Italian neutrality was an academic question. Blockade rationing would force Mussolini into the war; at best Italy would be a 'malevolent neutral' until Poland was defeated. Even Neville Chamberlain agreed: 'It would be wise to assume that Italy would be in the war against us. She was so tied up with Germany that it was un-likely she could adopt any other course.'[38] Earlier, the C.I.D. had inclined to the view that Italy should be forced into the war, even if the allies had to attack it.[39] However, because of the increasingly confused global situation, the issues of Italy's attitude and of England's European strategy were referred back to the Service chiefs for a final · consideration.

Six weeks before the outbreak of war Britain's strategic position seemed far more obscure and dangerous than it had in April and May. At that time the European situation had had precedence, an attractive,

36 A.F.C./13th mtg., 3 May 1939. Cab.29/160.
37 *D.B.F.P.* ser. 3, V; pp. 703—6; also Loraine to Halifax, 16 May 1939. F.O. 800/319.
38 C.I.D./368th mtg., 24 July 1939. Cab.2/9.
39 C.I.D./360th mtg., 22 June 1939. Cab.2/8.

aggressive strategy for dealing with Italy had been adopted, apparently with French agreement, and America had seemed willing to assist by keeping Japan at bay. By July, however, the Far Eastern situation had come unhinged, America had stayed aloof,[40] and Australia had mounted a campaign to keep London to its Commonwealth obligations. Moreover, because the French and British staffs had been unable to formulate a joint Mediterranean strategy, the prospects for eliminating Italy had dimmed. The global equation now proved itself insoluble.

It was within this radically changed context that the Committee of Imperial Defence met on 24 July 1939 for the last peacetime discussion of grand strategy. England's political leadership learned for the first time of the changed French policy in North Africa, and that 'there could be no early knock-out' of Italy. If the allies could so threaten Italy that its defeat seemed likely before Poland's, then Germany might divert its attention to the south; but this was speculative and improbable. The Chiefs of Staff had also concluded that a genuine Italian neutrality would be 'decidedly preferable to her active hostility'. The Mediterranean would remain open to supply Egypt, Turkey and Greece; the allied navies would enjoy wider freedom of movement; Spain would be more likely to stay neutral; and Japan would be less likely to join Germany. Italian neutrality would impede the application of a naval blockade of Germany and Turkey might sit on the fence with the Duce, but these did not outweigh the military liabilities of a Mediterranean war. If Italy looked like a genuine neutral, the Chiefs of Staff had recommended, no attempt should be made to force it to declare its position. 'On the contrary it would be worth our while to pay the high price, which she would doubtless demand, in order to avoid this contingency.'[41]

The false bottom of grand strategy had fallen out. The politicians present at the meeting received this advice with dismay and incredulity. The conclusions were 'disconcerting', 'disappointing'; there 'appeared little we could do'; the offensive action the allies could take seemed 'very meagre'; once it became clear that England and France would not defend their commitments in East Europe the effect on neutrals, especially America, would be 'deplorable'. As usual, there was a temptation to blame the French and Hore-Belisha wanted to use the

---

[40] Washington denounced its commercial treaty with Japan in July, an act that gratified the British but made no appreciable difference to their strategy.

[41] Chiefs of Staff, 'The Attitude of Italy in War and the Problem of Anglo–French Support to Poland', D.P.(P) 65 (Revise). Cab.16/183A.

threat to move the Mediterranean Fleet as a lever in co-ordinating strategy. But nothing would sway the Service chiefs from their opinion that 'it would not be possible to relieve German pressure on Poland by action against Italy, nor would such action have any appreciable effect on improving the situation in the Far East'. They had gone on to out-line the alternative courses of air action that could be taken against Germany in order to relieve the Poles, but the meeting had conveniently concluded that this 'would inevitably be solved by the Germans'. Apart from deciding that better inter-allied co-ordination was needed, the C.I.D. took special note of the revised opinions of the Chiefs of Staff regarding action against Italy.[42]

Little wonder that General Ironside, who had recently conducted staff talks with both the French and Poles, was by now 'profoundly depressed' and 'appalled' by the ignorance of his own government in the face of Britain's dilemmas and commitments.[43] By virtue of the decisions of 24 July the C.I.D. made it certain that British strategy at the outbreak of war would be determined by the Axis: in Europe by Hitler; in the Mediterranean by Mussolini's decision whether or not to go to war. This abdication of initiative was not inconsistent with earlier plans for a 'long war' strategy, but it is still surprising because the domestic and foreign political implications of a 'phoney' war were clearly understood by those present at the C.I.D. The unresolved crisis in the Far East was certainly a key theme of this discussion and a major restraint acting on policy-makers as the showdown with Hitler approached. War Office planners thought that war would surely come on three fronts against three first-class powers, and there is no evidence that a more optimistic opinion prevailed among Cabinet members. The situation only improved – and it improved radically – in late August when Mussolini stood out against Hitler and the Far Eastern situation eased.

'The greatest thing we have to fear', the First Lord had warned

---

42 C.I.D./368th mtg., 24 July 1939. Cab.2/9.

43 Colonel R. Macleod and D. Kelly (eds.), *The Ironside Diaries 1937–1940* (London, 1962). Ironside, recently home from talks in Warsaw, was not even invited to the 24 July meeting: 'I had not sent in a report and none of them had had anything but the haziest of conversations with me. It never dawned on any of them that I ought to be there to tell them what I had learnt' (p.83). Later he discovered that 'The French plan is *purely* defensive. There is no sign of an offensive either against the Siegfried Line or against the Italian frontier . . . The French have lied to the Poles in saying that they are going to attack' (p. 85).

Halifax during the debates on the Russian alliance, was a German—
Soviet combination. But Lord Stanhope appeared to fear an English—
Soviet alliance almost as much, and he had argued against alignment
with Stalin[44] – thus helping to realize his own worst fear. All of
Britain's strategic plans in 1939, including those for the Balkans, had
been based on the assumptions of Italy's probable hostility and Russia's
active assistance or friendly neutrality. But on 23 August Loraine wired
that he was 'confident' that Mussolini would stand aside,[45] and this –
added to the revolutionary development in German—Soviet relations –
vitiated the basic assumptions of strategy on the very eve of war and
necessitated an eleventh-hour review of military plans.

On 24 August the Chiefs of Staff convened and 'strongly adhered' to
their earlier opinion that Italy's neutrality was a prize worth sacrifice;
they mentioned the possibility of concessions to Italy on the issues of
Djibouti and the Suez Canal Company. Although reasonable precautions
should be taken in the Mediterranean, they recommended, nothing
provocative should be done to force Italy to declare its position.[46] Both
the Services and Foreign Office worked on their French counterparts to
dissuade them from any hostile gestures towards Rome, and in this they
were entirely successful; the French were also strongly in favour of a
neutral Italy.[47] The issue was deemed so important that all plans for
action in the Balkans were suspended in early September while the War
Cabinet waited for the intentions of Mussolini and Stalin to be clarified.

Thus had the debates on grand strategy come full circle back to the
policy of Mediterranean appeasement, back to a policy designed to
reduce global liabilities, buy time and relieve the strain on limited
resources. Once at war with Hitler England would quickly become
dependent upon the United States, and this in turn would rule out any
bilateral settlement with Japan. It was remarkably similar to the
situation as it had seemed in late 1937, only those earlier events and

---

[44] Stanhope to Halifax, 19 May 1939. Premier 1/409. Stanhope worried that an
alliance with Russia would result in Spain and Japan throwing in their lot
with the Axis.
[45] Dilks, *The diaries of Sir Alexander Cadogan 1938–1945*, p. 200.
[46] C.O.S. minutes, 24 August 1939. Cab.53/6.
[47] Cf. Ismay's note to General Jamet, 23 August 1939, and Ismay's minute of
24 August embodying the French reply. Cab.21/565. Also, Halifax to Sir R.
Campbell (Paris), tel. No. 241; and Campbell to Halifax, tel. No. 537, both
dated 22 August. *Ibid.* On the earlier views of Daladier and Bonnet, cf.
Gamelin, *Servir*, I, p. 444; and Minney, *The private papers of Hore-Belisha*
(London, 1960), p. 216.

dilemmas now looked like a tame rehearsal for the real dénouement. In both instances the crises in the Far East and Mediterranean interacted to paralyse policy and to rule out coercive solutions, such as the Mediterranean offensive or a naval demonstration against Japan. On both occasions too, tension in the Far East underlined England's growing dependence on American decisions; failing active U.S. support there, Britain fell back on Mediterranean appeasement in the last resort. The evidence goes far to suggest, in fact, that the Far East played a vital role in deciding British strategy in Europe and the Mediterranean at the outbreak of war; but historians have virtually ignored this aspect of decision-making.

Since neither Britain nor France intended to take the offensive against Germany, aside from limited actions to complement the blockade, the cancellation of plans for a 'second front' in the Mediterranean meant that Hitler once again had complete strategic initiative. Those plans would in any event have done little to help the Poles, whose fate was a foregone conclusion after the Nazi—Soviet pact. This grim fact only reinforced the Services in their determination to conserve military resources for the expected lengthy war instead of dissipating them in what they saw as a futile exercise. This had the virtue of caution, but it also looked to many like a cynical retreat from the commitments accepted earlier in the year. It was not lost on world opinion that the allies were dropping leaflets instead of bombs on Germany while Hitler and Stalin carved up Poland. Historians will one day balance the strategic gains against the political costs of this deliberated inactivity. But they will have to begin from the unfamiliar premise that the real 'unfought battle' of September 1939 occurred not in Europe, but in the Mediterranean where a new and ultimately un-successful period of appeasement was already under way when the Poles capitulated.

Conclusions

It has been argued, probably at too much length and with an excess of emphasis, that Britain's pre-war Mediterranean policies – and this applies to any aspect of its foreign policy – can only be understood against the background of an ever-deepening global predicament and an ever-diminishing margin of relative power. 'We are a very rich and a very vulnerable Empire', wrote Neville Chamberlain in early 1938 when the strain of interlocking problems was especially acute, 'and there are plenty of poor adventurers not very far away who look upon us with hungry eyes.'[1] To resolve Britain's imperial dilemma without precipitating the violence that would surely destroy the Empire must sometimes have seemed to Chamberlain a task akin to squaring the circle, but, whatever else he may have been, he was not a man who shirked his duty as he saw it. It bears repeating too that he did not invent, but rather inherited, the essential outlines of the policy of appeasement as it was practised in both Europe and the Mediterranean; and to interpret his coming to office in 1937 as a break with the diplomacy of his predecessors is a convenient but distorted luxury. A recent reassessment of appeasement argues that the policy

> was one of long standing, and that it was not personal to Chamberlain; that the task of meeting Germany, Italy and Japan in war was beyond the resources of Britain unless she had allies stronger than France; that the Far Eastern situation could not be contained or retrieved without the assistance of the United States; that the balance of naval power in the North Sea and the Mediterranean precluded Britain from diverting to the Far East a sufficient force of capital ships until she had at least defeated Italy, and preferably Germany as well; and that the responsibilities of those who do not hold office are distinctively different from those of ministers.[2]

And the same author concludes that it is 'unhistorical and unjust, and therefore wrong both in the factual and in the moral sense of the word, to heap the blame on the predilections and the follies of the few'.[3]

[1] Keith Feiling, *The life of Neville Chamberlain* (London, 1946), p. 336.
[2] D.N. Dilks, 'Appeasement revisited', *The University of Leeds Review*, 15:1 (May 1972), 48.
[3] *Ibid.* p. 56.

Conclusions

There is wisdom and historical sense in this. The great Croce remarks somewhere that it is not the business of historians to bustle about as judges, condemning here, giving absolution there. This must rule out the apologist's platform as much as the prosecutor's, however, for they are equally tempting culs de sac. The historian who has immersed himself in the documents of appeasement can easily be overwhelmed by the immensity and apparent insolubleness of the global predicament of pre-war England. It is but a small step from there to the conviction that its foreign policy was 'necessary', 'inevitable' or 'right'. Though they make them in circumstances they inherit and cannot fully control, statesmen and policy-makers do make choices and do influence the direction of their own history: a fact which even Marx acknowledged. The range of choices for Britain's pre-war diplomatists and strategists was, because of weakness and interdependent commitments, often very narrow, and in many cases decisions were taken in conditions of great uncertainty and unpredictability. Nevertheless, choices were made; opportunities were missed; avoidable injustices were committed; and the influence of certain key personalities on policy decisions cannot be denied. Which is to say that although Britain's pre-war dilemma was certainly intractable and perhaps insoluble, there was nothing predetermined or inevitable about its foreign policy.

Undoubtedly, however, the critics and apologists of appeasement will continue their partisan and pointless debate, each side using the available documentation much as a lawyer selects evidence to support his brief. The historian who is interested in the business of explanation, interpretation and re-interpretation can do little but hope that his own work will be used in the same spirit in which it is offered.

Our interpretation of appeasement stresses the role of imperial and extra-European influences on British policy-makers. It is by no means suggested that these were the only factors or that they were present in every decision-making situation. But we have argued that they did often figure in the calculations and actions of the policy-making élite — and to a far greater and more important extent than most historians have acknowledged. In Mediterranean policy the imperial and European perspectives were constantly at work, interacting in such a way as to be almost inseparable. The Mediterranean indeed was central to England's global crisis, and Britain's failure to restore its lost security there after 1936 was, we would argue, central to its inability to resolve its world-wide predicament.

199

Bibliography

I. PRIMARY MATERIALS

A. Unpublished

(*i*) *Official documents*

British Government Archives, Public Record Office, Chancery Lane and Portugal Street, London.

(*ii*) *Private documents*

Baldwin, Stanley. Papers and correspondence. Dept. of MSS. Cambridge University Library. Cambridge.

Buchan, John. (Lord Tweedsmuir). Papers and correspondence. Douglas Library, Queen's University, Kingston, Canada.

Caldecote, Viscount. Personal papers and correspondence. Dept. of MSS. British Museum.

Chatfield, First Baron. Papers and correspondence. (By permission of the present Lord Chatfield and Professor A. T. Patterson.)

Cunningham of Hyndhope, Lord. Papers. Dept. of MSS. British Museum.

Dalton, Hugh. Diaries. British Library of Economics and Political Science. London School of Economics and Political Science.

Drax, Admiral Sir R. A. R. Plunkett-Ernle-Erle-. Papers and correspondence. Churchill College Library, Cambridge.

King, W. L. M. Papers and correspondence. Public Archives of Canada, Ottawa.

Liddell Hart, Captain Sir B. H. Personal papers and letters. Medmenham, Bucks.

Pound, Admiral Sir Dudley P. R. 'A Brief Diary of Important Events (March 1936 to March 1938).' (This document, written by Pound while Mediterranean C-in-C., was shown to me by the late Donald MacLachlan.)

Simon, First Viscount. Diaries and papers. (By permission of the present Viscount Simon.)

Templewood, Viscount. Personal papers and correspondence. Dept. of MSS. Cambridge University Library. Cambridge.

Vansittart, Lord. Personal papers. Churchill College Library, Cambridge. (By permission of the Lady Vansittart.)

Bibliography

B. *Published*

(i) *Official documents*

France (Ministère des Affaires Etrangères). *Documents diplomatiques français. 1932–1939.* 2nd series. vols. I–III. Paris.
Germany, Auswärtizes Amt. *Documents on German foreign policy,* 1918–1945. Washington, D.C. U.S. Government Printing Office, 1949–. Ser. C, 5 vols.; ser. D, 13 vols.
Great Britain, Foreign Office. *Documents on British foreign policy, 1919–1939.* E. L. Woodward and R. Butler (eds.). London, HMSO, in progress, 1946–.
Italy, Ministero degli Affari Esteri. Commissione per la Pubblicazione dei Documenti Diplomatici. *I Documenti diplomatici italiani.* Roma, 1954. 9th series. 5 vols.
United States. U.S. Department of State: *Foreign relations of the United States.* (Yearly.)

(ii) *Private documents*

Aloisi, Pompeo. *Journal, 25 juillet 1932 – 14 juin 1936.* Plon, Paris, 1957.
Dilks, D. N. (ed.) *The diaries of Sir Alexander Cadogan 1938–1945.* London, 1971.
Harvey, J. (ed.) *The diplomatic diaries of Oliver Harvey.* London, 1970.
Macleod, R., and Kelly, D. (eds.) *The Ironside diaries, 1937–1940.* Constable, London, 1962.
Minney, J. R. *The private papers of Hore-Belisha.* London, 1960.
Muggeridge, Malcolm. (ed.) *Ciano's diary.* 2 vols. Heinemann, London, 1947 and 1952.
Ciano's diplomatic papers. London, 1948.

II. SECONDARY MATERIALS

A. *Memoirs and biographies*

Avon, The Earl of. *The Eden memoirs: facing the dictators.* Cassell, London, 1962.
Barros, James. *Betrayal from within.* Yale University Press, New Haven, Conn., 1969.
Birkenhead, The Earl of. *Halifax: the life of Lord Halifax.* Hamish Hamilton, London, 1965.
Bullard, Sir Reader. *The camels must go.* London, 1961.
Chatfield, (Alfred E. M.) First Baron. *The Navy and defence. Vol. 2: It might happen again.* Heinemann, London, 1947.
Churchill, Sir Winston. *The Second World War.* Vol. 1: *The gathering storm.* London, 1948.

Connell, John. *Wavell, scholar and statesman.* Collins, London, 1964.
Cunningham of Hyndhope, Lord. *A sailor's Odyssey.* Dutton, New York, 1951.
Feiling, Keith. *The life of Neville Chamberlain.* London, 1946.
Fergusson, Bernard. *Wavell: portrait of a soldier.* Collins, London, 1961.
Gamelin, General Maurice. *Servir.* 3 vols. Paris, 1946—7.
Ismay, General Lord. *Memoirs.* London, 1960.
James, Admiral Sir W. M. *Admiral Sir William Fisher.* Macmillan, London, 1943.
   The sky was always blue. London, 1951.
Kelly, Sir David. *The ruling few, or the human background to diplomacy.* London, 1951.
Kirkpatrick, Ivone. *Memoirs: the inner circle.* Macmillan, London, 1959.
   Mussolini: a study in power. Hawthorn, New York, 1964.
Knatchbull-Hugessen, Sir Hughe. *Diplomat in peace and war.* London, 1949.
Lawford, Valentine. *Bound for diplomacy.* London, 1963.
Leith-Ross, Sir L. *Money talks.* London, 1970.
Liddell Hart, B. H. *Memoirs.* 2 vols. Cassell, London, 1965.
Londonderry, Marquess of. *Wings of destiny.* London, 1942.
Macleod, I. *Neville Chamberlain.* London, 1961.
Magistrati, Count Massimo. *L'Italia a Berlino (1935—1939).* Mondadori, Milan, 1956.
Massigli, R. *La Turquie devant la guerre, mission à Ankara, 1939—1940.* Paris, 1964.
Middlemas, R. K. and Barnes, J. *Baldwin; a biography.* Weidenfeld & Nicolson, London, 1969.
Norwich, Viscount. *Old men forget.* London, 1955.
Peterson, Maurice. *Both sides of the curtain.* London, 1950.
Rendel, Sir G. W. *The sword and the olive.* John Murray, London, 1957.
Roskill, S. W. *Hankey, man of secrets.* Vol. 1. Collins, London, 1970.
Simon, Sir John. *Retrospect.* London, 1952.
Slessor, Sir John. *The central blue.* London, 1956.
Sykes, C. H. *Orde Wingate.* London, 1959.
Templewood, Lord. *Nine troubled years.* Collins, London, 1954.
Thompson, Geoffrey. *Front-line diplomat.* Hutchinson, London, 1959.
Vansittart, Lord. *The mist procession: the autobiography of Lord Vansittart.* Hutchinson, London, 1958.
Wilson, Field Marshal Lord. *Eight years overseas, 1939—1947.* London, 1950.
Wood, Edward, First Earl of Halifax. *Fulness of days.* London, 1957.
Wrench, Sir J. E. *Geoffrey Dawson and our times.* Macmillan, London, 1955.

B. Selected monographs and background studies

Antonius, G. *The Arab awakening.* London, 1939.
Baer, George W. *The coming of the Italian—Ethiopian war.* Harvard

University Press, Cambridge, Mass., 1967.

Barker, A. J. *The civilizing mission: a history of the Italo–Ethiopian war of 1935–1936.* New York, 1968.

Bitello, Prince Carlo Cito de. *Mediterranée-Mer Rouge: routes imperiales.* Grasset, Paris, 1937.

Blythe, Henry. *Spain over Britain.* Routledge, London, 1937.

Bolloten, Burnett. *The grand camouflage.* London, 1968.

Bono, Emilio de. *Anno XII: the conquest of an empire.* Cresset Press, London, 1957.

Boveri, Margaret. *Mediterranean cross-currents.* London, 1938.

Brenan, Gerald. *The Spanish labyrinth.* Macmillan, New York, 1943.

Collier, Basil. *The defence of the United Kingdom.* London, 1957.

Colvin, I. *Chamberlain's Cabinet.* London, 1970.

Connell, John. (J. Robertson). *The 'Office', a study of British foreign policy and its makers.* Taylor Garnett Evans, London, 1958.

Dawson, Rear-Admiral Lionel. *Mediterranean medley.* London, 1935.

Deakin, F. W. *The brutal friendship: Mussolini, Hitler and the fall of Italian Fascism.* Weidenfeld & Nicolson, London, 1962.

Boca, Angelo del. *The Ethiopian war 1935–1941.* Milan, 1965.

Domville, Admiral Sir Barry. *Look to your moat.* London, 1937.

East, Gordon. *Mediterranean problems.* Nelson, London, 1940.

Edwards, Kenneth. *The grey diplomatists.* Rich and Cowan, London, 1938.

Gott, Richard, and Gilbert, Martin. *The appeasers.* Lowe and Brydone, London, 1963.

Grenfell, Russell. 'The Navy and the Spanish war', *The Nineteenth Century and After*, 125 (May 1939) 567–74.
  Main fleet to Singapore. Faber, London, 1951.

Gwynn, Major General Sir C. W. *Imperial policing.* Macmillan, London: rev. 2nd edition, 1939.

Hancock, W. K. and Gowing, M. M. *British war economy.* H.M.S.O., London, 1949.

Higham, Robin. *Armed forces in peacetime: Britain 1918–1939.* New Brunswick, N.J., 1963.
  The military intellectuals in Britain: 1918–1939. Rutgers University Press, New Bruncwick, N.J., 1966.

Hirszowicz, Lukasz. *The Third Reich and the Arab East.* Routledge & Kegan Paul, London, 1966.

Howard, Michael. *The Mediterranean strategy in the Second World War.* Weidenfeld & Nicolson, London, 1968.

Hurewitz, J. C. *The struggle for Palestine.* New York, 1950.
  Diplomacy in the Near and Middle East. Princeton, 1956.

Johnson, Franklyn Arthur. *Defence by committee.* London, 1960.

Kirby, S. W. *The war against Japan, I: the loss of Singapore.* London, 1957.

Liddell Hart, B. H. *Paris, or the future of war.* 1925.
  The defence of Great Britain. London, 1939.
  Europe in arms. London, 1939.

When Britain goes to war. Faber, London, 1944.
Thoughts on war, 1919–39. Faber, London, 1944.
Lowe, C. and Marzari, F. *Italian Foreign Policy 1870–1940.* London, 1975.
Macartney, M. and Cremona, P. *Italy's foreign and colonial policy, 1914–1937.* Oxford University Press, London, 1938.
McElwee, William. *Britain's locust years.* Faber, London, 1962.
Mansergh, P. N. S. *Commonwealth affairs, problems of external policy, 1931–39.* London, 1952.
Marlowe, John. (pseud). *Rebellion in Palestine.* London, 1946.
The seat of Pilate. London, 1959.
Arab nationalism and British imperialism. London, 1961.
Anglo–Egyptian relations 1800–1956. London, 1965.
Martelli, George. *Whose sea? a Mediterranean journey.* Chatto & Windus, London, 1937.
Marzari, Frank. *Mare nostrum.* (Forthcoming.)
Monroe, Elizabeth. *The Mediterranean in politics.* Oxford University Press, London, 1938.
Britain's moment in the Middle East, 1914–1956. Chatto and Windus, London, 1963.
Namier, L. B. *Diplomatic prelude, 1933–1939.* 1948.
Europe in decay, 1936–1940. 1950.
Nolfo, Ennio di. *Mussolini e la politica estera italiana, 1919–1933.* Cedam, Padua, 1960.
Northedge, F. S. *The troubled giant.* Longon, 1969.
Petrie, Sir Charles. *Lords of the Inland Sea: a study of the Mediterranean powers.* Lovat Dickson, London, 1937.
Playfair, Major-General I. S. O. *The War in the Mediterranean.* Vol. I. H.M.S.O. London, 1954.
Richmond, Admiral Sir Herbert. *Sea power in the modern world.* G. Bell, London, 1934.
The Navy. London, 1937.
Statesmen and sea power. London, 1946.
Robertson, E. M. (ed.) *The origins of the Second World War.* Macmillan Student Editions, London, 1971.
Roskill, Captain S. W. *Naval policy between the wars:* I: *The period of Anglo–American antagonism, 1919–1929.* Collins, London, 1968.
Rowan-Robinson, Major-General H. *Imperial defence: a problem in four dimensions.* London, 1938.
Rowse, A. L. *Appeasement: a study in political decline.* New York, 1961.
Royal Institute of International Affairs. *Great Britain and Egypt, 1914–36.* Info. Dept. Papers, No. 19, London, 1936.
Great Britain and Palestine, 1915–1945. Info. Dept. Papers, No. 20 (Revised). London, 1946.
Slocombe, George. *The dangerous sea: the Mediterranean and its future.* Hutchinson, London, 1936.

Bibliography

Taylor, A. J. P. *The origins of the Second World War*. London, 1961.
Toscano, M. *The origins of the pact of steel*. Johns Hopkins University Press, Baltimore, 1967.
    Designs in diplomacy. Johns Hopkins University Press, Baltimore, 1970.
Thomas, Hugh. *The Spanish Civil War*. Penguin edition, London, 1965.
Thorne, C. *The approach of war, 1938–1939*. Macmillan, London, 1967.
Van der Esch, P. A. M. *Prelude to war: the international repercussions of the Spanish Civil War, 1936–1939*.
Watkins, K. W. *Britain divided. The effect of the Spanish Civil War on British political opinion*. Nelson, London, 1963.
Watt, D. C. *Personalities and policies*. London, 1965.
    Too serious a business: European armed forces and the approach to the Second World War. London, 1975.
Wiskemann, Elizabeth. *The Rome–Berlin axis*. London, 1966.

C. Selected articles

Askew, W. C. 'The secret agreement between France and Italy on Ethiopia January 1935', *Journal of Modern History*, 25. 47–8 (March 1953).
Burnett-Stuart, T. 'Future of the Empire: imperial defence', *The Spectator* (27 January 1939).
Bywater, H. C. 'The Franco–Italian naval situation', *The Nineteenth Century and After*, 109 (March 1931), 305–16.
    'Britain on the seas', *Far Eastern Review* (February 1938).
Carr, E. H. 'Britain as a Mediterranean power', *The Gust Foundation Lecture*. University College of Nottingham (November 1937).
Catalano, F. 'Les ambitions mussoliniennes et la realité économique de l'Italie', *Revue d'histoire de la deuxième guerre mondiale* (October 1969).
Cowie, D. 'Arms and the Empire overseas', *Quarterly Review* (October 1939).
Federzoni, Luigi. 'Hegemony in the Mediterranean', *Foreign Affairs*, vol. 14 (April 1936).
Germains, V. W. 'Some problems of imperial strategy', *National Review* (June 1938).
Gibbs, N. H. 'British strategies doctrine, 1918–1939', in Michael Howard (ed.). *The theory and practice of war*. Cassell, London, 1965.
Hosbins, H. 'The Suez Canal in time of war', *Foreign Affairs*, 14, 93–101.
Jouin, Lt. Col. Yves. 'La participation française a la résistance ethiopienne', *Revie Historique de l'Armée*, no. 4. Paris, 1963.
La Bruyère, R. 'Le Problème mediterranéan', *Revue des Deux Mondes* (1 September 1937).
Lestonnat, R. 'L'Activité de la marine française depuis le début de la

guerre espagnole', *Illustration.* (25 December 1937).

Liddell Hart, B. H. 'Armies of Europe: Britain', *The Spectator*, 158 (1 January 1937), 8–10.

'Defence of the Empire', *Fortnightly Review*, 149 (January 1938), 20–30.

'European crisis and Britain's military situation', *Contemporary Review*, 155 (January 1939), 26–36.

Longworth, F. 'Italy's new Red Sea base: the possibilities of Assab', *Great Britain and the East* (24 February 1938).

Marder, Arthur. 'The Royal Navy and the Ethiopian crisis of 1935–36', *The American Historical Review* (June 1970), 1327–56.

Marzari, Frank. 'Western–Soviet rivalry in Turkey, 1939', *Middle Eastern Studies* (January and June 1971).

Medlicott, W. N. 'Britain and Germany: the search for agreement 1930–1937', *The Creighton Lecture in History.* London, 1969.

Pinon, R. 'La Conférence de Nyon', *Revue des Deux Mondes* (1 October 1937).

Popper, D. H. 'Strategy and diplomacy in the Mediterranean', *Foreign Policy Report* (1 June 1937).

Pratt, L. R. 'The Anglo–American naval conversations on the Far East of January 1938', *International Affairs* (October 1971).

Robertson, E. M. 'Mussolini and Ethiopia: the prehistory of the Rome agreements of January 1935', in M. S. Anderson and R. Hatton (eds.), *Essays in diplomatic history, in memory of D. B. Horn*, London, 1970.

Robertson, J. C. 'The origins of British opposition to Mussolini over Ethiopia', *Journal of British Studies.* Vol. 9, no. 1 (November 1969).

Rougeron, C. 'L'Angleterre, l'Italie et le probl'eme naval en Mediterranée, *Illustration* (21 August 1937).

'Strategic centre: the Near and Middle East', *Great Britain and the East* (8 June 1939).

Toscano, Mario. 'Eden's mission to Rome on the eve of the Italo–Ethiopian conflict', in A. O. Sarkissian (ed.), *Studies in diplomatic history and historiography in honour of G. P. Gooch.* Barnes & Noble, New York, 1961.

Usborne, C. V. 'British links through the Mediterranean', *Great Britain and the East* (19 August 1937).

Watt, D. C. 'Gli accordi mediterranei anglo–italiani del 16 aprile 1938', *Rivista di Studi Politici Internazionali* (1959).

'The Secret Laval–Mussolini agreement of 1935 on Ethiopia', *Middle East Journal* (Winter 1961).

'Appeasement: the rise of a revisionist school?' *The Political Quarterly* (1965).

Index